THE
NEW
RUTHLESS
ECONOMY

THE

NEW

RUTHLESS

ECONOMY

**WORK & POWER
IN THE DIGITAL AGE**

SIMON HEAD

*A Century
Foundation Book*

OXFORD
UNIVERSITY PRESS
2003

OXFORD
UNIVERSITY PRESS

Oxford New York
Auckland Bangkok Buenos Aires Cape Town Chennai
Dar es Salaam Delhi Hong Kong Istanbul Karachi Kolkata
Kuala Lumpur Madrid Melbourne Mexico City Mumbai Nairobi
São Paulo Shanghai Taipei Tokyo Toronto

Published by Oxford University Press, Inc., 2003
198 Madison Avenue, New York, New York 10016

www.oup.com

Oxford is a registered trademark of Oxford University Press

Library of Congress Cataloging-in-Publication Data
Head, Simon.
The new ruthless economy: work and power in the digital age/Simon Head.
    p. cm.
"A Century Foundation book."
Includes bibliographical references and index.
ISBN 0-19-516601-9
    1. United States—Economic conditions—2001—Moral and ethical aspects.
2. Capitalism—Moral and ethical aspects—United States.
3. Business ethics—United States.
4. Industrial management—Moral and ethical aspects—United States.
5. Compensation management—Moral and ethical aspects—United States.
6. Labor economics—Moral and ethical aspects—United States.
7. Globalization—Moral and ethical aspects—United States.
I. Title.
HC106.83.H4 2003
330.973—dc21

                                                            2003051715

1 3 5 7 9 10 8 6 4 2

Printed in the United States of America
on acid-free paper

For Sigrún Svavarsdóttir
and in Memory of
Emile de Antonio—D.

CONTENTS

FOREWORD

Although many find change difficult to deal with, new ideas in technology, much like fashions in art, food, music, and clothing, tend to sweep along everything in their path. The effects of these new developments complicate not only social interactions but also the ways we earn our daily bread and spend our leisure time. Before bemoaning the rapid passing of "the good old days," however, we would do well to remember that those days themselves incorporated changes that almost certainly displaced some even older "good" days. The truth is that humankind has lived through eras that probably were neither as good nor as special as we tend to reimagine them.

After all, as agricultural communities, rich in social capital, gave way to the world of cities and anomie, most everyone also ended up better fed, better housed, and better educated than before. Dickens's London, for all its dreadful features, carried the germ of today's much more benign capitalism. But even if we can be optimistic about the general trend toward progress over time, this does not mean that we must celebrate every change or accede to it.

In this volume, Simon Head, former correspondent for the *Financial Times* and the *New Statesman* whose writings have also appeared in *The New York Review of Books,* analyzes change and reminds us of our opportunity and even our obligation to influence its course. While most of those who interpret economic and business trends "fight the last war" by focusing on manufacturing and the labor movement of the past, Head calls our attention to the modern economy, in which 80 percent of Americans are employed in the service sector. His important insight is that the technologies that produced such rapid progress in manufacturing—"Fordism," a rationalization of the production process centered on constant pressure on workers to increase output per hour—

have taken hold in the services as well. Enabled by information technology, employers are now able to monitor the performance of employees, resulting in the elimination of what are considered unnecessary interactions with customers, tightening one bolt on each client, as it were, before quickly moving on to the next. Whether in customer service or health care delivery, the pressures of the assembly line have moved from the factory floor to the office.

Despite the progress economists have made in understanding how economies work, their analyses often miss important parts of the picture. Preoccupied with numerical data, they by and large have failed to notice that many service sector professions—including their own—have evolved in ways that characterized manufacturing since the days of the assembly line: minimization of the time devoted to each task, intense supervision of activity, standardization in the processes used to conduct work. Based on his painstaking research, Head argues that the organization of work in such sectors as health care, customer service, software, and even the funeral industry have subjected workers to many of the same pressures that a Ford employee experienced a hundred years ago. As Head takes readers inside the workplaces that are among the fastest-growing sources of new jobs, many of which make use of the most advanced technology, his observations about parallels with turn-of-the-(previous)-century Taylorism resonate.

Head concludes that the extension of Taylorism to the service sector has unquestionably helped the U.S. economy grow more rapidly than most of its developed counterparts. But he also devotes considerable attention to its negative aspects, including the likelihood that it has contributed to the stagnation of wages among the bottom 80 percent of the income spectrum over the past thirty years, which also may explain why what has been happening in workplaces over that time has received so little notice.

With this book, The Century Foundation continues a long tradition of exploring the changing character of the American economy and the significance of these alterations for American workers and families. In recent years, we have supported such studies as Jeff Madrick's *Why Economies Grow;* Alan Blinder and Janet Yellen's *The Fabulous Decade;*

Edward Wolff's *Top Heavy: A Study of the Increasing Inequality of Wealth in America;* James Galbraith's *Created Unequal;* Paul Osterman's *Securing Prosperity: The American Labor Market: How It Has Changed and What to Do about It; What's Next for Organized Labor? The Report of The Century Foundation Task Force on the Future of Unions;* and Stephen Herzenberg, John Alic, and Howard Wial's *New Rules for a New Economy: Employment and Opportunity in a Post-industrial America.*

Much has been written about the culture that celebrates corporate leadership and about the greed that drives special deals for those with power as well as their cozy relationships with boards that might well be expected to police some of these matters. There also is a strong literature indicating the relative weakness of organized labor over the last generation and its difficulties weaving through the complex legal structure that makes even those protections on the books hard to enforce. But Head's special focus is on how changes in the structure of business have influenced inequality. Whatever the rate of growth in the economy as a whole, whatever the rate of productivity, however competitive forces come to bear, he argues that changes in the way businesses are organized, many of them driven by systems management and computers, have given management greater leverage than ever before. This leverage, he believes, can be quantified in one fairly compelling way: management's wages have grown while workers' have not.

On behalf of The Century Foundation, I thank Simon Head for this contribution to one of the central debates of our time: the causes of increasing inequality in the United States and what can be done to mitigate their effects.

> *Richard C. Leone, President*
> *The Century Foundation*
> *March 2003*

PREFACE

This book grew out of a piece I did on the "new economy" for the *New York Review of Books* in February 1996. I wrote the piece at a time when the mass layoffs of corporate "downsizing" and "restructuring" seemed to suggest that, however great the reliance of businesses on advanced information technologies, businesses were also still relying on workplace practices characteristic more of the late nineteenth century than the late twentieth. What has been so striking about the U.S. economy of both 1996 and 2003 has been that, although the economy has been growing steadily throughout most of the past thirteen years, the inflation-adjusted wages and benefits of most Americans have stagnated, rising at an annual average rate of less than 1 percent between 1990 and 2003.

The incomes of the rank-and-file majority remained virtually flat between 1992–1995, and so had not recouped the losses suffered during the Gulf War recession of 1990–1991. Even during the golden years of 1995–2000 real wages and benefits still rose at an annual average rate of less than 1 percent, falling far behind the growth of U.S. labor productivity and of U.S. Gross Domestic Product. In the *New York Review* piece I argued that there was a strong connection between these stagnant incomes and the corporate work practices then being introduced under the rubrics of "lean production," "reengineering," and "enterprise resource planning" (ERP). These practices drove the mass layoffs of the early and mid-1990s. But for most workers these corporate practices also reduced the role of skill in both factories and offices, subjected employees to an unprecedented degree of monitoring and control, and exposed them to wave upon wave of corporate restructuring. This harsh and unstable work regime, I argued, undermined the security of employees and weakened their bargaining power in the workplace.

The economy's strong performance from 1995 onward pushed aside such doubts about the "new economy." But the exuberance of the late 1990s faded away during 2001 and 2002. By mid-2001 a collapse of business investment, led by the information technology industries, was already dragging the economy downward. The terrorist attacks of September 11, 2001, further weakened the economy, pushing it toward recession in the third quarter of the year. Enron's multiple scandals and the ensuing corporate crime wave then brought to light some of the more insidious aspects of contemporary capitalism. A rapacious corporate leadership was able to accumulate great power and then use that power ruthlessly on its own behalf, and at the expense of its own employees and shareholders.

There is now therefore a need to pose some neglected questions about the "new economy." It is not simply that issues which seemed important five or six years ago are now making a comeback. It is rather that those issues never went away. They were simply overlooked during the golden years of 1995–2000. The performance of the U.S. economy during those five years approached the economy's post-war best, with labor productivity growing at well over 2 percent. But there was still this virtual stagnation of most American incomes, with a statistical gap opening up between the efficiency of labor, as measured by the growth of labor productivity, and its rewards, as measured in the growth of real wages and benefits. It is hard to believe that most Americans had barely been getting ahead during a period of such high growth and low unemployment, but government statistics are unequivocal on this score, and I analyze them in some detail in chapter 1.

As the late-1990s boom soared, so did this divide between the output of labor and its rewards, and I was convinced that the key to this paradox was still to be found in those work practices which already accounted for the stagnation of real wages in the early and mid-1990s. In the late 1990s practices such as reengineering were still an essential part of corporate restructuring, even though these practices no longer attracted the kind of the media attention they had a few years before. I believed that the only way to make sense of what was going on was to go out to factories and offices and start looking around.

As a journalist, I had been making such visits since the early 1990s, and thanks to the generous support of The Century Foundation from 1997 onward, I continued to make such visits. I have been to machine shops and auto assembly lines; to semiconductor plants and design bureaus; to software startups, call centers, hospitals, outpatient clinics; to management consultants in health care, reengineering, high technology, and "complex systems." I was able to spend three months in Silicon Valley and Cambridge, Massachusetts, trying to understand how software engineers go about developing and implementing their systems.

Without such field work it is, I believe, difficult if not impossible to understand how technologies are actually being used in the workplace and how they are changing the lives of countless Americans. In my field work I found again and again that information technology was being used to renew a long-established industrial culture whose values had supposedly been displaced by those of the "new economy." These established practices included the standardization, simplification, and measurement of tasks; the preoccupation with monitoring and control; the persistence of hierarchical relationships between managers and employees; and the unceasing efforts to speed up "business processes" with "business process reengineering."

These practices have not only survived in U.S. manufacturing, where they have been embedded for over a century, but they have also crossed over and colonized the service industries which now dominate the U.S. economy. The most spectacular example of this colonization is the rise of "managed care," which is essentially the industrialization and reengineering of health care. How information technology has renewed these industrial methods and eased their transfer from manufacturing to services is the dominant theme of this book. Such a view of information technology requires us to look at the familiar objects of IT—computers, servers, software operating systems—in the context of the work practices which have grown up around them, just as a century ago the practices of mass production grew up around Henry Ford's machines, presses, and assembly lines.

Evidence that contemporary practices may have old roots led me

back a century and more to the formative decades of American industrial history. There I found a clear line of descent linking our contemporary practices with those of mass production and scientific
management—the twin foundations of modern American industrialism pioneered a century ago by Frederick Winslow Taylor and Henry
Ford. To demonstrate this continuity I have included a chapter on the
roots of mass production in America. After this time travel I return to
the present and look at some of the contemporary strongholds of the
old industrial culture in the manufacturing and service industries. I end
by discussing the social and political significance of this history, and also
the politics of reform.

ACKNOWLEDGMENTS

I owe a great debt of gratitude to The Century Foundation, without whose generous support the field work which forms the basis of this book could not have taken place. I would particularly like to thank Richard Leone, president of The Century Foundation; Greg Anrig, vice president for programs; Beverly Goldberg, vice president, Publications; and Ken Emerson, my editor at the foundation.

It is a common complaint of authors that they do not receive the editorial support from their publishers which they think they deserve. This has not been my fate, and I have been very fortunate to work with Steve Fraser, the original commissioning editor of this book, and Tim Bartlett, my editor at Oxford University Press. I am also grateful to Rob Tempio and Catherine Humphries, and Tara Kennedy of Oxford for their editorial support.

I have also been very fortunate to have worked with Zoë Pagnamenta of the Wylie Agency, who has been a wise and reassuring guide through all the vagaries of authorship. I would also like to thank Andrew Wylie and Sarah Chalfant for their support.

Some of the writing and research for this book was done in England, and I would like to thank my brother and sister-in-law, Richard and Alicia Head, and my sister, Tessa Haddon, for their unfailing hospitality and encouragement.

Like many books this one has its origins in the columns of the *New York Review of Books,* and I would like to thank Robert Silvers for opening up the subject matter of this book in ways I had never thought of.

In my journeys across America I was overwhelmed by the attention, support, and encouragement I received from so many people, among them:

In Los Angeles, San Francisco, and the Bay Area: Charles Ackerman,

Danny Bobrow, Michael Borrus, Sandy Close, John Hummer, Sandy Kurtzig, AnnaLee Saxenian, Franz Schurmann, Harley Shaiken, Marc Trachtenberg, Bob Treuhaft, Jack Whalen, Horace Wood, and John Zysman.

In Cambridge, Mass.: Richard Freeman, Michael Porter, and Shoshana Zuboff. In Fairhaven, Mass.: Gary Johnson. In Boston: Frederick Reichheld. In Madison, Wisc.: Frank Emspak and Joel Rogers. In Milwaukee: Ellen Bravo. In Iowa City: Dick Greenwood, Marc Linder, and Clara Olsen.

In London: Robert Oakeshott. In New York City: Roger Alcaly, Nelson Aldrich, Dee Aldrich, Steven Aronson, Elizabeth Baker, Annabel Bartlett, Helen Bodian, Bill Bradley, Ernestine Bradley, Susanna Duncan, Ed Epstein, Frances Fitzgerald, Andrea Gabor, Edward Garmey, Joann Haimson, Alexandra Howard, Philip Howard, Bokara Legendre, Valerie Lucznikowska, Sidney Morgenbesser, Constancia Romilly, Richard Sennett, Sigrún Svavardsdóttir, and Lou Uchitelle.

Simon Head
New York City
April 2003

I

A NEW ECONOMY?

A T THE TURN OF THE MILLENNIUM, the U.S. economy was widely celebrated as a "new economy," one sustained by strong investment and low inflation, by steady growth throughout virtually the entire previous decade, by the monetary fine-tuning of the Federal Reserve, and by the renewed global supremacy of U.S. technology. Investment in new information technologies was the great driving force of the expansion. Between 1994 and 2000, investment by business in computers, allowing for deflation, increased sixfold and at an annual average rate of 43 percent, a growth of investment unmatched in U.S. peacetime history. In the same six-year period, investment in software tripled, growing at an annual average rate of 18 percent.[1]

The economic slowdown that began in 2001 has severely tarnished the economy's lustrous image, and not least because the great drivers of the 1990s expansion, the information technology (IT) industries themselves, have led the economy downward. Even before the terrorist attacks of September 11, 2001, weakened the economy, the IT industries had already become a severe drag.[2] Investment in sectors such as telecommunications and the Internet had collapsed, and companies like Cisco, Lucent, and Nortel, once flagships of the IT revolution, were laying off tens of thousands of workers and writing off tens of billions of dollars worth of inventory. It's now clear that the "new economy" and its industries have not been immune from the excesses of investment that have always driven the business cycle.

In the space of two and a half years, the near boundless optimism of Bill Clinton's second term has given way to this new age of anxiety, surely among the most dramatic changes in the U.S. economic climate to have taken place since the Harding-Coolidge boom gave way to the Hoover bust between 1928 and 1930. In 2001 and 2002, the transgressions of a whole slew of U.S. corporations, with Enron, Tyco, and WorldCom to the fore, added a new dimension to this turn-of-the-century malaise. But despite the upheavals of recent economic history, there exists a hard vein of continuity that also helps define the economic present. This continuity is bound up with what Americans earn, not with what they produce. Since the early 1990s, even at the height of the late-1990s boom, the wages and benefits of most Americans have stagnated, as if the economy were already mired in a crisis of low growth and high inflation. Now that the economy may actually be entering a period of lower growth, this phenomenon of earnings stagnation is likely to persist.

This stagnation has affected the earnings of the 80 percent of Americans that the Labor Department classifies as falling outside the higher executive, managerial, and professional ranks. Between January 1990 and January 2003—a period that takes in the Gulf War recession, the late 1990s boom, and the phase of lower growth beginning in 2001— the average hourly wage of these American workers, allowing for inflation, rose by just 6 percent.[3] But this figure actually overstates the annual increases in their incomes because it does not allow for the declining value of benefits provided by employers, notably in health care. In 2002, research sponsored by the Kaiser Family Foundation found that, for a family with an income of $30,000, the added health care costs incurred by the loss of health care benefits absorbed more than half of their average annual pay rise.[4]

The Economic Policy Institute of Washington D.C. has extended this analysis to cover the boom years of the late 1990s. There was some improvement in the earnings of the poorest Americans during those years, as many left the unemployment rolls and entered the workforce for the first time. But this trend reversed itself in 2001 as unemployment increased and the nation's shrinking safety net reduced the nonwage incomes of the poor.[5] For most Americans even the late-1990s boom was a lean period. Between 1995 and 2000 the American worker's average annual wage increase of 1.2 percent fell to an increase of .7 percent, a fall of 42 percent, when the impact of declining benefits was factored in. These statistics confirm a history of weak earnings growth for most Americans which reaches back to the early 1970s.[6] By comparison, between 1995 and 2000 the total compensation of the average CEO increased at an average annual rate of 25 percent, from $3.44 million in 1995 to $10.44 million in 2000. The ratio by which this CEO pay exceeded the pay of the average worker increased from 100 in 1995 to 350 in 2000. As recently as 1978 the ratio had been a mere 36.5.[7]

The notion that technology itself may be a leading cause, if not *the* leading cause, of this income stagnation runs strongly counter to a very widely shared view of recent U.S. economic history. If the golden years of the late 1990s were technology driven, then how possibly could this same information technology also be responsible for something so negative as the stagnation of most American incomes? For the past five or six years it has been the pervasive yet amorphous concept of "globalization" that has most often been cited as the chief driver of American inequality. Globalization has many meanings and can refer to the overseas investments of multinational corporations, the growth of free trade, or even the ideological hegemony of U.S.-style capitalism. But it has been globalization defined as a sharpening of international competition that is most often seen as a threat to U.S. jobs and wages, and so as a leading cause of inequality in the United States.

In the mid-1990s the Asian tiger economies such as South Korea and Indonesia displaced Germany and Japan as the United States' global nemesis, threatening U.S. jobs and incomes. But then the Asian financial crisis of 1998–1999 exposed major flaws in the Asian tiger economies, and these economies also faded as agents of competitive globalization.[8] However, even before the Asian financial crisis cut the ground from under competitive globalization, many economists had concluded that this variant of globalization could not account for the stagnation of U.S. wages and the growth of inequality in the United States.[9] Competitive globalization is overwhelmingly a phenomenon of manufacturing, with U.S. workers supposedly losing jobs and earnings to makers of cheap imports in the developing world, or to multinational corporations relocating their plants overseas.

So the percentage of the U.S. workforce exposed to these global pressures could not much exceed 12 percent, the percentage of the total U.S. workforce employed in manufacturing. Yet earnings stagnation affects up to 80 percent of the U.S. workforce, the great majority of whom are employed in service industries and are therefore largely beyond the reach of competitive globalization. These incontrovertible statistics led economists back to technological change as a force at work throughout the economy, and so of sufficient magnitude to account for an economy-wide phenomenon such as earnings stagnation.

To question the economic role of information technology is not to deny the contributions IT can make to the economy's productivity or to the quality of working life—whether as a device for shifting goods in factories and warehouses; a research weapon for scientists and physicians; an information processor for workers in industries such as banking and insurance; and, thanks to search engines such as Google, a tool for resolving many problems of everyday life. But there is also a vast sprawling gray area where the relationship between men and digital machines is less clear cut and where outcomes depend on decisions taken by executives and managers as to how technologies will actually be used in the workplace. To make sense of this gray area the definition of technology itself has to be opened up to include more than just the familiar objects of technology—computers, servers, processors, lasers, and software operating systems.[10]

"Technology" also embraces the workplace practices that new technologies engender, just as a century ago the practices of mass production grew up around the machines, presses, and assembly lines of Henry Ford's Detroit plants. For the tens of millions of Americans who work in offices and factories, this is the definition of technology that counts. From the early 1990s onward, the twin phenomena of "reengineering" and "enterprise resource planning" (ERP) have been prime examples of workplace practices built around new information technologies. Relying on computers and their attendant software, reengineering and ERP automate, simplify, join together, and speed up business processes. Reengineering and ERP do this by imposing upon these processes the standardization, measurement, and control of the old industrial assembly line. Despite their heavy reliance on advanced digital technologies, the two practices therefore remain profoundly "old economy" phenomena.[11]

Reengineering was a buzz word of management theorists in the early and mid-1990s and then, like so many management fads, it seemed to fade away. But businesses have kept reengineering their business processes. In 1995, when the reengineering tide was high, a survey conducted by two of the Big Six accounting firms found that between 75 and 80 percent of America's largest companies had already begun reengineering and "would be increasing their commitment to it over the next few years."[12] By 2000, when the practice had morphed into ERP, the leading IT consultancy, AMR Research of Boston, could state that "most companies now consider core ERP applications as part of the cost of doing business, a necessary part of the organization's infrastructure."[13]

There is scarcely a business activity that has escaped the attention of the reengineers. In their early years, they targeted such mundane activities as the ordering, storing, transporting, and billing of goods. But over the past ten years, reengineers have steadily widened the scope and ambition of their activities to include sales, marketing, customer relations, accounting, personnel management, and even medicine—"managed care" being essentially the reengineering of health care. For the 80 percent of Americans now employed in these service occupations, reengineering in its various forms has become a dominant force in their working lives.

In the mid- and late 1990s, reengineering evolved into ERP, a form of hyper-reengineering that brings together single business processes and tries to weld them into giant mega-processes. Led by the German software maker SAP, the reengineers of ERP are inspired by a vision in which business processes great and small—from the ordering of office furniture to the drawing up of strategic plans—all can be made to operate together with the smooth predictability of the mass production plant. But getting these ERP systems to work is turning out to be much more difficult than corporate reengineers had expected, and the subversive figure of Rube Goldberg and his fantastic machines keep peeping out from ERP's sprawling, unwieldy structures.

The emergence of this white-collar industrialization since the early 1990s is highly paradoxical. At a time when the percentage of the U.S. workforce actually employed in manufacturing has shrunk to 12 percent, work methods born in machine shops and on assembly lines have crossed over and colonized the offices, call centers, hospitals, and conference rooms of the nonmanufacturing economy. At the very heart of the "new" economy, therefore, are practices that are already a century old. The four pillars of industrialism—standardization, measurement, monitoring, and control—were already at work in the early 1900s when Henry Ford and Frederick Winslow Taylor created the organization and methods of the mass production plant. Today we are living in a new age of mass production and a new age of "scientific management," always the chief operating doctrine of mass production.

In a famous article that appeared in the 1929 edition of the *Encyclopaedia Britannica,* Henry Ford defined mass production as "the focusing upon a manufacturing project of power, accuracy, economy, system, continuity and speed." In this list of attributes, "speed" is paramount.[14] Between 1908 and 1916, Ford's great achievement as a production engineer was to increase a hundredfold the number of automobiles turned out each day in his Detroit plants. It was the economics of speed that ensured that, by the late 1920s, mass production had become dominant within the American industrial economy. For a business like Ford's, with high capital costs and a large labor force, the spectacular increases in output made possible by mass production so lowered Ford's cost per unit of output that the retail price of his first mass production automobile, the Model T, fell from $850 in 1908 to $360 in 1916.[15] Without this fall in price a mass market for automobiles could never have developed.

Ford's account of mass production reflects the times in which he lived and bears the imprint of the primitive technologies he had to use. In his *Britannica* piece, Ford himself says that the object of mass production was the "single standardized commodity."[16] When Ford first achieved mass production in his Highland Park plant in 1913, he and his engineers believed that it was impossible to mass produce the Model T without the complete standardization of that vehicle and its components. Every alteration of the product required altering the machines used to make the car, and this changeover was time-consuming and interfered with the flow of production. The Highland Park plant was therefore dedicated to the manufacture of the Model T alone. But as early as the mid-1920s, Ford's chief competitor, General Motors (GM), was experimenting with more flexible forms of mass production.

The progress of mass production over the next eighty years can be measured by its capacity to make products of ever greater complexity, building into them as much variety as the market might require without sacrificing speed or the simplification of work. This regime applies not only to automobiles, machine tools, computers, consumer electronics, paper mills, steel mills, and chemical plants, but also to sales and customer service, banking, money management, insurance underwriting, credit rating, medical treatments, and decisions about the length of a patient's hospital stay. Mass production long ago crossed the frontier separating the manufacturing and service industries, and with the coming of reengineering and ERP, this crossing over has become a full-scale invasion.

The methods used by today's reengineers to revamp a business "process" such as customer service provide compelling examples of how the patterns of the past keep turning up in the present. These methods are virtually identical to those used a century ago by Frederick Winslow Taylor, who was, with Ford, the joint founding father of mass production in America. As with today's executives, Taylor and his fellow "scientific managers" wanted his workforce of machinists, assemblers, and laborers to be more productive. Taylor achieved this by examining the workers' routines, strictly analyzing "time and motion"—the time each task took, the motions involved—a process that could last for months. Having worked out which among a variety of routines was the most productive, managers would then draw up a master plan laying out the exact routines to be followed by every worker.

Allowing for the greater sophistication of today's technologies and workers, this is exactly what happens when a team of software engineers descends upon a business process such as customer service, subjecting it to "business process reengineering." First the software team observes in minute detail exactly how these employees go about their work. Usually the team seeks out the ablest workers and debriefs them at length to determine why some workers are more productive than others. Like Taylor's scientific managers, the software team then goes away and draws up a plan describing how the process ought to be reengineered, focusing upon the best practices of the best workers. Having obtained a final go-ahead from senior management, the team will then incorporate its ideas into workflow software, and thereafter that software will govern the routines of all those engaged in the process.

These are the assembly lines of the digital age, complete with their own new digital proletariat. But this industrialization of white-collar work is not confined to workplaces in which tasks are routine and repetitive. The new industrialism is invading the territory of the skilled worker, with the reengineer trying to impose factory discipline on the work of even those classified by economists as "very skilled." With the coming of ERP, managers as well as frontline workers are finding themselves increasingly subject to industrial discipline. Another skilled worker who has had to cope with this expanding industrialization is the physician.

There are technologies that supplement the skills of the physician in the same way that design software supplements the skills of engineers: diagnostic systems that speed the identification of illness, scanners that provide visual images of disease, and Internet search engines such as Medline that can give the physician immediate access to a mass of specialized literature. But medical reengineers have also developed technologies that circumscribe the physician's expertise and subject him or

her to industrial disciplines. The physician does not control these technologies. They are the tools of medical directors and case managers
employed by managed care organizations (MCOs).

Databases incorporating decision-making algorithms "decide" on
the proper length of a patient's hospital stay, set out the appropriate
length of time for a physician to spend with his or her patient, and rule
on the treatments that patients should or should not receive. There are
also software systems that set targets for each physician's "clinical productivity" and then monitor whether physicians are meeting their goals.
Unlike most reengineered workforces, the medical profession has the
power and prestige to fight these attempts to industrialize its work,
and every day this battle between physicians and MCO administrators
is being fought in the medical workplace.

There are also white-collar workplaces where industrialization un-
dermines the opportunities for middle- and lower-income workers to
do skilled work. Economists have singled out the "front office" as a
place in which less-skilled workers can exercise "non-routine, cognitive,
interactive skills."[17] As the arm of the corporate bureaucracy that in-
tersects with the customer in areas such as marketing, sales, and customer service, the work of the front office requires an irreducible
minimum of human interaction that is not easily susceptible to the advanced automation of the corporate "back office."

The archetypal front office worker is the call center agent enclosed
in his or her cubicle, communicating with customers via telephone,
E-mail, and the Internet. As with the physician, an array of technologies now surrounds the call center agent. There is so-called knowledge
management and data warehousing software that provides information
about a customer's dealings with the company, along with a history of
the customer's own tastes and preferences. These information-
gathering technologies could be used to enhance the skills of the call
center agent. As the focus of all these information flows, the agent
could be left to decide how best to persuade the customer to place an
order or renew a contract.

But the operative word here is "could," because, as with the physician,
reengineers have developed technologies for the front office that sub-

ordinate the skills of the call center agent to an industrial, assembly line discipline. "Decision-support" software pre-decides for the agent which products he or she should promote, and how. Scripting technologies display on the computer screen the exact conversation, word for word, line by line, that agents must follow in their dealings with the customer. Above all, monitoring technologies track every facet of the agent's work, whether via telephone, E-mail, or the Internet. Armed with this data, supervisors can know from moment to moment whether agents are doing their jobs exactly as prescribed by workflow software, and whether they are meeting their production targets—minutes spent per call, minutes spent between calls, percentage of calls that result in a sale, minutes spent going to the bathroom.

Economists use the term "skill complementarity" to describe how information technology enhances the skills of high-income workers such as architects and engineers. They speak of "skill substitution" when technology eliminates the jobs of telephone operators or bank tellers. The examples of the physician and the call center agent add a third dimension to this interaction between employees and digital machines, which I shall call "skill debilitation." Skill debilitation occurs when management tries to apply the principles of industrialization to skilled work, whether the skilled work of a high-income worker such as the physician, or the skilled work of a lower-income worker such as the call center agent. Within the elite of college-educated workers, "skill debilitation" and "skill complimentarity" are therefore working at cross purposes: One limits skill, while the other enhances it. For the workforce as a whole, the practice of skill debilitation shows that some of the oldest practices of the old economy still have a very strong presence within the new.

Computer business systems are of recent enough origin that there is a need to go out to the highways and byways of the economy and look closely at how these systems are actually being used. Economists too often neglect these investigative tasks and as a result their work can have an abstract, detached quality which fails to capture the spirit and meaning of a critical period in American economic life. This book draws upon information gathered during visits to plants and offices over the past ten years. In the early 1990s, I was particularly interested in the global automobile industry and visited the U.S. and western European plants of Japanese companies such as Toyota, Nissan, and Honda, then thought to be posing a serious threat to the health of the U.S. and western European industries. From 1997 onward, I widened the scope of my investigation to include visits to machine tool plants, steel works, call centers, hospitals and doctors offices, insurance companies, business consultancies, IT hardware companies, and IT software companies specializing in areas such as reengineering and ERP.

But, however worthwhile, my visits to American companies could cover only a minute fraction of the hundreds of thousands of workplaces in the $10 trillion U.S. economy. So although my visits yielded plenty of hypotheses, these always ran up against the problem of "generalizability": How could I be sure that my findings were valid for more than just the handful of firms I had actually visited?[18] In this book I have relied heavily on sources that I believe do enable one to go beyond this handful of firms. These sources consist of the books, professional journals, trade journals, and product manuals put out by companies and their trade associations.

Trade literature shows industries facing inward and talking to themselves. In the privacy of their own trade journals, managers will often say things to each other that they tend not to say when, with spin doctors and human resource experts on hand, they face outward and address the wider world. I first learned about this particular feature of trade journals from the late, great Jessica Mitford, author of *The American Way of Death* (1963), still the definitive work on the American funeral business.[19] In field work for her book, Jessica Mitford visited many funeral parlors in the San Francisco Bay area and beyond. But it was from the industry's trade journals, notably "Casket and Sunnyside," that she came across the singular mix of piety, manipulation, and greed that characterized the industry's in-house dialogue.

These two kinds of evidence—the evidence of the trade literature and the evidence of one's own eyes—run strongly counter to one of the most common claims made on behalf of the new economy, that the "old economy" businesses that make use of IT are coming more and more to resemble the new economy businesses that create and supply that technology, so that the skill, proficiency, and flexibility of the Silicon Valley workforce is showing up all over the economy and at all levels of skill. In 1989 the MIT Commission on Industrial Productivity wrote of "new patterns of workplace organization" in U.S. manufacturing that required the "creation of a highly skilled workforce" and that was incompatible with "the ways of thinking and operating that grew out of the mass production model."[20]

In 1995 Louis Csoka, then research director for human resources/organizational effectiveness at the Conference Board, a leading corporate lobbyist, described how throughout the economy employees are "working in concert with others, [forming] work groups that become high performing teams through teambuilding, teamwork and interdependence."[21] In 1999 human resource experts surveyed by economists Timothy Bresnahan, Erik Brynjolfsson, and Lorin Hitt also claimed that "IT use is complementary to a new workplace organization that includes broader job responsibilities for front line workers, decentralized decision making, and more self-managing teams."[22] In 2000 economist Paul David of Stanford, now professor of economics at Oxford, wrote of the "process of transition to a new information-intensive techno-economic regime" with "new kinds of workforce skills" and "new organizational forms" that would "accomplish the abandonment or extensive transformation . . . of the technological regime identified with Fordism."[23]

Neither the plant and office-level evidence, nor the evidence of the trade literature, supports this vision of a newly skilled workforce empowered by information technology going about its business within autonomous, self-directed teams. At the upper echelons of "old economy" companies, new and advanced skills may be required of those who oversee the implementation of reengineering and ERP projects. But the sponsors of these systems habitually use them to simplify the work of middle- and lower-level workers, surrounding their tasks with elaborate regimes of business rules, and setting up all-seeing systems of digital monitoring to make sure that the rules are being obeyed. Perhaps the chief error of those who have proclaimed the coming of the autonomous, self-managed workplace has been their failure to allow for the sheer intrusiveness of the digital workplace and its technologies. With the reengineering of health care and the coming of ERP, skilled workers such as physicians and managers are themselves no longer beyond the reach of this all-seeing industrialism.

The alliance of information technology and the white-collar assembly line raises issues of society and ethics that have preoccupied social thinkers since the times of Adam Smith, John Stuart Mill, and Karl Marx—issues that exist quite independently of the economist's concern about the impact this alliance might have upon output, productivity, and wages. Does the new industrialism devalue employee experience and skill? Does it hand employers and managers too much power? Does it subject employees to a degree of supervision and control that is excessive and demeaning? And how should the U.S. economy be judged if it has a poor record on all these counts, yet still manages to achieve annual growth rates of 3 percent or better? These issues will be as much a part of the subject matter of this book as the strictly economic issue of whether "skilled biased technological change" can account for the recent stagnation of most U.S. incomes.

Nonetheless, the analysis of this relationship and its impact on the behavior of real wages and benefits can provide a precise measurement of how the information economy affects the lives of most Americans, which may be why so many leading economists have paid so much attention to the subject. Perhaps the most convincing way to demonstrate a causal link between "skilled biased technological change" and the stagnation of wages and benefits is to provide case histories of industries and groups of industries, each documenting the links in the causal chain with detailed and conclusive statistical evidence. But at a time when economists are only just beginning to define what computer business systems actually are, a body of research with the critical mass to demonstrate such connections simply does not exist.

Yet even without such detailed evidence, data for the economy as a whole provides strong circumstantial evidence of a causal link between technological change in the form of practices such as reengineering and ERP, and the stagnation of most U.S. wages and benefits. Employee insecurity is a good proxy for the effect of technological change on an employee's ability to bargain. Employees who are uncertain of their skills and their jobs are not well placed to press their employers for a raise. A 1999 poll carried out by Survey Research indicates that 37 percent of workers feared losing their jobs, three times the percentage who had such fears at the depth of the 1981 recession, when unemployment was double the rate of the late 1990s.[24] Another survey, conducted in 1998, found that, despite declines in the rates at which employees were actually being laid off during the 1990s, employee insecurity remained high by historical standards.[25]

Employee insecurity in the workplace has many causes, some of which may seem to have nothing to do with technological change. Many employees must deal with a steady whittling away of the value of their health and pension benefits, the declining protection of labor unions, and the determination of employers to pursue workplace "flexibility"—that is, the right to treat labor exactly like a commodity, even if loyal and experienced employees must be let go. Yet what Professor Paul David calls the "techno-economic regime" stands at the pinnacle of the causal hierarchy, and without its commanding presence, the impact of these lesser causes would be much diminished. To show why this is so, let us assume for a moment that the account of the new workplace provided by Bresnahan, Brynjolffson, and Hitt's "human resource experts" is in fact the right one.

If "computer business systems" had indeed produced such a decentralized, skill-intensive workplace then "skilled biased technological change" would be working in favor of middle- and lower-income employees and not against them, as at present. If "decentralized decision making" and "responsibility" really were the order of the day, then the judgment of experienced, loyal employees would be assets of great value to employers. The balance of power in the workplace would be quite different from what it is now, with employers looking for ways to cement the loyalty of such key workers. Employees, for their part, would have more leverage in defending their benefits, their jobs, and their ability to influence how computer business systems might be used. But it is because the "techno-economic regime" actually devalues the experience of front line workers and diminishes their role in production that many employers believe they can treat the employee more and more as a white-collar proletariat.

While Professor David's "techno-economic regime" contributes indirectly to employee insecurity, it also has a direct and visible impact as well. There are the phenomena of skill substitution and skill debilitation themselves bringing about, in Alan Greenspan's words, "a perception that skills are becoming redundant at a rate unprecedented in human history."[26] There is the manner in which skill substitution and skill debilitation are taking place, with much of the workforce finding itself the passive tool of elite management and reengineering teams with virtually unlimited powers. There is also the power of computer business systems to bring to white-collar work the kind of monitoring and control that factory workers have had to live with for a century. Once a white-collar worker turns on his or her empowered computer at the beginning of the workday, then from that moment the employee must reckon with the possibility of managerial monitoring, even though at any given moment the employee cannot know for sure whether monitoring is actually taking place.

These workplace practices make up a business culture whose origins go back a long way in American history, and this culture must be given its due. We will therefore begin by looking at the rise of mass production and scientific management during their formative century, a period that began as long ago as the 1820s and ended in the 1920s, with the early use of "flexible mass production" by General Motors. This is overwhelmingly a history of U.S. manufacturing, since the origins of mass production and scientific management are to be found in the machine shops and along the assembly lines of American manufacturing.

We will then move forward and trace the influence of mass production and scientific management in our own times. Since both practices have their origins in manufacturing, one of the best ways to trace their contemporary influence is to look at a leading manufacturing industry whose history has been entwined with the histories of scientific management and mass production. In manufacturing, the automobile industry perhaps satisfies this criterion better than any other. For almost a century, the automobile industry has led all others as a testing ground for the most advanced methods of mass production. In the final six chapters of the book, we will look at the colonization of the service economy by these twin practices of mass production and scientific management.

How information technology has renewed these industrial methods and eased their transfer from manufacturing to services is the dominant theme of this book. But can methods rooted in the tight disciplines of the mass production plant be adapted well to situations in which human agents talk, listen, argue, and bargain, as they habitually do in service industries? Can transactions between agents and their customers be governed by the rigid dictates of the digital script? Can consultations between doctors and patients be squeezed into the rushed, eight-minute encounter of the reengineered clinic? Can the unpredictable life of a business be forced to conform with the machine-like routines of enterprise resource planning? Whether it is right to treat employees as cogs in the digital wheel is a question of ethics. But whether it is efficient to do so is very much a question of economics.

2

THE ROOTS OF MASS PRODUCTION

THE PAST MAY CAST A LONG SHADOW over today's U.S. economy, but the economy's manufacturing and service industries relate to this past in different ways. Once the methods of contemporary U.S. manufacturing are set alongside those worked out a century ago by Ford and Taylor, the descent of the one from the other becomes very clear. The historical stepping stones that link past and present can also be identified. First, there was the triumph of the mass production model during World War II when its methods, applied to the U.S. armaments industries, made possible President Franklin D. Roosevelt's arsenal of democracy. Then there was the widespread application of these methods to the civilian, consumer economy in the late 1940s and the 1950s. Finally, there was the renewal of the mass production model by Japanese manufacturers such as Toyota in the 1970s and 1980s.

With the service industries, the link with the past is less an unbroken sequence, and more a contemporary rapprochement made possible by information technology. The early attempts to apply the methods of mass production scientific management to the U.S. service industries date from the 1920s and 1930s. But by mid-century it was evident that much white-collar work resisted the standardization and control of scientific management, and white-collar Taylorism did not have the same record of success as its blue-collar counterpart. However, with the coming of the networked computer and its workflow software in the

1990s, managers now had at their disposal formidable new powers of measurement and control that overcame many of these obstacles. In the past decade there has therefore been a "Great Leap Forward"—or more accurately a "Great Leap Backward"—in the application of scientific management to service industries.

But to show that the past exerts such strong influence on the present, we need to define exactly what that past is. An account of the relevant past may also help explain why old practices have had such remarkable staying power, remaining a dominant force in U.S. business throughout the twentieth century, and now beyond. By looking at these practices in the context of their entire life span, we might also gain some insight into why some aspects of this business heritage are more susceptible to change and reform than others. The history of mass production in the United States stretches back to the first decades of the nineteenth century, which is where our chronology begins. But this history entered a critical phase in the last decade of the nineteenth century and the first three decades of the twentieth, which will be the focus of this chapter.

The roots of mass production run deep in American history. In *The Visible Hand*, his seminal history of American business, Alfred D. Chandler gives many examples of the Victorian origins of mass production. In the 1870s John D. Rockefeller was already producing petroleum with a continuous flow of oil through his refineries that "eliminated nearly all manual movements" of oil or petroleum. With these methods Rockefeller achieved a tenfold increase in production, and a halving of production costs per barrel of oil. Also by the 1870s Andrew Carnegie achieved a continuous manufacture of steel with the integration of blast furnaces, converters, and rolling mills. By the turn of the century, a modern, integrated mill could roll as many tons of steel in a single day as a mill of the 1850s could roll in a year.[1]

This early wave of mass production was not confined to the commanding heights of American industry. By the 1880s the American home was being transformed by the new methods. The Heinz, Campbell, and Borden companies were adding tops and bottoms to their soup and milk cans at the rate of four thousand an hour. The Diamond Match Company had machines that could turn out and package matches by the billions, while machines owned by the tobacco magnate James B. Duke could produce cigarettes at the rate of 120,000 an hour. Thirty such machines could supply the entire American market for cigarettes. Also in the 1880s George Eastman pioneered the mass production of photographic film with the use of gelatin emulsion, and Proctor and Gamble introduced a "high volume mechanical crusher for soap making."[2]

But in the nineteenth century, the greatest influence on the American model of mass production was exerted by a varied and somewhat eccentric group of industries which went under the heading of "metal working": the manufacture of firearms, sewing machines, reapers, clocks, locks, bicycles, and, eventually, automobiles. At mid-century the economy's largest concentration of skilled workers was to be found within these industries, a consequence of the difficulties of working with metals such as iron and steel. It was within these industries that the conflict between men and machines was most acute, with the success of mass production marked by the advance of the automatic machine and the retreat of the craft worker.

In the nineteenth and early twentieth centuries, methods of mass production in the metal-working industries developed at the levels of both technology and organization. The *technology* of mass production consisted of the development of automatic machines that could achieve a very high volume of output of metal components, and also a very high degree of precision in their machining. Components could then be rapidly assembled into finished goods. The *organization* of mass production consisted in the measuring and coordinating of all the activities of the manufacturing plant so that the speed and efficiency of these activities could match the efficiency of the machines themselves. These activities included the purchase and delivery of raw materials, the routing of work through the factory, the deployment of the workforce, and the final testing of the product. All these phases of production had to be joined together in a single, continuous flow.

But these methods of organization did not begin to emerge until the end of the nineteenth century, and did not become widely diffused in

American industry until the first two decades of the twentieth. This chronology largely coincides with the rise of Taylor and his doctrine of scientific management. Taylor was, by profession, an engineer, and the experiments and inventions that formed the basis of his theories were mostly carried out in the 1880s and 1890s, when he worked as an engineer in the Pennsylvania machine shops. It was only at the turn of the century, when Taylor, his friends and disciples became the dominant group within the American Society of Mechanical Engineers, that scientific management became a coherent doctrine, one that these pioneer consultants could then go out and sell to U.S. companies.

However, while Taylor and his collaborators were working out the organization and management of mass production, the technologies of mass production had already existed in the metal-working industries for at least seventy years. Here the critical breakthroughs had been achieved by the U.S. federal armories in the 1820s and 1830s—a very early example of a fruitful partnership between government and industry in the field of military procurement. The greatest success was achieved at the Harpers Ferry armory between 1819 and 1828, where John Hall was the armory's chief engineer. In his invaluable study of Harpers Ferry, Merritt Roe Smith makes a convincing case that Hall should be seen as one of the "pivotal figures" of the industrial revolution in America, whose achievements "formed the taproot of modern industrialism."[3]

By 1824 Hall had suceeded in manufacturing muskets whose nearly identical components could be fitted together without skilled craftsmen. Hall's achievement consisted in the methods he used to do this. In 1828 Hall wrote to the War Department that he was ready for "large scale" production at Harpers Ferry, using a "minute subdivision of Labor."[4] This "minute subdivision of Labor," however, was not the labor of craftsmen, but of machines. Hall developed a series of special-purpose machines for the cutting, drilling, shaping, and smoothing of metal components. In the course of its manufacture, the component would be moved from one machine tool to another, with each machine performing a distinct operation.

Already visible at Harpers Ferry was the existence of a "direct" and "indirect" workforce, whose skills and roles in production were quite distinct. The indirect workforce still comprised skilled machinists and mechanics who maintained, repaired, set up, and even built machines, since Hall put together many of his own machines. The "direct" workforce consisted of workers engaged hour by hour in production—those operating forges, tending machines, and assembling the final product. Hall boasted that his machines were so efficient that they could be operated by youths with no previous experience in machining:

> The best person, decidedly so, that has ever worked with the cutting machine is a boy of but eighteen years of age, who never did a stroke of work in his life previous to commencing with them a few months since.[5]

Hall's joining of machine tools and unskilled labor marked a historic departure. In the early nineteenth century, England was the world's dominant industrial power, and in English practice the machine tool was used primarily as as a flexible, versatile instrument that, controlled by a skilled machinist, could perform a sequence of operations needed to complete the manufacture of a single component. It was therefore the machinist who had the power to decide when work should be done, how it should be done, and how much time should be spent doing it. With the coming of the automatic machine tool and the unskilled machine operator, these powers were transferred from the machinist to the supervising engineer and manager. It was for the engineer to decide how each machine tool should be configured to perform its particular task and how fast the machine tool should then be set to operate. The machine operator had no part in any of these decisions. In the metal-working industries, this was an American innovation and marked the beginning of what has come to be known as the American System of Manufacture.

From its modest beginnings at Harpers Ferry in the 1820s, the American System took root in a growing number of privately owned industries. This was a history of gradual, steady advance. Then in 1913, at his Highland Park plant, Henry Ford pulled together the successful technologies and organization of the nineteenth century, added immeasurably to their scale and complexity, and made them the dominant forms of American industrial life for at least the next sixty years. However, the road from Harpers Ferry to Highland Park was often meandering, with the new technologies applied to industries that did not seem to belong to the commanding heights of their times: among them, revolvers, sewing machines, reapers, clocks, and bicycles. What these industries had in common was not a shared strategic importance, but the character of the engineering problems that had to be overcome if mass production was to be achieved.

Hall's successors used special-purpose machinery on a scale far surpassing anything seen at Harpers Ferry, and they achieved huge increases in production. Between 1860 and 1885 McCormick of Chicago increased its production of reapers, mowers, binders, and other agricultural implements from 4,000 to 49,000. Between 1856 and 1885 Singer's annual production of sewing machines increased from 2,500 to 500,000.[6] However, in their use of automatic machines, Hall's successors found it difficult to achieve his standards of precision. Prominent among these successors was Samuel Colt, who boasted that his Hartford Armory was the largest and most modern factory of its kind in the world. But by the 1850s Colt had not fully introduced Hall's system of gauges, fixtures, and jigs at Hartford, and so had not achieved Hall's standards of precision.[7]

The Singer Sewing Machine Company is an example of a business that had relied heavily on European craft methods, and that converted to the American System in order to meet increased demand. In his detailed account of Singer's early history, Geoffrey Hounshell shows how slow and difficult this conversion was. Although Singer began its conversion to the American System as early as the 1850s, it was not until the 1890s that Singer achieved full proficiency in automatic machining.[8] By then, however, the history of mass production could no longer be seen simply as a progress marked by the development of ever more sophisticated machinery. The technology of mass production had already given birth to the organization and management of mass production.

The movement to reform the management of the industrial enterprise had its beginnings in the 1880s. Its immediate cause had been the very severe recession of the 1870s, which had squeezed the revenues and profits of American manufacturing, including the metal-working industries. In response to these hard times American managers began for the first time to look for ways to organize and manage their businesses more effectively. Their chief target was the old contract system of management, whereby day-to-day management of the shop floor was delegated to skilled mechanics or craftsmen. The powers vested in these workers was instead to be concentrated in the hands of management. From the start, this reform movement was dominated by engineers, with Taylor eventually becoming preeminent among them. As we have seen, Taylor and his collaborators believed that the machine and its method of operation provided a model of efficiency for the operations of the entire plant and its workforce.

The ideal of scientific management was to achieve machine-like standards of speed and reliability with the routines of the workforce, whether of laborers, machinists, inventory clerks, purchasing agents, supervisors, or managers. The task of the scientific manager was to study the routines of all these employees, work out the simplest and fastest way for them to be done, and, finally, set a standard time for their performance. The worker was then required always to follow this "one best way" and to do so within the allotted time. Taylor dreamed that the workforce of scientific management might become so proficient in following its standard routines that a modern plant could virtually run itself: "The daily routine of running the entire works should be carried on by the various functional elements . . . so that, in theory at least, the works could run smoothly even if the manager, superintendant and their assistants . . . were all to be away for a month at a time."[9]

Taylor began his career in 1878, at the Midvale Steel Company in Philadelphia, and although scientific management was a system geared to the very special circumstances of the metal-working industries, Taylor and his disciples were always ready to apply their ideas to any kind of work, however menial: the scraping of boilers, the laying of bricks, the sweeping of factory floors, and, most notoriously, the shoveling or loading of sand, clay, and pig iron in the backyards of the Bethlehem Steel Company. Taylor believed that one way of promoting scientific management was by showing how it could increase the productivity of workers engaged even in such basic activities as shoveling and loading. Between 1899 and 1901, therefore, Taylor and his assistants spent months analyzing and timing the routines of the loaders and shovelers in the Bethlehem backyards. Taylor, for example, took the "process" of shoveling and broke it down into fifty or sixty "small elements." "Stage F" designated time taken "dropping barrow and starting to shovel." "Stage W" was "walking one foot with loaded shovel," and "Stage W-1" was "resting one foot with empty shovel."[10]

Taylor then seized upon a particularly productive Bethlehem worker called Noll ("Schmidt," in Taylor's writings). Taking Noll or another such model worker as his guinea pig, Taylor and his assistants timed each of the fifty or sixty "small elements" of shoveling and then "re-assembled" them to come up with a target time for the shoveling or loading operation as a whole. The Bethlehem workers were then expected to "hit" the target time, receiving a bonus if they did so consistently. But as with all of Taylor's projects, there had to be an elaborate system of supervision both to keep the workers up to speed and to make sure that they really made their times and earned their bonuses. Taylor's focus on shoveling and loading took him far from the finer points of engineering, and it may have been because his 1911 book *The Principles of Scientific Management* devoted so much space to the activities of the Bethlehem laborers that the engineering grandees of the American Society of Mechanical Engineers were unwilling to publish it.[11]

But Taylor's faith in this dumbed-down version of his doctrine was well placed, though this did not become fully apparent until his death in 1915. The methods of time-and-motion study pioneered by Taylor in the Bethlehem backyards have shaped the industrial workforce of the twentieth century. Beginning with Henry Ford's Highland Park plant in 1913, every worker who has ever worked on an assembly line, whatever the industry, and whatever the economy, has to some degree been an object of scientific management and an heir of the Bethlehem laborers. This remains as true today as it was eighty-five years ago, and looks set to remain true well into the twenty-first century. But in his own career Taylor himself was first and foremost an engineer and a metallurgist, and for him the Bethlehem laborers were never more than a side interest. For him the chief target of scientific management was always the skilled machinist.

When Taylor began his career as an engineer at the Midvale Steel Company in 1878, he found a machine shop dominated by its craft workers:

> As was usual then, and in fact as is still usual in most of the shops in this country, the shop was really run by workers and not by the bosses. The workmen together had carefully planned just how fast each job should be done, and they had set a pace for each machine throughout the shop, which was limited to about one-third of a good day's work.[12]

Taylor was determined to improve the productivity of his workforce, but in trying to do so he immediately ran up against the entrenched powers of the craft worker. Writing of himself in the third person, Taylor

> found . . . that his efforts to get the men to increase their output were blocked by the fact that his knowledge of just what combination of depth of cut, feed, and cutting speed would in each case do the work in the shortest time was much less accurate than that of the machinists who were combined against him.[13]

Taylor's conviction that "the men were not doing half as much as they should" was so strong that he obtained the permission of the management to conduct a series of experiments to "investigate the laws of cutting metals with a view to obtaining a knowledge at least equal to that of the combined machinists who were under him." In his experiments, Taylor was always searching for mathematical formulas that could express the relationship between each of twelve variables and the machinists' final decisions, formulas that could then be used to put these decisions on an objective, scientific basis. As early as 1883 Taylor had developed a formula that linked the speed of a tool's rotation with the length of time the tool could be used before wearing out. By the turn of the century, in collaboration with the Norwegian-born metallurgist Carl C. Barth, Taylor had worked out a series of formulas linking all twelve variables to the machinists' final decisions. Then, between 1899 and 1902, Taylor and Barth developed a slide rule whose use could automate the highly complex, twelve-dimensional calculations that had to precede these decisions.

With the slide rule, these calculations could be made quickly and accurately by someone without any special knowledge of mathematics or machining. The Taylor-Barth slide rule was in fact one of the nineteenth century's most advanced examples of what we today call "business applications software." Taylor and Barth's slide rule lacked the support of Intel's Pentium chips and Microsoft's Windows NT operating system, but in every other respect their slide rule performed exactly the same kind of functions as a software product put out by SAP or Oracle, the global economy's leading suppliers of these specialized products. Just as today's factory manager uses Oracle software to find out how best to schedule a month's worth of production, so in Taylor's time the slide rule was used to find out how best to perform a complex machining operation.

The expertise embodied in the slide rule was not, however, to be used to enhance the knowledge and skill of the machinist. Taylor conducted no experiments to find out if machinists who used the slide rule might become more productive than those who did not. With the slide rule, Taylor at last was within reach of the goal he had been working toward since 1880, that of "taking the control of the machine shop out of the hands of the many workmen, and placing it completely in the hands of management, thus superseding 'rule of thumb' by scientific control."[14] In his 1906 paper for the (ASME) "On the Art of Cutting Metals," Taylor, therefore, laid out very precise instructions as to how the slide rule was to be used on the shop floor: "The slide rules cannot be left at the lathe to be banged about by the machinist."[15]

A system of management had to be set up to operate the slide rules and convey their findings to the worker at the machine. The actual use of the slide rule was to be the responsibility of a clerk in the planning department, management's outpost on the shop floor. This man "with reasonably clean hands, and at a table or desk" had to write up the detailed instructions that issued from his use of the slide rule.[16] Then another representative of management, the gang boss, went to the machine with these written instructions and explained them to the machinist, who then carried them out. The slide rule would show the worker "how many cuts to take, where to start each cut, the depth of the cut, the best feed and speed."[17]

Taylor also created an elaborate bureaucracy of "functional foremen" who, fanning out from the planning department, could keep the worker at the machine under close surveillance. There was an order of work and route clerk, who "laid out the exact route which each piece of work [was] to travel through the shop."[18] There was a time and cost clerk providing the men with all the forms needed for recording their times. There was also a shop disciplinarian who, in cases of insubordination or impudence, took the workman or bosses in hand and applied "the proper remedy." The "bosses" were the four functional foremen who patrolled a segment of the shop floor to make sure that the planning department's instructions were followed.

With its proliferation of clerks and bosses, each generating an unending flow of new paperwork, Taylor's system of shop floor control had a Rube Goldberg quality that could alienate employers as well as workers. This part of the Taylor system was rarely introduced in full, even by companies that had hired Taylor as a consultant. At the Bethlehem Steel Company, where a fairly full-blooded version of the Taylor system was put into effect between 1899 and 1902, even Taylor's close collaborator Henry Gantt described its operation as overly "elaborate and autocratic."[19] From 1910 onward resistance to scientific management increasingly took the form of strikes. David Montgomery has written of a "Great Fear" of scientific management that seized the metal crafts from 1910 onward, comparable to the mass anxiety of the French peasants at the outbreak of the French Revolution in 1789.[20]

While the resistance of the metal crafts to scientific management grew from 1910, the ensuing years, paradoxically, were also the years of scientific management's greatest success. In these years craft workers were not so much defeated by scientific management as bypassed by it. In the century's second decade the practice of scientific management broke out of the confines of Taylor's machining world so that by the early 1920s, in Alfred Chandler's words, "the practice of systematic and scientific management had become standard for the management of the processes of mass production in industries using increasingly complex technologies."[21] The operative words here are "mass production," because it was the application of scientific management to these fast-expanding industries that freed them from Taylor's obsession with the craft machinist, also making obsolete the over-elaborate structures of control that Taylor had developed specifically to ensnare the machinist. In these mass production industries, managers found that Taylor's goals of standardization and control could be secured with a simpler structure of management.

With these industries we are, for the most part, back in the world of the American System, in which standard products were manufactured in large quantities, the automatic machine was the workhorse of production, and, for the workforce directly engaged in production, the skilled machinist was being replaced by the machine operator. This new and wider constituency of scientific management included the Royal and the Remington Typewriter Companies, the Winchester Arms Company, and multiplant companies such as General Electric, Westinghouse, and International Harvester. In the emerging automobile industry, there was the Dodge Brothers Plant at Detroit, which turned out engines for both Oldsmobile and Ford. But the recruit to scientific management whose importance dwarfed that of all of these others combined was the Ford Motor Company.

Between 1904 and 1914 Ford underwent one of the most remarkable transformations in American business history. In 1904 Ford was not much more than a job-shop operation, using methods that were in some ways less advanced than those used by John Hall at Harpers Ferry in 1824. In 1904, for example, there were no automatic machines at Ford. In that year Ford made 1,745 automobiles with a workforce of less than 500. Nine years later, at his Highland Park Factory, Ford was employing 14,000 workers and turning out his first mass-produced car, the Model T, at a rate of 189,000 a year. By 1916 Ford employed 40,000 workers and was turning out 585,000 Model T's a year.[22] This stupendous increase in production was made possible by a record of innovation that makes the rise of Ford perhaps the pivotal event in the history of mass production.

Ford deployed the automatic machinery of the American System on a scale far surpassing anything seen in the nineteenth century. At his Highland Park factory, to which he moved in 1910, he had 15,000 machines, the great majority automatic.[23] With every group of machines timed to move in harmony with its neighbors, Ford's goal was to have parts and components moving through the machine shops in a seamless flow. Ford was also the first to use the assembly line to put together as complex a product as an automobile. With axles, engines, and the automobile itself moving inexorably down the line, the tasks of assembly could be performed with a machine-like efficiency hitherto seen only in the machine shops. Ford also developed a system of management that could keep the vast agglomerations of steel, glass, and rubber moving in the right directions and at the correct pace.

Scholars disagree about the relationship of "Taylorism" and "Fordism." Some, such as Geoffrey Hounshell, have accepted Henry Ford's own claim that he had invented a "wholly new method" of production that the "efficiency movement . . . early in the 20th century" had not foreseen [24] But the values and practices of scientific management so permeated the Highland Park plant that Stephen Meyer is surely right in arguing that "Ford managers and engineers . . . followed the general principles" of scientific management.[25] Foremost among these principles was to find the simplest and fastest way to do a job, make that the standard, and see to it that the job was always done in this right way, and within the allotted time. Such basic principles of Taylorism ruled at Highland Park. In his machine shops, moreover, Ford could rely on the automatic machine to help enforce the disciplines of scientific management, something that Taylor had rarely been able to do.

From John Hall's time onward, the use of the automatic machine tool had simplified the tasks of the machine operator, but at Highland Park, Ford carried this simplification to new lengths. Machines were specially configured to reduce the role of the operator to the minimum. Horace Arnold, a journalist who visited Highland Park in 1914, noted this aspect of Ford's machine design:

> While the machine tools used are all regular commercial productions, the fixtures used are most elaborate, carefully designed to save movements as far as may be, and are well made so that the workman need exercise no care or scrutiny in operating and working them.[26]

Ford also simplified the machine operator's tasks by shortening them, sometimes to a matter of seconds, and here Arnold's account is particularly helpful because it lists the timings of virtually every machining operation carried out at the Highland Park plant. In the machining of the Model T's front axle, for example, a sequence of turning, pressing, facing, and drilling operations were each timed to last thirty-four seconds. With these precise timings it was then easy for the Ford engineer to work out the standard output for each machine's working day, which the machine operator would have to achieve. In the case of the Model T's axle, the standard was fixed at 850 units for an eight-hour period.[27]

Ford's engineers also worked out a way of monitoring the operator's performance that much simplified the task of the shop floor supervisors and so eliminated the need for Taylor's elaborate bureaucracy of functional foremen. Ford linked its rows of automatic machines with a series of gravitational slides and slides with rollers, so that once an operator had finished his job, he would place the workpiece on the slides, and it would then arrive immediately at the next machine on the line, ready for the next machining operation. Arnold explains how this innovation simplified the tasks of supervision and control. Before the introduction of the slides and roll ways

> the straw boss could never nail, with certainty, the man who was shirking, because of the many workpiles and general confusion due to shop floor transportation. As soon as the [slides] were placed, the truckers were called off, the floor was cleared, and all the straw boss had to do to locate the shirk or operation tools at fault, was to glance along the line and see where the roll-way was filled up.[28]

At the Highland Park machine shops, Ford brought together the technology of the American System and the discipline of scientific management. With the assembly of the Model T, Ford went beyond the technology of the nineteenth century and introduced methods still used throughout American industry today. But it was always Ford's variant of scientific management that governed the routines of the assembly line worker. As a product with five thousand parts and components, the Model T's assembly posed problems of organization not found in the assembly of such products of the American System as the revolver and the bicycle. Before 1913 the Model T's chassis and major components, such as the engine, were assembled on stands or benches. Parts and components were stored in trays or bins positioned in the assembly area. Unskilled workers known as component carriers kept the trays and bins full.

In his memoirs, Charles Sorensen, a leading production engineer at Ford, claimed that the idea of the assembly line came to him in the summer of 1908. But from the early 1860s onward there was already a trend toward using moving lines to "disassemble" pork and beef carcasses in midwestern slaughter houses, and in his memoir *My Life and Work,* Henry Ford himself refers to this squeamish precedent. According to Ford, the concept of the assembly line came "in a general way from the overhead trolley that the Chicago packers used in dressing beef."[29] Whatever the exact origins of the assembly line, its first use at Ford dates from April 1913, when the Model T's magnetos were first put together using this novel method. An engine assembly line was in operation by November 1913, and an assembly line for the Model T's chassis by April 1914. In early experiments with the new methods, Ford achieved spectacular increases in worker productivity.

Using the old, stationary methods, a single worker had put together between thirty-five and forty magnetos in a nine-hour day. Working on the line, and as part of a fourteen-man team, the same worker could assemble ninety-five magnetos in a day. Under the old methods it took twelve and a half hours of a worker's time to put together a single chassis, on the line it now took a little under two hours.[30] On the assembly line, as in the machine shops, Ford took the methods of scientific management and adapted them to the demands of a new workplace. Just as the use of automatic machines made it possible for Ford to subject the machine operator to the disciplines of scientific management in a way that Taylor had never been able to do with the skilled machinist, so the use of the assembly line enabled Ford to do the same with workers of even less skill.

Ford's assembly line workers were subjected to time-and-motion studies no less rigorous than those used by Taylor with the Bethlehem laborers. An example drawn from Ford's memoirs illustrates the importance of such studies for Ford and the use to which he put them. Ford describes how pistons and rods were assembled before and after the application of scientific management to the tasks of assembly. Under the old system one workman "pushed the pin out of the piston, oiled the pin, slipped the rod in place, put the pin through the rod and piston, tightened one screw, and opened another screw." This was a "very simple operation," but it still took three minutes. A foreman was ordered to analyze all these motions with a stopwatch, the essential tool of all scientific managers. The foreman found that four hours out of the assembler's nine-hour day were spent walking. The assembler did not go anywhere, "but he did shift his feet to gather in his materials" and to "push away his finished piece."

The solution was to make a simple job very much simpler by creating two mini-assembly lines. In Ford's words:

> The foreman . . . split the operation into three divisions, put a slide on the bench and three men on each side of it, and an inspector at the end. Instead of one man performing the whole operation, one man then performed only one-third of the operation—he performed only as much as he could do without shifting his feet.[31]

In April 1914 the final assembly of the Model T's chassis and interior began to be done "on the line." This was the most ambitious and elaborate of all of Ford's assembly lines. Once again, Horace Arnold has done posterity a service by leaving a detailed description of the division of labor on the final assembly line.[32] Assemblers worked alone or in small groups ("teams," in today's language) of two or three. The task of every worker or group of workers was timed to last exactly seven minutes and thirty-six seconds. Horace Arnold gives a detailed description of two assembly line jobs (numbered "3" and "4") and shows how this dividing up of tasks worked. He also gives a feel for the dense effort of a routine repeated by workers day in and day out:

> (3) Three men. Two men place and fix the rear axle, connecting the rear spring to the rear-axle spring shackles; one man working simultaneously with the other two places and fixes the front-axle assembly under the chassis frame. (4) Two men. One completes the fixing of the front axle, places the two combined lamp-brackets and front mud-guards, and catches nuts on, while the other man places and fixes the mud-guard bracket truss-rods.[33]

On the assembly line, discipline and control could be enforced by the line itself, and so there was no need for Taylor's elaborate army of functional foremen. Once again, Ford relied on technology to refine and improve the methods of scientific management. Having timed each job on the chassis assembly line to last exactly seven minutes and thirty-six seconds, Ford's engineers could fix the line's speed so that the chassis would remain within the "territory" of a worker or group of workers for precisely that amount of time and no more. In such a setting the worker becomes a link in a chain of production, a link that, "if it does not function properly is quickly noticed by management and by other workers."[34] If the worker failed to do his job in the allotted time, the line carried him beyond his "territory," and he would start getting in the way of other workers.

Meanwhile, the next workpiece on the line rolled onward unattended. If the worker tried to make up time by leaving part of his task undone, his incomplete work was visible to foremen and fellow workers as it paraded down the line. The invention of the assembly line also gave management the power to accelerate the pace of work whenever it wanted. All it had to do was throw a switch and the line moved faster. A history of the near-seventy-year relationship between the United Auto Workers (UAW) and the Detroit Big Three could be written largely as a prolonged dispute about "speed up." A journalist who visited Highland Park in 1914 has well described the temptations—for management—of "speed up":

> Under these conditions of production, is it any wonder that the move-
> ments of men become practically automatic and that output is regu-
> lated by the speed at which the travelling chains are operated? Speed
> up the electric motors a notch and—presto! Ford production has in-
> creased another hundred cars per day without the necessity of hiring a
> single workman.[35]

In the mid-1920s the market turned against Henry Ford and he had to
rely more and more on speed up and pay cuts to keep profits from
falling. In the post-war world, American consumers had become more
demanding and were beginning to tire of what Emma Rothschild has
called the "functional and uncomfortable" Model T.[36] Ford's U.S. market share fell from 55 percent in 1921 to 30 percent in 1926, and to 25
percent in the first half of 1927, when Henry Ford announced the dis-
continuation of the Model T.[37] Those months in 1927 were significant
for another reason. It was then that production at General Motors'
mass market division, Chevrolet, exceeded Ford's for the first time.
Chevrolet's production rose from 280,000 in 1924 to 732,000 in
1926, and to over a million in 1927.[38]

The technical architect of Chevrolet's success was William S. Knudsen, a former production engineer at Ford who joined General Motors
in 1921 and was appointed general manager at Chevrolet by Alfred P.
Sloan in 1924. Sloan and Knudsen understood, as Henry Ford did not,
that the consumer's changing desires had to be met. To this end, Knudsen pioneered methods of flexible mass production that both accommodated the consumer, and also kept the workforce still largely
subjected to the rule of scientific management. This principle of industrial organization dominates U.S. manufacturing to this day, and as its
originator, Knudsen must rank with John Hall, Frederick Winslow Taylor, and Henry Ford in mass production's hall of fame.

In Knudsen's first years at GM, "the appearance of the Chevrolet did
not change appreciably from one year to the next," according to *Fortune*. But each year, Knudsen was in fact making small improvements to
the Chevrolet that chipped away at the Model T's market share. *Fortune* refers to the Chevrolet's "three inch longer wheel base, standard

transmission, and . . . annual new styling" that "made the Chevrolet, priced near the Model T, look like more money."[39] But Knudsen was also planning more radical changes. By the late 1920s Sloan's strategy for all of GM was not simply to restyle its cars every year, but also to introduce a completely new model every third year.

In gearing up for this new production regime, Knudsen moved beyond the hyper-specialization of Ford's Highland Park plant, in which most machines were dedicated to the production of just one model. Knudsen's approach was to introduce a new kind of machine, one that had a "standard tool base, easy for the tool builders to manufacture," but also had a superstructure that could be altered to accommodate the changed specifications of any new model.[40] Knudsen's machines combined the flexibility of the old general-purpose machine with the high productivity of Ford's automatic machines.

However, this innovation did not require any significant change to the workforce of mass production common to both Ford and General Motors. The reconfiguration of the machine's superstructure was skilled work, but it was performed by a small indirect workforce of skilled workers that, at GM, as at Ford, represented between 10 and 15 percent of the total workforce. The routines of the assemblers and machine operators remained as they had been at Highland Park. A contemporary account drew attention to this aspect of Knudsen's engineering. His machines would meet the "special needs of the automobile industry" because

> the feeds and speeds cannot be changed at the will of the operator but can be transformed at the will of the executive by the transposition of gears. These machines permit adjustments, but only by the set-up man.[41]

Driven by the innovations of Taylor, Ford, and Knudsen, the American System of mass production achieved some of its greatest advances in the first three decades of the twentieth century. But it was in mid-century that the system really entered its golden age and exerted an influence that reached well beyond the machine shop and the assembly line. During World War II the application of mass production methods to armament production, and particularly to the aircraft industry, helped bring about the soaring output of Roosevelt's "arsenal of democracy." Taking their cue from Ford and GM, the U.S. armament industries, and the aircraft industry in particular, organized their production around giant plants employing huge numbers of workers. In the aircraft industry this expansion created a two-million-strong workforce with very little previous experience of aircraft production. Of the twenty-five thousand workers at Curtiss-Wright's Lockland, Ohio, plant, only 2 percent of job applicants had any such experience.[42]

The management theorist Peter Drucker, a close observer of the wartime economy, has written of how U.S. industry took such "totally unskilled workers" and, relying heavily on Taylor's methods, "converted them in sixty to ninety days into first rate welders and ship builders."[43] Boeing geared the production of the B-29 bomber, perhaps the most complex weapon system of the war, to the requirements of this mostly unskilled workforce. Large sections of the B-29 fuselage "had the same measurement and fabrication characteristics," making the plane easier to build. Subassemblies were then shipped to a final assembly line where "less experienced workers could literally bolt everything together more quickly and with fewer mistakes."[44]

With the end of the war this powerful engine of production began catering to the needs of the civilian economy, and in the late 1940s and 1950s an American middle class emerged whose lives were surrounded at every turn by the artifacts of mass production emerged. There were families living in mass-produced, Levittown houses; families tending their new homes with mass-produced appliances; families driving to work in mass-produced cars, eating and drinking in the mass-produced establishments of the roadside strip. The power of American mass production seemed all the greater when set alongside the penury of European economies still recovering from the devastation of war. On the management side, the unchanging routines of mass production seemed best served by a management structure in which executive suite and assembly line were linked in a single, seamless hierarchy.

Among economists it is very widely accepted that this system began to break down starting from the late 1960s onward. In their influential book *The Second Industrial Divide* (1983), Charles Sabel and Michael Piore argued that, just as the consumer of the 1920s had grown tired of the Model T, so the consumer of the 1960s had tired of the standardized goods of the post-war era.[45] By the late 1960s technologies were coming on line that could satisfy the consumer's desire for ever greater variety. But this new regime of "flexible specialization" differed in important respects from the old system of mass production that, in the view of Sabel and Piore, was now obsolete.[46] The new technologies were complex and difficult to operate and so could no longer be handled by workers trained in the simple routines of scientific management. Sabel and Piore looked forward to a revival of the craft tradition in U.S. manufacturing.[47]

But Knudsen's working out of "flexible mass production" in the mid- and late 1920s had already shown how resilient the mass production model could be in the face of consumer demands. Flexible technologies could *both* satisfy the consumer *and* keep in place the workforce of scientific management. In the 1970s and 1980s the mass production model pulled this off yet again. However, now the agents of renewal were no longer to be found in the midwestern heartland of Ford and GM, but rather thousands of miles away in Japan.

3

THE PAST ALIVE: AUTOMOBILES

IN JANUARY 1994 I visited the chief European engine and assembly plant of Nissan, then the number two Japanese automaker after Toyota. In 1981 Nissan had built its European plant in the heart of Sunderland, an industrial city in the north-east of England whose roots go back to the industrial revolution itself, but whose fortunes had been in decline for most of the twentieth century. Amid the rotting remains of Sunderland's abandoned shipyards and steel mills, the gleaming, mile-long workshops of the Nissan plant stood out as sleek symbols of renewal and hope for the people of Sunderland. The plant's two thousand shop floor workers were drawn mostly from the surrounding public housing projects, where unemployment rates of 20 percent or more were common.

With the Japanese economy mired in a decade of stagnation from which it shows no sign of recovery, these references to a once-feared symbol of Japanese industrial power sound like recollections of ancient history. But the coming of these Japanese "transplants" to the United States and western Europe in the 1970s and 1980s played a pivotal role in the U.S. debate on the relationship between technology and work in factories and offices. So many of the concepts—multiskilling, flexible specialization, worker empowerment, worker autonomy—used to define the role of employees in the "new economy" had their origins in the methods of Japanese companies like Nissan.

As we have seen, in 1989 the MIT Commission on Industrial Productivity wrote of "new patterns of workplace organization" pioneered by Japanese corporations that were "different in almost every feature from Detroit's mass production system" and that required "the creation of a highly skilled workforce."[1] In 1990 another influential commission on U.S. manufacturing, headed by Bill Clinton's future health care czar, Ira Magaziner, described in detail what would be required of workers in the new, Japanese-style workplace: "The new high performance forms of work organization . . . rather than increasing bureaucracy . . . reduce it by giving front-workers more responsibility. Workers are asked to use judgment and make decisions. . . . Management layers disappear as front line workers assume responsibility for many of the tasks . . . that others used to do."[2]

The big loser in this manufacturing revolution was thought to be, in the words of the MIT Commission, the "ways of thinking and operating that grew out of the mass production models."[3] The Magaziner Commission argued that, since the "Taylor model of work organization . . . did not require skills from the vast majority of its workers," the model could not survive in a workplace in which "workers are asked to use judgment and make decisions."[4] For most of the twentieth century, the U.S. industrial workforce had lived in the shadow of mass production, with its regimentation, standardization, and control. Here were new methods of production that could restore to the industrial worker the skill, dignity, and independence of the craft tradition.

This early theorizing about the new economy and its benefits for employees was heavily focused on the manufacturing sector, in which Japanese companies like Toyota and Sony were active. Then, in the 1990s, the great surge of IT investment in the United States shifted attention increasingly toward service industries, in which a rising proportion of IT investment was now concentrated. With this change of perspective, the whole body of theorizing about a workplace revolution was simply transferred from manufacturing to services. The success of the Japanese revolution in manufacturing paved the way for similar practices to be set up in the service industries.

Thus, Professor Paul David, writing in 2000 about the impact of IT investment on the whole economy, could use language very similar to the language used by the MIT Commission in its 1989 study of U.S. manufacturing: "a process of transition to . . . new organizational forms . . . with new kinds of workforce skills . . . which would accomplish the abandonment or extensive transformation . . . of the technological regime identified with Fordism."[5] The leading practitioners of service sector reengineering also used the language of the new workplace. Thomas Davenport wrote of how reengineering created "a more empowered and diversified work force, eliminating levels of hierarchy, creating self-managing work teams, combining jobs and assigning broader responsibility, and upgrading skills."[6]

Few would want to oppose a workplace revolution that could enhance the role of employee judgment and skill. Employees so empowered can command good wages, are well placed to form unions, and can have a real say in how technologies are used in the workplace. But has such a revolution really taken place? The use of "new workplace" rhetoric by a leading reengineer such as Thomas Davenport should have given us pause. Similarly, the prevailing view of Japanese production methods espoused by (among others) the MIT and Magaziner Commissions, and the whole body of theory derived from this account were both deeply flawed.

Companies like Toyota and Nissan did not abandon the mass production model, they strengthened and renewed it. They drew heavily on the legacy of Ford and Taylor, and added some new refinements of their own. The adoption of Japanese methods by U.S. corporations such as Ford and GM was also therefore a renewal of the mass production model, whose U.S. variant had lost much of its edge in the 1960s and 1970s. With the IT surge of the mid-1990s a transfer of methods from manufacturing to services did indeed take place, but not the kind of transfer envisaged by the theorists of the new workplace. Emboldened by the renewal of U.S. mass production at the hands of the Japanese, leading reengineers such as Michael Hammer, James Champy, and Thomas Davenport, along with business consultancies such as Andersen Consulting (now Accenture) and Ernst and Young, all simply applied this industrialism lock, stock, and barrel to the service industries.

A whole superstructure of theory has been built upon the shaky foundation of these Japanese production methods, or, more accurately, upon a particular interpretation of them. We now need to look at this Japanese model methods more closely.

Even from the perspective of Japan's industrial heyday in the late 1980s, I doubted that the methods being used by Japanese corporations amounted to a repudiation of the mass production model, still less to a revolution in manufacturing. As a financial journalist in East Asia in the late 1960s and early 1970s, I had watched the early stirrings of a new Japanese "Co-Prosperity Sphere" in the region. Japanese corporations such as Panasonic and Sony began building plants in Hong Kong and South Korea, and then in more developed Southeast Asian countries such as Malaysia and Thailand. There they turned out basic electronic goods like radios, tape recorders, and TVs.

In postwar Japan, early generations of industrial workers were drawn mostly from rural areas, and Japanese industrialists such as Eiji Toyoda of Toyota had to adapt their methods to allow for the limited skills of a peasant workforce in much the same way that Henry Ford had done with immigrant laborers in Detroit. These postwar lessons were applied throughout East Asia. Work on the Asian assembly lines was reduced to its simplest elements. Time-and-motion studies were rigorously carried out and teams of supervisors closely observed the line. Workers were allowed to suggest ways in which the line might be speeded up, but management always retained full power to decide whether and how these suggestions might be used.

When I stood alongside the Nissan plant's main assembly line in January 1994, what I saw revealed that little had changed in two decades and that Japanese corporations such as Nissan were uncertain bearers of a revolution in manufacturing. For there before me was a cleaner and no doubt less noisy version of the scene that Horace Arnold had described eighty years before at Ford's Highland Park plant. Hordes of young workers swarmed over scores of cars as they moved slowly along the assembly line. Workers performed the same simple tasks over and over again, and there was a palpable sense of stress as workers struggled to get their tasks done within the amount of time it took for the vehicle to pass through their segment of the line.

As I toured the line I noticed piles of blue, plastic-lined books scattered in the workers' rest areas. Each worker had his or her own blue book, and these provided a detailed description of his or her job. The books' contents revolved around a concept known in Japanese industrial parlance as "tac." Tac comprises the exact amount of time allowed for every job in the factory. Tac for my conducted tour of the the plant was ninety minutes. Tac for each assembly line job at Nissan in January 1994 was one minute and ten seconds. Each seventy-second job was further divided into three or four sub-jobs, precisely timed to last twenty-three or seventeen seconds each. As at Ford's Highland Park plant, the assembly line worker's job consisted of such tasks as tightening screws, fixing wires, putting in seats, and adjusting windshields.

In their descriptions of these jobs, the blue books followed the example set by Taylor with the shovelers and loaders of the Bethlehem backyards. In the minutest detail, the blue books specified the exact movements to be followed in performing these tasks and sub-tasks, each movement timed to the nearest fraction of a second. Here is a description of a sub-job, drawn from Workshop Management, a compendium of Nissan work practices: "unit of factor action: extend the right hand, pick up screw, insert through seal: take a screw in right hand, insert screw through the seal."[7] Each blue book also contained a chart that recorded the worker's progress toward doing his job in the alloted time and at an acceptable level of quality.

An "I" on the worker's chart meant that he or she still had to refer to a written worksheet while doing the job, and an "L" meant that the worker had dispensed with the sheet, but could not yet do the job within the alloted tac. A "U" on the worker's chart meant that he was "up to speed" and meeting his tac, but that the quality of his work was still deficient. A square on the chart meant that speed and quality of work were both acceptable, and finally—the ultimate accolade—a square with a dot in the middle meant that the worker himself had suggested ways of doing his job in still less time. In the blue books I examined, most workers had managed to learn two seventy-second jobs up to "square" standard.

A few workers had learned three or four such routines, and these had usually become, or were in line to become, "team leaders." At Nissan the phrase "multiskilled" was often used to describe workers with two or more squares to their name. But this was misleading. Although Nissan managers were reluctant to admit it, throughout the plant there was a clear distinction between workers who were genuinely skilled and those who were not. The former are known in the United States as "skilled trades," and they are exactly the kinds of skilled, craft workers Taylor came up against at the turn of the century: pipe fitters, electricians, tool and die makers, skilled machinists, and machine repairmen. To do their jobs they had to have served multiyear, German-style apprenticeships or acquired an equivalent qualification in a technical school. At the time I visited the Nissan plant, "skilled trades" made up 9 percent of the work-force—less than their strength at Highland Park in 1914.

All the Japanese automakers, including Nissan, had, and still have, a policy of trying to shrink the "skilled trades" workforce over time. This they do by outsourcing to nonunion shops as much "skilled trades" work as they can, and also by relying on the outside manufacturer to undertake major machine maintenance and repair. For the great majority of unskilled or semiskilled workers in the Nissan plant's machine shops, on its assembly lines, and in its body and paint shops, there was a dwindling number of better paying, skilled trades jobs to which they could aspire. By adding to their personal inventory of seventy-second routines—by becoming "multiskilled" in the company sense—these workers were getting no nearer to the acquisition of real skills. Indeed, what they were doing fell comfortably within Taylor's definition of the "higher class of work" that, with scientific management, the unskilled or semiskilled worker could perform: "A man with only the intelligence of an average laborer can be taught to do the most difficult and delicate work if it is repeated enough times."[8]

The organization of work along the Nissan assembly line is a striking example of how the methods of scientific management can thrive in a contemporary setting. But the modern consumer's demands for product variety and choice have also obliged Nissan to add to its inheritance from the past—just as Sloan and Knudsen had done at Chevrolet in the 1920s. On the Nissan assembly line there was a small object that symbolized this latest coming together of "flexibility" and mass production. Attached to the front bumper of each car body as it reached the head of the assembly line was a small, plastic box shaped like a playing card. The box contained an electronic device that communicated with a nearby computer. On receiving the box's message, the computer printed out a legal-sized document that was then attached to the car's body.

The document told the assemblers which among a variety of seats, dashboards, radios, carpets, or door handles was to be fitted to that particular car. The plant's system of supply ensured that the right variety of components reached the right point on the assembly line at exactly the right time. Nissan's design engineers explained to me that this "mass customization" of their automobiles was always governed by the principle of "manufacturability." Manufacturability meant that every variety of seat, dashboard, door handle, or radio had to be designed in such a way as to minimize any variation in the assembler's routine as he or she installed that particular component.

I asked personnel managers at Nissan, and later also at Honda's European plant, what importance they attached to the education and vocational qualifications of their prospective shop floor employees, and whether the introduction of this mass customization had led them to give more importance to such qualifications. Their answer was that, with or without mass customization, "very little importance" was attached to such qualifications outside the skilled trades. What they were looking for in most applicants, the managers explained, were dexterity, enthusiasm, stamina, and an ability to "fit into the team." Thus in one of Honda's job tests candidates were shown piles of nuts and screws of various sizes. They were then asked to match up the fitting pairs as quickly as they could.

With this "flexible mass production" Nissan was treading a path opened up seventy years before by Sloan and Knudsen at General

Motors. Nissan had "mass customized" its cars so as to accommodate consumer tastes, but it had done this without giving up the workforce of mass production bequeathed by Ford and Taylor. Speed and efficiency on the shop floor were still achieved through the endless repetition of simple tasks, and not through the enhancement of worker training and skills. Whatever the economic value of this increased productivity, success still depended on methods that required workers to be adjuncts of the machine and assembly line. But perhaps the most important contribution of Japanese manufacturers to the theory and practice of scientific management has been to develop what can be called its participatory side. Taylor himself envisaged that workers themselves could suggest ways of adding to the speed and efficiency of their routines, provided that management always had the final say in deciding whether an employee's suggestion was acceptable and exactly how the design and timing of tasks should then be altered. In the *The Principles of Scientific Management* Taylor wrote:

> Every encouragement . . . should be given him [the worker] to suggest improvements, both in methods and in implements. And whenever a workman proposes an improvement, it should be the policy of the management to make a careful analysis of the new method, and if necessary conduct a series of experiments to determine accurately the relative merit of the new suggestion and of the old standards. And whenever the new method is found to be markedly superior to the old, it should be adopted as the standard for the whole establishment. The workman should be given the full credit for the improvement, and should be paid a cash payment as a reward for his ingenuity.[9]

In Taylor's lifetime the fierce resistance of the skilled machinist to scientific management so poisoned Taylor's own view of the workforce that this participatory aspect of his doctrine was largely ignored by Taylor and his disciples. Their view was that improvements to the "one best way" were decided by management and then had to be imposed on a reluctant workforce: Thus Taylor's elaborate bureaucracy of planners and supervisors. It has been left to modern Japanese corporations such as a Toyota and Nissan to develop the participatory side of scientific management. To best understand how participatory Taylorism works at a company like Nissan, one must first describe the corporation's unending campaign to improve productivity by speeding up the pace of operations.

At Nissan the workers' "blue books" laid down, as we have seen, standard operating procedures (SOPs) governing every aspect of their work, along with the mandated tac for the completion of a job. But this working out of SOPs and tacs was only the opening shot in a permanent campaign to shave seconds and fractions of seconds off both and so speed up the line. For assembly line workers, with their tac of seventy seconds, management's goal with this time shaving was always to shave a total of seventy seconds from all the members of the work team, so that an entire job could be eliminated and the redundant worker's tasks distributed among his or her surviving neighbors on the line. In this permanent campaign for speed up the pivotal figure was the supervisor, management's frontline representative on the shop floor.

The supervisor's job combined many of the tasks of Taylor's old functional foreman. Nissan's company handbook, *Workshop Management,* said that the supervisors first task was "to establish the standard approach" for each job on the line. It was also the supervisor's task to "research for a better procedure" so that the worker's routines could be speeded up. This involved keeping the workers in their zone of responsibility under close surveillance, so that "abnormalities" in performance could be identified. Workers who had discovered a faster way of performing a task but had failed to share their discovery with the supervisor or the other members of the "work team" were as guilty of "abnormality" as those whose work was shoddy or slow.[10]

But managers at Nissan were ready with abundant evidence that workers on the line had willingly collaborated with their supervisors in suggesting ways to speed up the pace of production—just as Taylor had envisaged in the *Principles of Scientific Management.* There were sheets of statistics giving the number of suggestions received and their rate of growth over the years, and interviews were easily arranged with leading workers. I have visited a score of Japanese and Japanese-style plants in Europe and North America and this emphasis on the self-improving role of the workforce was a staple of all of them. Stories of self-improvement also feature prominently in the many books and articles published in the United States that commend Japanese production methods and claim that they represent a clean break with the Ford/Taylor tradition.

It was puzzling to me why employees at a place like Nissan should willingly collaborate in speeding up their work routines, particularly since it was and is company policy not to reward workers who come forward with suggestions that are acted upon. It was clear that employees on the line were already working under great pressure. At the time I visited the Nissan plant there was a story going around about a visiting delegation of managers and trade unionists from BMW's Munich base. After being shown the line, the visiting Germans were asked what they thought. After an awkward silence, one of the unionists remarked "Well, some of our people are over fifty." It was indeed hard to see how anyone much over forty, let alone fifty, could long survive the pace at Nissan. So why should Nissan employees be thinking of ways to make the line even faster?

One obvious explanation was that there has been no strong union at Nissan to place checks on management's drive for "speed-up." In auto assembly plants, resistance to speed up has been the a chief task of unions since the 1930s. It was the cause of the UAW's first great strikes against Ford and GM in the 1930s and a leading cause of the UAW's strikes against GM in the winter of 1997–1998. But the "big three" Japanese automakers—Toyota, Honda, and Nissan—have kept the UAW out of their U.S. plants, and Toyota and Honda have kept their British-based European plants union-free. At its Sunderland plant, Nissan deals with a weak union, the Amalgamated Engineering and Electrical Union (AEEU), once Margaret Thatcher's favorite union. Representing about a third of the shop floor workforce, the AEEU at Nissan acts much like a company union that has given management carte blanche to run the plant as it sees fit.

But while the absence of a strong union can explain why the Nissan workers had not put the brakes on management's relentless pursuit of speed up, the absence of such a union could not adequately explain why

employees had been willing collaborators in participatory Taylorism.
Even without strong unions, workers could have met management's demand for suggestions about speed up with silence. Interviews with assembly line workers at Nissan shed some light on this mystery. Two of
the workers I talked to had come up with suggestions that had been accepted and put into effect, a process known in Japanese corporate parlance as *kaizan*. The first worker's job consisted of fastening the front
bumper to the car body. His innovation was to place the tools and fasteners needed for the job on a tray that he then hitched to the assembly line itself. As the car body traveled down the line, the worker's tray
traveled with it so that he did not have walk back and forth to a stationary and increasingly distant tray each time he completed one sub-
job and needed different tools or fasteners for the next.

The second worker used a heavy automatic wrench to fasten part of
the car body to the chassis. His improvement was to rest the wrench on
an elevated metal tripod so that he would not have to bend to pick up
and put down his tool for every sub-job. Surrounded by the toil and
stress of the line, one did not need to ask these two workers why they
had thought of these innovations and why they had reported them to
the supervisor. The innovations made their jobs easier. But this was by
no means the end of the story. Once such suggestions were made
known to the supervisor, they became enmeshed in the machinery of
scientific management, just as Taylor had envisaged: "It should be the
policy of the management to make a careful analysis of the new method,
and if necessary conduct a series of experiments to determine accurately the relative merit of the new suggestion and of the old standard."

This is exactly what happened with all but the most minor of the employees' suggestions once they were made known to the supervisor.
Elaborate time-and-motion studies had been conducted to work out exactly how much time the proposed change of routine could save, with
SOPs and tacs then having to be changed. At Honda's European plant
these investigations could take between four and six months, depending on the magnitude of the proposed change. The greater the change,
the more senior the managers involved in these deliberations. At Honda
a notice posted on the shop floor spelled out the complex protocol of

kaizan. Neither at Honda nor at Nissan could shop floor teams operate as autonomous, empowered teams, free to think up and implement their own improvements.

At Nissan the tiny parcels of time saved through *kaizan* were much prized by management because it was through their steady accumulation that the magic figure of seventy seconds could be reached and one less man employed on the line. Superfluous workers could be assigned to another department or simply laid off. Every three months engineers met to pull together all the savings and "rebalance" the line—either by reducing standard tac for all jobs on the line, or by cramming more sub-jobs into jobs with their existing, seventy-second tac. For the worker, therefore, this participatory Taylorism involves a trade-off between the convenience of doing the job in a simpler, less burdensome way, and the inconvenience with speed up, of also having to do the job just a little bit faster. From the perspective of the assembly line, this saving of effort through *kaizan* can easily loom larger than the price to be paid with the seconds, or fractions of seconds, of speed up. However, over time these seconds and fractions of seconds can pile up.

Nissan is but one Japanese corporation, and its assembly line is but one of several processes used in the manufacture of automobiles. Toyota, however, is perhaps the most successful and innovative automaker in the world. Toyota has also pioneered the transformation of a process that, among all those of automobile production, is usually considered the most demanding of skill. This is the task of adapting the setup of machines for the manufacture of the varied parts and components of "flexible production"—a process that takes place in the machine shop, and so before the components are transported to the line for final assembly. The reconfiguration of machines is perhaps the core activity of manufacturing flexibility, as important to theories of flexibility and skill as the routines of the pin factory once were to Adam Smith's theory of the division of labor.

In the United States, Toyota has a mystique and influence that Nissan, as an imitative number two, has always lacked. Toyota's reputation has also survived Japan's decade-long crisis largely intact. Perhaps the most influential American account of Toyota's production methods is to be found in *The Machine that Changed the World* (1990) by James P. Womack, Daniel T. Jones, and Daniel Roos.[11] The book was based on an exhaustive study of the world automobile industry conducted by the International Motor Vehicle Programme of the Massachusetts Institute of Technology (MIT), a close cousin of MIT's earlier Commission on Industrial Productivity.

The MIT book states that what it calls "the concept of lean production" was pioneered after World War II by "Eiji Toyoda and Taiichi Ohno at the Toyota Motor Company."[12] Throughout their account of lean production, the three MIT authors repeatedly cite Toyota as providing examples of Japanese "best practice." However, along with *The Machine that Changed the World* there is a second book that is of equal importance in understanding the Toyota system and its impact on the world. This book is as obscure as the MIT work is famous. The book's unpromising title is *A Revolution in Manufacturing, the SMED System,* and its author is Shigeo Shingo. SMED stands for Single Minute Exchange of Die.[13]

Whereas the changing of a die on a press or stamping machine, pre-Shingo, had taken hours to perform, it could now be done in minutes. The importance of this SMED is best explained by taking another look at the concept of flexibility itself. In industrial production there is a distinction to be drawn between "hard" and "soft" flexibility. Soft flexibility involves changes to the appearance and styling of a product, such as occurred on the auto assembly line at Nissan, with its variety of dashboards, seats, radios, and carpets. This flexibility can easily be accommodated by a work regime that remains wholly Taylorist in design. Hard flexibility refers to something much more ambitious, the ability to vary not merely the outward appearance but the basic engineering structure of a product, so that a single machine shop or assembly line can turn out, within a single day, more than one model of an automobile, computer, or video recorder.

Though SMED itself refers literally to a single kind of procedure involving a single kind of machine, Shingo's book deals with a huge variety of setup operations involving every conceivable kind of machine. The hard variant of flexibility was therefore widely achieved in the Japanese engineering and electronics industries, and wherever it was practiced, engineers could adapt the output of machine shops and assembly lines to allow for sudden and unexpected fluctuations in demand. In Shingo's words, "We must recognize that flexible production can come about only through SMED."[14] However, Shingo's writings and his life work are notable for another reason. Together they represent perhaps the most important restatement of the principles of scientific management in recent times.

In his curriculum vitae at the end of his book, Shingo refers to the moment in 1931 when he read Taylor's *Principles of Scientific Management* and "decided to make the study and practice of scientific management his life's work."[15] These are mere words, but it becomes clear from the very first page of *A Revolution in Manufacturing* that Shingo, who died in 1990, was indeed a true disciple of Taylor, someone steeped in the world of the Midvale and Bethlehem Steel Companies, the Watertown Arsenal, and the American Society of Mechanical Engineers. But as a scientific manager, Shingo does more than reiterate past doctrines. He adapts and renews them for the age of flexibility.

Shingo felt toward craft workers and their skills much as Taylor had felt toward the skilled machinists at the Midvale Steel Company in the 1880s. Shingo thought that the much-vaunted "intuition" that was so much a part of their skills gave rise to error and inefficiency: "In my frequent visits to factories, I often tell the foremen: since you are so convinced of the value of determining settings by intuition, do it three times on the same machines. If you get the same results each time, then there's no problem. If you get good results only twice, then the method has to be abandoned."[16] A better alternative, Shingo believed, was to find ways of simplifying and standardizing the work so that it could be performed by virtually anybody:

> It is generally and erroneously believed that the most effective policies for dealing with setups address the problems in terms of skill. Although many companies have setup policies designed to raise the skill level of the workers, few have implemented strategies that lower the skill level required by the setup itself.[17]

Indeed, as recently as 1990, Womack, Jones, and Roos, writing in *The Machine that Changed the World*, could claim that SMED needed an "extremely skilled" workforce.[18]

In the full spirit of scientific management, Shingo was confident that higher productivity could be achieved by the simplification and standardization of tasks. As a scientific manager he also believed that the chief responsibility for working out these new, simplified routines lay with managers and engineers, and not with frontline workers. Like Taylor, Shingo is often critical of these workers, whom he sees as the authors and defenders of inefficiency on the shop floor. For example, after discussing a problem involving the transport of dies, Shingo comments, "This example illustrates a tendency of people on the shop floor to be distracted by small efficiencies while overlooking bigger ones. Considered on a deeper level, it shows the need for front line managers to understand internal and external setup thoroughly." And again: "The workers had often made errors of subtraction, and this in turn had necessitated repeated checks of their arithmetic."[19]

As with all systems of scientific management, managers had to conduct "a detailed analysis of each elemental operation" so that the fastest and most efficient way of doing the job could then be worked out. Thenceforth, this "one best way" would be followed by frontline workers. In words that could have been take directly from Taylor's *Principles of Scientific Management,* Shingo explained:

> To implement function standardization, individual functions are analyzed and then considered one by one. That is, general operations are broken down into basic elements, for example, clamping, centering, dimensioning, expelling, grasping and maintaining loads. The engineer must decide which of these operations, if any, need to be standardized.

Once the system was up and running, "quality . . . improves, since operating conditions are fully regulated in advance."[20]

Thus *A Revolution in Manufacturing* contains many examples of those minutely timed and detailed worksheets that are such a feature of Taylor's writings. One particularly revealing sheet describes a die-changing operation to be carried out by two operators working in tandem. The job is timed to last exactly seven minutes and fifty seconds. It is further subdivided into sixteen sub-tasks, each timed to last between fifteen and forty seconds. For the second task, timed to last twenty seconds, the first worker "removes front mounting bolts securing upper die" while the second "removes rear mounting bolts securing upper die."

For the thirteenth task, timed to last fifty seconds, the first worker "tightens front mounting bolts securing upper die," while the second "prepares to tighten rear bolts securing upper die." The worksheet also has a column that specifies exactly when one worker must use a buzzer to signal to the other that he has completed his task. Shingo comments that in the past, managers had complained that a shortage of sufficiently trained manpower had prevented them from conducting such two-man operations. But with his SMED system, this problem was eliminated because "only a few minutes" assistance will be needed, and "even unskilled works can help, since the operations are simple ones."[21]

A Revolution in Manufacturing has many descriptions of arcane setup procedures whose common feature is that they had once been performed by skilled workers but, thanks to Shingo, could now be performed by virtually anybody. Thus, machine setup for making television picture tubes was once highly skilled work requiring "tremendous accuracy and considerable time." With SMED, "the intermediary jig was standardized and positioning was now performed very easily."[22] With the setup of a hobbing machine for gear grinding, the alignment of the jig and the workpiece required "a great deal of skill." But with SMED, "the setup was simplified and alignment made easier."[23] Setup for the machining of camera bodies had previously required a high level of skill because of the very high tolerances involved. Again, Shingo found a way of standardizing the operation so that "even an ordinary machine operator [could] take charge of the set up."[24]

Shingo and his U.S. clients also provide examples of the use of his methods by American companies. The manager of Ford's Cleveland engine plant testifies that "because of Dr. Shingo's direction, we have been able to reduce changeover time from 4 to 5 hours to an average of 2.5 to 4 minutes."[25] A vice president of Omark Industries, an engineering company in Portland, Oregon, wrote to Shingo that "we had always assumed that a set up change had to be performed by a specially skilled worker and that it had to take several hours." The company overcame this "conceptual blind spot" and was able to reduce to one minute and thirty seconds a setup operation that had previously taken two hours.[26] Shingo's dealings with Federal Mogul, a U.S. manufacturer of auto components, reveals the scientific manager's concern with the minutest details. Under Shingo's supervision, Federal Mogul had developed a screw that, used in machine setup, could be fastened or unfastened with a single turn.[27]

In its exhaustive 1993 study *Manufacturing Productivity*, the McKinsey Global Institute gives a contemporary U.S. account of this renewed scientific management, tailored to the needs of McKinsey's U.S. corporate clients struggling to match the superior productivity of their Japanese counterparts.[28] The McKinsey study therefore has a significance that goes beyond the persuasiveness of its recommendations. Whatever their intrinsic worth, these recommendations embody the advice that McKinsey, among the largest and most influential of U.S. consulting groups, has been giving its clients. At one time or another these clients have included virtually the entire Fortune 500, including the "big three" U.S. automakers, General Motors, Ford, and Chrysler (now DaimlerChrysler).

Manufacturing Productivity has separate chapters on the automobile assembly, and the automobile parts and components industries. However, common to both chapters is the assumption that Japanese manufacturers set the standards of high productivity with methods that their U.S. competitors need to emulate. In automobile assembly, McKinsey found that in 1990 Japanese companies had a productivity advantage of 16 percent over the Detroit Big Three, and a lead of 24 percent in components manufacture.[29] McKinsey also singled out Toyota and its production system as the model to be emulated not only by competing automakers but by companies in other industries that it surveys, including steel, machine tools, and consumer electronics:

> All of the characteristics of the Japanese management system described
> above are epitomized by Toyota, which serves as a model of labor pro-
> ductivity both inside and outside Japan for the automotive as well as

other industries. In fact more is to be learned from studying Toyota as a company, than by studying Japan as a country with regard to labor productivity in the automotive assembly industry.[30]

McKinsey's account of the Toyota system is fully consistent with Shingo's account in *A Revolution in Manufacturing* and also with the version of the Toyota system that I saw in operation at Nissan's Sunderland plant. The production system that McKinsey describes and commends in *Manufacturing Productivity* is an advanced system of scientific management, firmly based on Taylor's original theories and practices, as refined by Shigeo Shingo and Taiichi Ohno. McKinsey, however, is not notably sympathetic to the point of view of organized labor, and so issues of speed up do not feature prominently in its account. Neither McKinsey, nor indeed Shingo, offer any support for the claims of Sabel and Piore, and of the MIT and Magaziner Commissions—that flexibility of production requires a workforce with "very high skills," including craft skills.

Indeed, what McKinsey has to say about the modest skill requirements of the Toyota system echoes what I was told by Nissan and Honda managers at their European plants. McKinsey shares the insouciance of these managers about worker skills, viewing lack of skill as a common characteristic of a modern industrial workforce, and one that does not disqualify such a workforce from meeting the requirements of flexible, lean production. In McKinsey's account, it is German industry, with its elaborate hierarchy of craft workers, that is the odd man out.

In its chapters on the automobile assembly and components industries, McKinsey sets out to explain why the productivity of the Toyota system should be so high. It focuses on two factors: "Our causality analysis suggests that differences in design for manufacturing and the organization and function of tasks drive a large proportion of the differences in labor productivity."[31] "Design for manufacturing" and the "organization of functions and tasks" in turn set the standards for shop floor skills. McKinsey's definition of the organization of functions and tasks draws heavily on the language of scientific management:

> It is the accumulation of thousands of small changes, to the point
> where the placement of every small part and every machine and the
> movement of every worker are optimized for productivity. It . . . in-
> cludes the optimization [not only] of time and motion, but also [of]
> the management structure.[32]

The organization of functions and tasks remains "essentially a management decision," but, in the tradition of participatory Taylorism,
workers can suggest ways of improving and speeding up production.
Toyota, for example, "was able to reduce its employment in one paint
shop from eight to three employees over the course of four years simply by following employee suggestions with regard to cutting down
worker walking distances."[33] McKinsey also strongly emphasizes "design for manufacturability" as a way to simplify the tasks of shop floor
workers and so add to their productivity. McKinsey defines design for
manufacturing as "ease of assembly and low complexity": "In designing products, firms in Japan remain very conscious of how such designs
affect the manufacturing functions, and attempt to simplify them so that
they are easy to produce and assemble."[34] Among American-owned assembly plants, McKinsey singles out Ford's Taurus plant in Atlanta as
one that has suceeded through "excellent . . . design for assembly, and
design for manufacturability."[35]

In its analysis of skill, McKinsey draws a distinction between the
basic skills that are the "pre-hiring skills" of prospective employees,
and their "post-training skills" that the employer must develop.[36] Mc-
Kinsey's unequivocal finding is that for auto manufacture, high productivity can be achieved with a workforce armed with the most basic
of basic skills, and this is because post-training worker skills are so undemanding. McKinsey's post-training skills are the very same skills that
I was told about at Nissan and Honda. According to McKinsey, Japanese companies screen applicants to find those with "attitudinal factors
that make [them] more flexible, less likely to call in sick, and committed to remaining on the job for a long period of time."[37]

McKinsey does not include "craft-based individual excellence"
among these skills. Indeed, McKinsey regards the craft tradition of German industry as an obstacle to the achievement of high productivity, re-

porting "In Germany the focus on specialization has led to excessively high complexity in the production process."[38] McKinsey then goes on to question whether the attitudinal factors that it so commends should be described as skills at all: "Others often define these attributes as skills. . . . In our study employee screening and motivation are captured under the 'organization of functions and tasks.' "[39] But as we have seen, McKinsey's concept of the organization of functions and tasks leans heavily on the theory and practice of scientific management, in which functions and tasks are simplified, standardized, and repeated, so that workers with few skills can easily learn them.

It is because these post-training workers' skills are so undemanding that the basic, pre-hiring skills that employers are looking for among prospective employees are equally undemanding, and are therefore easy to come by. Though McKinsey does not say so, these are presumably the skills of basic literacy and numeracy that, in the words of the Magaziner Committee, enable an employee to "read a production schedule or follow an instruction card."[40] McKinsey found that in the United States, Japan, and Germany, companies did not have any problem finding recruits with these basic skills. McKinsey concludes therefore that "basic labor skills are not an important causal factor for explaining productivity differences" in any of the nine industry case studies it carried out. The "important causal factor" was whether companies were able to take those with these basic, pre-hiring skills and then add the modest skills—the skills of scientific management—needed for the organization of functions and tasks.[41]

The Japanese have taken a long-established *American* system of production that had been showing its age and have given it a new lease on life. This has been a restoration, not a revolution, and one that has enabled American manufacturers to improve their performance while holding onto a workplace regime that has existed for most of the twentieth century. These Japanese methods have unquestionably improved the output per worker, or labor productivity, of both Japanese and American manufacturing corporations. But as I argued in chapter 1, there is a social and ethical dimension to issues of productivity, technology, and work that must not be overlooked. The new Taylorism developed by the Japanese, like the old, undervalues employee skill and experience, surrounds employees with a pervasive regime of monitoring and control, and encourages an all-powerful management to treat its workforce as a commodity.

These enduring characteristics of scientific management diminish the quality of working life, and historically it has been the role of labor unions to shield the industrial workforce from the more egregious aspects of the system, notably its unending quest for speed up. But the renaissance of scientific management at the hands of the Japanese has come at a time when American labor has been in severe decline. In 2001, 14.6 percent of the manufacturing workforce in the United States belonged to labor unions, compared with 27.8 percent in 1983—a near halving in eighteen years.[42] The "big three" Japanese automakers, Toyota, Nissan, and Honda, have all fought hard and successfully to keep the UAW out of their U.S. plants.[43] In their invaluable research, Mike Parker and Jane Slaughter have shown that the kind of harsh work regime that I saw at Nissan's Sunderland plant is to be found throughout Japan's union-free "transplants" in the United States.[44] The extension of such methods to U.S.-owned businesses is therefore the very reverse of the benign revolution heralded by admirers such as the MIT and Magaziner Commissions.

Where the rhetoric of revolution can be better employed is with the transfer of this renewed scientific management from U.S. manufacturing to the U.S. service economy, which took place with the IT investment surge of the 1990s. This was partly a matter of historical accident. The revival of the mass production model by the Japanese took place on the very eve of the IT explosion in the United States, so that, chronologically, the new Taylorism was ideally positioned to influence how IT would be used in the U.S. service economy. But there was also an operational affinity between the Japanese approach to scientific management and the qualities that computers and their attendant software could, in the hands of the reengineers, bring to the control of business processes in the service industries. In the timing and monitoring of industrial processes, the Japanese pushed the disciplines of scientific management to new highs (or lows).

With the surge of IT investment in the 1990s, reengineers could now try to apply this rigorous discipline to the more elusive processes of the service industries. But whereas in manufacturing the frontline worker on the shop floor had been the prime target of the new Taylorism, in service industries, reengineers have extended the reach of the practice upward to middle management and beyond, as we shall now see.

4

THE RISE OF THE REENGINEERS

WHILE THE NAME FREDERICK WINSLOW TAYLOR still holds its prominent, if ambivalent position in any hall of fame of American business, it is safe to say that the name William Henry Leffingwell (1876–1934) is almost totally forgotten. Yet it was Leffingwell who took the lead in working out how the principles of scientific management might be applied to the activities of service industries—to the routines of banks, accounting firms, insurance companies, and mail-order houses. In the years following World War I, it was books such as Leffingwell's *Office Management: Principles and Practice, Textbook of Office Management,* and *Better Office Management* that described in immense detail how the practices pioneered by Taylor and Ford could be used to improve the productivity of American clerks, messengers, and typists.

As a management theorist, Leffingwell always saw himself as a disciple of Taylor, and this modesty may help account for his present obscurity. His most influential work, *Office Management: Principles and Practice,* published in 1925 ten years after Taylor's death, is dedicated to the Taylor Society in appreciation of its "inspirational and educational influence." Leffingwell presented a copy of his book to Carl Barth, then one of Taylor's closest surviving collaborators and the coinventor of Taylor's machining software: "It is with deep appreciation of the honour of knowing one of management's greatest minds that I sit at your feet and sign my name."[1] Leffingwell's books contained frequent references to Taylor and his works, so that the reader could be assured that the disciple was never straying too far from the precepts of the master. Leffingwell acknowledges his debt to Taylor in the opening paragraph of *Office Management:*

> Many businessmen, after analyzing the remarkable results secured by applying Frederick W. Taylor's system of scientific management in factories, have asked whether or not similar betterments could not be obtained in offices with the system. Their question can now be answered, for the main principles of the Taylor system have actually been adapted and applied to office work.[2]

Despite this modesty, Leffingwell's texts are worth close scrutiny. They reveal what the service sector looks like after being subjected to the disciplines of scientific management. In these books, the language of Taylor, purged of the grease and noise of the factory, is applied to the cleaner, more genteel world of the office. But despite these changed surroundings, Leffingwell never loses the perspective of the industrial engineer. His ambition is always to have an office run as much like a factory as possible.

Leffingwell benefited from the gap of a generation that separated him from Taylor. At the turn of the century, Taylor had struggled to apply the methods of scientific management to a metal-working industries still strongly influenced by the craft tradition. Leffingwell's heyday came twenty years later, in the eleven-year period separating the end of the World War I in 1918 from the Wall Street crash in October 1929. During those years, the craftsman, along with the small and medium-sized plants in which he worked, was in full retreat before the advance of the giant, mass production plant, eptiomized by Ford's Detroit factories at Highland Park and River Rouge. In 1925 Leffingwell wrote of the Ford factories as models for scientific managers in the service as well as engineering industries:

> The progressive assembly plan, worked so effectively in the Ford automobile factories, where the component parts of a machine start from so many sources and pass from one operation to another, gradually

seeming to assemble, until finally a completed car rolls out of the factory on its own power, is a great modern principle of production, which applies with equal force to the production of office work.[3]

Just as Taylor's experiments and theories had been focused upon the routines of the Pennsylvania machine shops, so Leffingwell's were concentrated on the workings of mail-order driven business. Leffingwell's case histories therefore tell of companies such as Montgomery Ward and Curtis Publishing. The thousands of orders received each day by the mail-order houses triggered a business process that had to end in the dispatch of goods to the customer. This process presented problems of coordination and control that the methods of scientific management were well suited to resolve.

For Leffingwell, as for Taylor, the goal of scientific management was to set up routines that, once learned and remembered, could govern every aspect of office life. At the Curtis Publishing Company, Leffingwell boasted of having standardized "more than five hundred operations" and of having "accomplished results that were remarkable."[4] As with Taylor, Leffingwell's routines ranged from the exceedingly trivial—how best to open an envelope, to the lengthy and complex—how best to fulfill a customer's order. Yet all of Leffingwell's lesser routines had their places in a hierarchy of routines that, for a mail-order house, together made up the "business process" of order fulfillment. Thus, opening the envelope was part of the task of receiving an order. While receiving an order, along with operations such as credit checking and dispatch, was part of the overall process of order fulfillment.

At the very bottom of Leffingwell's hierarchy of office processes were the minute-by-minute routines by which the mail-order clerks performed their daily tasks. Here Leffingwell's obsessive attention to detail fully matches Taylor's second-by-second analysis of the shoveling of sand and clay in the backyards of the Bethlehem Steel Company. Thus in an office of scientific management there was no place for the blotter and "the thousands of useless motions" it caused. The use of blotters could be eliminated with a "fine pen" and "good, hard quality paper."[5] Leffingwell also commended a manager who had "made a time study of the evaporation of inks," so as to ascertain whether it would pay to buy non-evaporating ink wells.

With one dram of ordinary black ink evaporating every forty-eight hours, tests showed that inkwells of the non-evaporating variety would save $1 per inkwell per year.[6] Leffingwell also advised against too vehement use of the rubber stamp: "A clerk using a rubber stamp may use so much force that the stamp makes only a blurred impression." Less force meant less fatigue and better work, and also increased the life of the stamp.[7] The "rubbing or pounding" of a letter after its sealing should be treated in exactly the same way. In the opening of mail, a core micro-process of the mail-order business, Leffingwell reduced the necessary motions from thirteen to six and increased the output of mail opening from 100 to 200 items an hour. Further refinements in the methods pushed the rate up to 250 an hour, then to 300 an hour.[8]

There was, however, an interesting and important way in which the processes of Leffingwell's mail-order houses differed from those of Taylor's machine shops. Leffingwell's processes had to adapt themselves to the vagaries of the customer in a way that Taylor's did not. The customer orders that poured into the mail-order house each day could not be anticipated and classified with the same precision as the metal components that populated Taylor's machine shops. "In this work," Leffingwell wrote, "it is of course impossible to tell in advance just how long the letters are going to be, what sort of letters they will be, whether the writing will be plain or indecipherable, and whether each letter can be disposed of summarily or will require additional labor." Cash on delivery remittances that required practically no clerical work were mixed in with remittance letters that did. All of this "caused a great deal of confusion," and to find the proper time for each process seemed for the scientific manager almost impossible.[9]

Leffingwell solved this problem of the diversity of work by applying what he called the "exception principle," the process of weeding out "difficult" cases and sending them to an expert or team of experts whose sole job was to deal with exceptional cases. Leffingwell had used the exception principle to cut down the credit checking step in his revamping of an unnamed mail-order houses's order fulfillment process.

The majority of customers who were within 75 percent of their credit limit could have their credit worthiness passed by an "ordinary clerk." But the minority of customers who had used up over 75 percent of their credit limit, or had exceeded their limit, had their cases flagged to be handled by an expert, the "credit man." In *Office Management* Leffingwell remarked that this was but one application of a principle that could be used to management's advantage in many other ways.[10]

But one aspect of the exception principle was that employees were sometimes required to make decisions about what should be done with particular orders. Were they difficult and therefore to be handled by an expert such as the credit man, or were they routine and therefore to be handled by an ordinary clerk? "Decision being the most important factor in this work," Leffingwell wrote, "the girls were told to practice making quick decisions."[11] However, any mention of decision making by workers, however trivial the decisions to be made, was for Leffingwell a sensitive matter, since for him, as for all scientific managers, it was axiomatic that decisions should, wherever possible, be made by managers, and not by workers: "If the work is merely turned over to a clerk and he is told to go ahead and do the work, the result is almost certain to be a failure"; and again, "In some poorly organized offices the person who determines the time of doing [the work] is not the manager but the worker."[12]

In his discussion of the exception principle, therefore, Leffingwell was at pains to assure his clients that the decision making left to the worker could be so narrowed and simplified that it would not disturb the even flow of production along the clerical assembly line, nor would such decision making require any elaborate training of the worker. The clerk's decisions would "always be upon principles determined by management" and would "not demand profound original thought on the part of the worker."[13] Training for the work was brief but intensive: "Every motion is taught precisely, and the teacher is constantly at the side of the worker during the entire period of training." Although it might seem to the "casual observer that this method is expensive," it was in fact the cheapest possible method because "a worker becomes

highly productive in a very short time," by which Leffingwell meant between two and three weeks.[14]

Sometimes it was necessary to supplement this on-the-job training
with elementary education so that employees would have the proper literacy and numeracy to read and understand worksheets or customers'
orders. In 1917 Leffingwell noted that a large number of corporations
had already included such elementary education in their training
schools.[15] Leffingwell, like Taylor, had no use for the apprentice system,
whereby a young worker was employed by a business and spent up to
three years learning a substantive, craft skill. Under what Leffingwell
calls an "old-fashioned system," the apprentice "would work at low
wages, and then [be] allowed to dabble a little at a time in some of the
higher-priced [i.e., skilled] work." Leffingwell noted with disapproval
that, with this old way, it "often took years for an employee to become
worthwhile."[16]

For Leffingwell, as for Taylor, the efficient working of a business required an almost exclusive concentration of power in the hands of management. In the Leffingwellian office, management was personified by
the office manager, supported by his planning staff. "The office manager," wrote Leffingwell, "through his control or planning room will
actually control the production of the entire clerical staff."[17] It was for
the office manager and his staff to work out the precise routines, large
and small, that the clerical workforce had to follow throughout its
working day, including the exact amount of time each routine should
take.

The office manager and his staff were responsible for training each
worker so that he or she could do the work in the allotted time. It was
also for the office manager to assign the work and, assisted by his foremen, closely monitor the performance of the workforce so that it
achieved its planned output. Finally, it was the responsibility of the office manager to find ways of making the routines more efficient, of
speeding them up. The reverse side of managerial hegemony was employee subordination. For Leffingwell, as for Taylor, the cause of efficiency was best served when the scope for independent decision making

by employees was reduced to a minimum. In his *Textbook of Office Management,* Leffingwell writes that this "human element" was "notoriously variable and unreliable," when the human element in question was that of workers, not managers. Wherever possible this element should be "eliminated, or if not, minimized to the smallest possible degree."[18]

Leffingwell's reputation may have faded, but Leffingwell's project of applying the methods of scientific management to the service industries endured. By mid-century, numerous periodicals were devoted to the subject, among them *The Office, Office Management, Office Control and Management, Paperwork Simplification, Office Economist,* and *Office Equipment Digest.* Founded in 1951, The Methods, Timing, Measurement Association (MTM) carried on Leffingwell's work of applying time-and-motion studies to clerical work, "recognizing, classifying, and describing the motions used or required to perform a given operation and assigning pre-determined time standards to these motions."[19] In the late 1950s, handbooks of scientific management such as *The Manual of Standard Time Data for the Office* relied on movie cameras to refine Leffingwell's methods: "With slow-motion films . . . each motion [the clerk] goes through is filmed and then analyzed and timed against . . . an electric clock constantly within camera view."[20]

With the continued industrialization of white-collar work also came speed up and its discontents. In 1960 the International Labor Organization, a United Nations agency, reported that "clerical workers often complained of muscular fatigue, backache and other such ills as a result of the unaccustomed strain of operating machines."[21] But a more basic problem with white-collar Taylorism was that much white-collar work resisted the rigorous standardization and measurement of scientific management. Despite Leffingwell's assurance to his clients that a clerk's decisions would "always be upon principles determined by managers" and "would not demand profound original thought on the part of the worker," at mid-century and beyond, Leffingwell's successors were finding that many varieties of white-collar work were not easily subject to measurement, standardization, and control.

In 1970, for example, *Business Week,* reporting on research being done at the MTM Association, found that "those who seek a time fix on the work of, say, a loan processor will for some time to come have to accept far less precision than for a keypuncher." Work measurement was "tough" even in the case of lower-level workers such as "statistical clerks, mail girls and expeditors."[22] In 1972 GE published its own *Program for Clerical Cost Control* with "motion time studies" (MTS) tables enclosed, but it acknowledged that jobs such as receptionist and confidential secretary did not lend themselves to control.[23] Clearly, it was difficult to assign standard times to tasks that varied according to their content and according to the skills of those who performed them.

Another major problem for scientific managers was that the technologies of the office did not provide managers with immediate, up-to-date information about the performance of employees. Here the clerical assembly lines lacked one of the essential characteristics of the real thing. In Ford's factories, the primary source of real-time information about employee performance was the moving line itself. Supervisors could know when production was behind schedule, and who was responsible, just by looking at the line. But in the office there was no moving line, and office technologies such as the typewriter and the telephone were no substitute for one. Typewriters could record a typist's strokes per minute, but that information then had to be collected and analyzed. Similarly, supervisors could record their employees' telephone conversations, but calculating the average length of calls was laborious and time consuming.

The trade press carried stories about the limitations of scientific management in the office. In 1969 *The Office* told of a New Jersey company that, despite its use of "work management controls," had found that "at least 17 percent of the time employees were literally doing nothing except walking around and talking."[24] The rather mixed record of white-collar Taylorism helps explain why the reengineering movement of the 1990s took its cue less from Leffingwell's American heirs and more from the Japanese automakers, with their success in renewing scientific management's industrial model. But with the coming of the networked computer and its workflow software, Leffingwell's vision of a white-collar assembly line subject to the rigorous control of the factory floor was now within reach.

The modest word "process" is central to Leffingwell's career as a scientific manager, and the word is also omnipresent in today's business economy, revealing a continuity of business practice. The words "scientific management" themselves rarely appear in the business press or in the writings of management consultants. Today, no self-respecting consultant wants to be identified with a century-old practice widely thought to be primitive and archaic. The word "reengineering" has become a synonym for the practice of scientific management in the contemporary service economy. We have already come across the advanced reengineering of ERP, but reengineering's roots in scientific management are most clearly on display in the first-generation reengineering that emerged in the early 1990s. Like Leffingwell, reengineers seize upon business processes, simplify them, and speed them up.

In Leffingwell's mail-order world, the dominant business process was, as we have seen, order fulfillment, the sequence of tasks that had to be performed for a written order to become goods dispatched to the customer. Order fulfillment also features prominently in the texts of today's leading reengineers, among them Michael Hammer and James Champy, authors of the best-selling book *Reengineering the Corporation* (1993), and Thomas H. Davenport, whose first textbook on reengineering, *Process Innovation: Reengineering Work though Information Technology*, was published in 1993.[25] There is a remarkable resemblance between Leffingwell's 1917 description of order fulfillment and Hammer and Champy's 1993 description of the process. First Leffingwell's 1917 account, somewhat abbreviated:

> Orders segregated from mail and stamped. Orders returned and divided by bookkeepers. Orders sent to treasurer for examination. Credit department passes credit. Copy of order sent to stock room to be filled. Order form returned from stock room after being filled, and priced. . . . Invoice made, checked and mailed. Order charged. Item posted.[26]

Hammer and Champy's 1993 account is remarkably similar, though nowhere do they cite Leffingwell:

> Someone in customer service receives the order, logs it in, and checks it for completeness and accuracy. Then the order goes to finance, where someone else runs a credit check on the customer. Next, someone in sales operations determines the price to charge. Then the order travels to inventory control, where someone checks to see if the goods are on hand. . . . Eventually warehouse operations develops a shipment schedule.[27]

Hammer and Champy and Leffingwell are describing unreformed, unreconstructed business processes. The steps that the scientific manager of eighty years ago and the reengineers of today recommend to rationalize and speed up their delinquent processes are also remarkably similar. At the very outset, both emphasize the importance of mapping the process that a business is actually following, how, for example, a business really goes about fulfilling its customer orders. There then follows the critical task of working out which steps can be shortened, amalgamated, speeded up, or eliminated altogether.

Both scientific managers and reengineers are also much concerned with the amount of time wasted by moving paperwork between different departments of a business, or between employees working within a business department. Both recommend the setting up of "cross-functional teams" as a way of cutting down this time, with groups of workers made up of different specialists. Both recommend the use of the exception principle to weed out difficult tasks that might hold up the worker and interrupt the flow of production, whether in factories or offices. Both also look to engineering or mechanical devices to speed up processes: the scientific manager to "conveyor belts, elevators, telephones, buzzers and horns," the reengineer to computers and their software.[28]

But while both the reengineered and the Leffingwellian offices trace their descent from the mass production plant, it is the modern-day reengineer who has come much closer to reproducing in an office setting the rigor and disciplines of scientific management. The reengineer owes this to information technology's prodigious powers of measurement, monitoring, and control, unavailable not only to Leffingwell but to all office managers of the pre-digital age. In the Leffingwellian and pre-digital office, for example, most monitoring had, of necessity, to be after the fact. At various times during the workday the office manager and his subordinates would examine the blizzard of work tickets and worksheets generated by the clerical assembly lines. In the Leffing-wellian office, "real-time" monitoring was for the most part confined to the foreman's patrolling the line and peering over the shoulders of the laboring clerks.

But with modern-day reengineering, the balance between this "real-time" and "after the fact" monitoring shifts dramatically, and the scope for real-time surveillance takes off in a way that the pre-digital office manager could only have dreamt of. Here the computer rivals the in-dustrial assembly line itself as an agent of surveillance and control. Man-agers can peer into subordinates computers with their own, time an employee's work to the nearest second, record and time workers' tele-phone calls, mark to the nearest second their every movement—to the toilet, the water fountain, or the lunch room. Graphs, statistical tables, pie charts—the latter illuminated with colored segments of green, yel-low, and red—all can analyze from every conceivable angle the per-formance of an employee or group of employees over a period of hours, days, weeks, or years, with up-to-the-minute analysis.

Thomas Davenport has provided a conceptual framework that well illustrates the scale and importance of present-day reengineering.[29] The subject matter of reengineering remains the business process, and Dav-enport draws a distinction between what he calls operational and man-agerial processes. Operational processes involve the "day to day carrying out of the organization's basic business purposes" and are the kind of routine activities that feature prominently in Hammer and Champy's reengineering case studies—order fulfillment, customer services, sales, and marketing. "Managerial processes" are those that "control, plan, or provide resources for operational processes," a definition that allows Davenport to include as managerial processes virtually everything man-agement does: strategy formulation, planning and budgeting, per-formance measurement and reporting, resource allocation, and human resource management.[30] The distinction between operational and managerial processes also largely demarcates the neighboring territories of basic reengineering, to be discussed here, and the more ambitious reengineering of ERP, to be discussed in chapter 9.

The use of information technology as a reengineering tool has three chief aspects. The first is the impact of information technology on the substantive tasks that make up the process to be reengineered: Does information technology require higher, "new workplace" skills from those performing these tasks, or does technology wholly or partially perform skilled tasks itself and leave employees with a residue of lesser skills? The second aspect is the impact of information technology on the structure of work: how tasks are divided between employees, and the degree to which tasks can be measured and timed. The third aspect is the impact of information technology on the control and monitoring of work by management: Does the manager-as-supervisor really disappear, as some "new workplace" advocates have claimed, or does IT simply replace the managerial eye with the electronic eye?

Reengineering has a long enough track record that we can look at these issues in the context of case histories. The reengineering of IBM's Credit Corporation in 1991 and 1992 features prominently in Hammer and Champy's *Reengineering the Corporation*.[31] With its headquarters at Stamford, Connecticut, the IBM Credit Corporation, a subsidiary of IBM, provides credit for clients who want to purchase IBM products. In the pre-reengineering era, specialists were responsible for each stage of the business. Specialists in one department logged in credit applications, those in another entered data specifying special conditions for particular clients. Another department fixed the appropriate rate of interest. Yet another gathered all the relevant information into a "quote letter" to be sent to the IBM salesman and his customer.

Reengineering teams descended on these specialized departments and swept them away. Aside from a few exceptional cases, which were still handled by a team of specialists, the functions once divided among the various departments now became the responsibility of a single employee, called the "deal structurer." He or she now handled the entire credit-granting process, from the moment that IBM received the customer's credit application to the moment that the company's "quote letter" was sent off by Federal Express. One does not have to look beyond Hammer and Champy's own texts to realize that the "deal structurer" is very far from inhabiting a "new workplace" world of autonomy, empowerment, and skill.

Writing of a "case manager" for an insurance company, someone whose reengineered job is comparable to the job of the IBM deal structurer, Hammer himself explains how it is that case managers and deal structurers can suddenly start performing whole sequences of tasks hitherto performed by entire departments of specialists: "Case managers are able to perform all the tasks associated with an insurance application because they are supported by powerful PC-based workstations that run an expert system and connect to a range of automated systems on a mainframe."[32] Expert systems are software programs that can automate much clerical decision making. In tough cases that might be beyond the capabilities of the expert system, the case manager calls for assistance from a senior underwriter or physician (one of Hammer's many uses of Leffingwell's "exception principle").

In *Reengineering the Corporation* Hammer and Champy themselves admit that the purpose of expert systems is to enable the less skilled to perform work that hitherto had been performed by the skilled: "The real value of expert systems technology lies in its allowing relatively unskilled people to operate at nearly the level of highly trained experts."[33] Davenport sheds further light on expert systems, citing the example of American Express, which set out to improve the cost, time, and quality of its credit authorization process. It did so by embedding the knowledge of its best authorizers in an "Authorizer's Assistant," an expert system. This redesign led to a "$7 million annual reduction in costs due to credit losses" and a 25 percent reduction in the average time for each authorization.[34]

The power of expert systems to absorb skills hitherto exercised by specialists defines the work of Hammer and Champy's deal structurers and case managers. The expert system authorizes or denies credit, comes up with the prices or rates of interest to be charged, and makes allowances for the client's "special circumstances." The deal structurer and the case manager are essentially competent computer operators who feed the right information into the machine, follow the machine's recommendations, and make sure that difficult cases that the machine might not be able to handle are forwarded to a team of human experts. All this is summed up by Hammer and Champy's statement that expert systems allow the unskilled to operate at the level of the expert. But this finding is not easily reconciled with their claim that employees such as the deal structurer "do richer and more demanding work" than their specialist predecessors.[35]

The second role of information technology as a reengineering tool is to change the structure of work. The tasks that make up a process are no longer broken down into a sequence of separate steps to be parceled out among workers, with each worker assigned his or her particular task. This classic division of labor, expounded by Adam Smith and practiced by Taylor, Ford, and Leffingwell, is, it is claimed, superceded. With information technology, the tasks of a process can be brought together and performed in their entirety by a single worker—for example, IBM's deal structurer. It is this "compression of tasks" that Davenport proclaims to be a "radical departure from the way we have organized work since the industrial revolution."[36]

These claims rest on shaky foundations. The tasks performed by the reengineered deal structurer cannot be compared with the tasks performed by their specialist predecessors, and it is therefore misleading for the reengineers to lump the two activities together under the same heading. Deprived of most elements of research, calculation, and judgment, the activities of the deal structurer/computer operator can best be described as "operations," comparable to the activities of machine tool operators working at computer-controlled machines. Without this substitution of "operations" for "tasks," the concentration of activity in the person of the deal structurer could not take place. Hammer and Champy's substitution of "relatively unskilled people" for the specialist could not take place either.

Once the deal structurer's operations have been separated from the specialist's tasks, it is not at all difficult to locate the former's job firmly within the traditions and practices of scientific management. In their characterization of Taylor's legacy, the reengineers often seem fixated upon the extreme atomization of work that was practiced in Ford's early machine shops, in which the job of the machine operator could often be measured in seconds. But they overlook Taylor's important dictum that "a man with only the intelligence of an average laborer can be taught to do this most difficult and delicate work if it is repeated enough times."[37]

With images on a computer screen replacing documents as the raw material of "process," workflow software, in Davenport's words, "defines the paths images follow through a process."[38] So just as the sequence and content of Taylor's machining operations could be varied according to the component to be machined, so workflow software can vary the sequence of operations that the deal structurer must perform according to the urgency or importance of the case or order to be processed. By 1900 Taylor's machining software, the Taylor-Barth slide rule, could be used to automate the substantive machining judgments involved in each machining operation. With reengineering, expert systems are available to automate the calculations and judgments formerly performed by specialists.

The third aspect of information technology as a reengineering tool is its impact on the relations between managers and employees. Hammer and Champy draw upon the rhetoric of the "new workplace" to describe this relationship: With reengineering, managers "stop acting like supervisors and become more like coaches." Similarly, Thomas Davenport writes of a "culture of facilitative management," in which "trust is extended whether or not direct management control is now exercised."[39] The layoffs of the early and mid-1990s were particularly hard on middle managers, and Hammer and Champy cite this downsizing as evidence of management's diminished role. But such evidence can bear more than one interpretation. The bloodletting can be taken as evidence of management's withering away, as the reengineers claim. But the culling of the cubicles can also signify that tasks of monitoring and control have been subject to partial automation, so that fewer managerial bodies are needed around the office.

In her *In the Age of the Smart Machine,* Shoshana Zuboff draws a distinction between the power of information technology to "automate" and its power to "informate." Automation "replaces the human body with a technology that enables the smart processes to be performed with more continuity and control"—as in John Hall's and Henry Ford's machine shops. But contemporary information technology "simultaneously generates information about the underlying productive and administrative process." It provides "a deeper level of transparency to activities that had been either partially or completely opaque." Zuboff coins the word "informate" to describe this "unique capacity" of IT to provide information about the tasks in which IT itself is engaged.[40]

Thus, workflow software can not only prescribe that tasks or operations be performed in a certain sequence, but also record whether the prescribed sequence is in fact followed. Expert systems not only come up with a price or rate of interest to offer, they also record how long it takes for an operator to carry out the pricing or credit-rating operations. If a task involves the use of the telephone as well as the computer, software can monitor the call according to the importance of the customer or the value of his order. Software can coordinate the monitoring of what the employee is saying on the telephone and the monitoring of what the employee is doing on his computer screen. Software can also record the times when employees are away from the telephone or computer.

Writing in the mid- and late 1980s, Zuboff leaves open the question of how this power of technology to "informate" might be used: whether it would be used by management to strengthen its supervision and control, or whether, as the reengineers argue, this power would be made available to employees, so that they could analyze and improve their own performance.[41] In the next chapter, we will address this issue by looking in detail at one of the fastest-growing of the lower, operational processes: the "customer-facing" side of business, the direct dealings a business has with its customers via telephone, fax, E-mail, and the Internet. But one does not have to look beyond the writings of the reengineers themselves to find strong evidence of management's determination to claim the "informating power" of technology for itself.

In *Reengineering Management,* James Champy writes of AT&T's Universal Card Services, where "the entire company is evaluated daily on over 100 different indicators." These range from "questions such as whether there has been any downtime on the computer to questions about the professionalism and courtesy of the customer-service people on the phone." The performance bar on each indicator is "raised steadily over time" and everyone in management . . . spends a certain number of hours a month monitoring telephone associates, listening to them do their job."[42] Rhetoric about "facilitative management" notwithstanding, Davenport also emphasizes the monitoring of employees in the overall management of process. With its equating of human, physical, and financial assets as equal inhabitants of the world of process, each to be monitored and controlled in its own particular way, Davenport's language recalls Leffingwell's earlier bringing together of the mechanical and the human:

> To optimize the use of key assets in processes—be they physical goods inventory, human resources, or financial assets—companies must be constantly aware of the location, availability and best use of those assets. "Smart warehouses" of physical goods track the movement of inventory in and out of company facilities; asset management, in the form of productivity management systems, measures and reports by computer the time it takes an employee to complete a task; and automated cash management applications help companies make optimal use of liquid financial assets.[43]

There is one final aspect of reengineering that qualifies the practice as a modern-day version of scientific management. This concerns the reengineers' methods, how they have actually gone about altering and speeding up processes. In the *Principles of Scientific Management,* Taylor wrote, "Only through the enforced standardization of methods can the faster work . . . be assured" and "the duty of enforcing the adaptation rests with management."[44] Similarly, Hammer and Champy write, "The push for reengineering must come from the top of an organization . . . because people near the front lines lack the broad perspective that reengineering demands. . . . it is axiomatic that reengineering never, ever happens from the bottom up."[45] Davenport writes:

> Process innovation is typically much more top down, requiring strong direction from senior management. Because large firms' structures do not reflect their cross-functional processes, only those in positions overlooking multiple functions may be able to see opportunities for innovation.[46]

Taylor also recommended that "all of those who, after proper teaching, either will not or cannot work in accordance with the new methods and their higher speed must be discharged by the management."[47] Here it is unquestionably Michael Hammer who has been the most hard-nosed of the reengineers, viewing the human objects of reengineering much as Taylor viewed the skilled machinists at Midvale in the 1880s. In his book *The Reengineering Revolution*, Hammer uses lurid language to warn his reengineering clients about the kind of resistance and obstruction they could expect from the enemies of reengineering.

Hammer warns of "naysayers" who might have been "carping and criticising from the beginning." "When change bites people," he writes, "they bite back."[48] Some of these resisters are "malicious," some "want to leach onto the reengineering effort in order to promote some vested interest of their own."[49] The resisters may employ a particularly dastardly strategem that Hammer calls the "kiss of yes": "Everyone vows, 'yes yes, yes, we are fully with you. We are going to do it,' but they don't do it. They lie."[50] Faced with such opposition, the reengineer must not falter: "Leniency toward those who refuse to cooperate with the reengineering effort gives the lie to the leader's pronouncements about reengineering's critical importance."[51]

"Extreme measures," writes Hammer, "are sometimes the only way to overcome entrenched opposition," while "slapping people's wrists" instead of "breaking their legs" is simply "a sign of weakness."[52] Hammer recommended "confronting resisters and making it clear that termination [as a] consequence of their behaviour is a very valid technique."[53] The reengineering team, led by a "czar" has to steel itself for these unpleasant tasks. "Only someone who is serious about reengineering, perhaps to the point of fanaticism, can send the right signals."[54] Hammer provides an example of such commendable fanaticism.

In the heat of battle one of Hammer's czars decided to remove a subordinate from the reengineering team on the grounds that the team member's wife was about to have a baby. However, the czar acted as he did not because the subordinate might be distracted from his duties by his family obligations, but because he might not be. The subordinate was consumed with Hammer's commendable fanaticism: "The czar knew that this man was so absorbed in the project that he would continue working virtually up to the moment his wife entered the delivery room; instead [the czar] forced him to to the right thing."[55] Hammer mentions greed as another important catalyst for leadership. Greed can communicate to management "the promise and potential benefits of reengineering."[56]

In *The Reengineering Revolution,* Hammer admits that the harshness of reengineering might lead employees to regard the practice "with much trepidation and anxiety," finding the experience "to be unsettling and dislocating." Some employees might even experience "utter panic" and "sheer terror."[57] But evidently, Hammer believed that such insecurity was a price worth paying for the enemies of reengineering to be pushed aside—the naysayers, malicious leeches, and practitioners of the "kiss of yes." Hammer's intolerance of opposition is not entirely a matter of personality and temperament. Like all scientific managers, reengineers believe that their "one best way" rests upon a foundation of objective, scientific truth, not of opinion and conjecture. Those who oppose the scientific managers' "one best way" are therefore refusing to acknowledge this truth, often willfully so, and this helps explain why scientific managers from Taylor to Hammer have been so intolerant of their opponents.

In a December 1996 piece on reengineering, *The Wall Street Journal* gave a revealing example of Hammerism in action. With Hammer as consultant, Levi Strauss and Co. the clothing manufacturer, had embarked on a $850 million reengineering project that included the reorganization of much of the workforce into "process groups," and the cutting of the order fulfillment process from three weeks to thirty-six hours. On the human resource side, Levi Strauss's reengineering czars acted very much in the spirit of Hammer's *Reengineering Revolution*. Levi Strauss launched a preemptive strike against the potential enemies of reengineering, ordering 4,000 white-collar workers to reapply for their jobs as part of "process reorganization." The turmoil that followed so unnerved Levi Strauss's senior managers that they had to promise not to discharge anyone because of the reorganization.[58]

Such case histories can give a vivid sense of reengineering's authoritarian side, its reliance on information technology to enforce an elaborate code of rules and procedures. But the full force of reengineering's alliance with information technology can only be grasped by going beyond particular case histories and looking instead at the record of an entire service industry, and one whose evolution epitomizes the changing relationship between man and digital machine. At the level of the lower, operational processes, the "customer-facing" side of business—sales, service, marketing—meets this criterion as well as any. All three activities are given pride of place in the rhetoric of the "new economy." They can engage the skills and judgments of employees, and they are all being subjected to a hefty double dose of technological and process reengineering.

5

THE CUSTOMER RELATIONS FACTORY

IN THE THEORY AND RHETORIC OF THE NEW ECONOMY, few subjects have received more attention than customer relations management, the analysis and then the reengineering of the processes that link a business to its customers. A 1999 survey carried out by Andersen Consulting and the *Economist's* "Intelligence Unit" found that customer relations management (CRM), was "moving to the centre of corporate strategy."[1] The Gartner Group, a leading consultant in high technology, describes the corporate call center as the "chief electronic meeting place between a business and its clients . . . a kind of customer intelligence center, breaking down any barriers between customer and company, fostering a sense of customer intimacy."[2] Anyone who is a habitual user of 1-800 numbers also knows something about the importance of CRM to a service economy.

The preeminence of customer relations management has been an insistent theme of recent business literature. The author of *Thriving on Chaos* and *Liberation Management,* and perhaps the best-known representative of what might be called the evangelical school of business consultancy, Tom Peters has enthroned the customer in his own inimitable way: "In short I contend that over the next 10 to 15 years the primary strategic battle, in virtually any industry you can name, will be the battle to see who can go the farthest in empowering customers." Like all battles, this one will be decided on the front line: "When it comes to customer service, it's the front line that counts. No doubt about it! (Never has been any doubt . . . to me.) But what sparks the front line is the obvious obsession for doing it right, making it right for the customer."[3]

In sober language more appropriate to a leading theorist of the Harvard Business School, Rosabeth Moss Kanter has also stressed the importance of CRM. With the shift from an industrial to an information economy "more people hold jobs involving human contact." These workers "must influence, affect, or satisfy other people, often in direct interactions in which they look customers in the eye or listen to their voices." These employees "are performing emotional work, not just technical work." The quality of the emotional experience in these human exchanges "often determines organizational success."[4] However, no endorsement or promotion of CRM is likely to carry more weight than the one given by Bill Gates in his book *Business @ the Speed of Thought*:

> More than anything, though, a company has to communicate with its customers and act on what it learns in that communication. This primary need involves all of a company's capabilities: operational efficiency and data gathering, reflexive reach and coordination, and strategic planning and and execution. The need to communicate effectively with your customers will come up again and again in his book.[5]

Customer relations management has also been a major preoccupation of reengineering and the reengineers, and indeed the whole activity of CRM is an integral part of the reengineering movement. In *Process Innovation,* Thomas Davenport writes that "processes at the customer interface are perhaps the most critical to an organization's success. They are essential to a firm's cash flow, customer satisfaction, and process efficiency."[6] In *Reengineering the Corporation,* Hammer and Champy define customer relations management as reengineering's chief task: "Companies today have customers—business customers and individual consumers—who know what they want, what they want to pay for it . . . customers such as these don't need to deal with companies that don't understand and appreciate this startling change in the customer-buyer relationship." Therefore,

> The best place for the reengineering team to begin to understand a
> process is on the customer end. What are the customer's real require-
> ments? What do they say they want and what do they really need, if the
> two are different? What processes do they perform with the output?
> Since the eventual goal of redesigning a process is to create one that
> better meets customer needs, it is critical that the team truly under-
> stand these needs.[7]

Estimates of total employment in call centers vary from a low of 3.5 million, or 2.6 percent of the nation's workforce, to a possible high of 6 million. By comparison, there are 11 million production workers in all of manufacturing. The *New York Times* has estimated that there are at least 60,000 call centers in the United States.[8] The corporate call center has become an enduring image of the information economy: a vast, football-field-sized space in which many hundreds of employees work, each enclosed within his or her cubicle, each equipped with telephone headset and computer screen. These are the "customer-facing" employees who, in the words of one report on the call center industry, act as the corporation's "voice to customers . . . the frontline warriors in the battle for customer loyalty."[9] Three strands of technology come together within the confines of the call center.

First, "knowledge management" and "data warehousing" software can illuminate each encounter between agent and customer with an almost infinite volume and variety of information. Data warehouses can include the entire history of the customer's relations with the business, the customer's own financial history, and any amount of information about those products of the company that may interest the customer. Knowledge management software presents this information to agents in whatever form management wishes. Second, a technology known as computer telephony integration (CTI) permits exchanges between agent and customer to take place using a combination of telephone, fax,

E-mail, and Internet. Third, information technology has the power to integrate the call center, often known as the corporate "front office," with the corporate "back office," the departments responsible for such concrete tasks as scheduling, purchasing, manufacturing, accounting, and repairing.

These technologies have the power to make the call center agent a truly skilled worker whose knowledge and judgment can be of great value to the agent's employer. With the full history of a customer's past dealings with the company before him on the computer screen, the agent needs to know how to assess that history and decide very quickly how best to go about persuading the customer to buy the company's products and services. With the complex products of banking, insurance, or health care, the agent needs to have a full understanding of these products and know how they might appeal to particular customers. In all transactions with the customer, the agent must also work toward the "soft" objective of cementing the customer's loyalty to the company.

In a survey of in-house corporate call centers carried out in March 1998 by IT consultancy Omnitech, 32 percent of call centers surveyed were devoted to banking, 27 percent to managed health care, 16 percent to retail brokering, and 14 percent to retail telecom—that is, the dealings between AT&T and Verizon, and their customers about billings or changes to service.[10] In the call center industry there is also an important distinction to be drawn between those call centers that are kept in house by companies, and those that are outsourced to independent service bureaus. The Omnitech survey shows a slow but steady trend toward the outsourcing of call centers. In 1991, about 90 percent of call centers were kept in house, but by 1996 this figure had fallen to 80 percent, and in 2002 the figure was estimated to fall by another 10 percent.[11] A graph published in the April 1999 issue of *Call Center Solutions*, also shows a spectacular increase from 1997 onward in the percentage of call center transactions conducted by means other than the telephone—principally by E-mail and the Internet.[12]

Call Center Solutions (CCS) is a good place to begin our study, because it is the industry's leading trade journal, with the largest circulation and the most comprehensive coverage of the industry's new products. While *CCS* does take an occasional editorial swipe at deficient software products, the majority of its features are written by executives of software companies, or by consultants who have advice to sell to the call center industry. This particular group of writers is not usually in the business of advertising a product's weakness or of questioning its purpose, and it may therefore be argued that *CCS* lacks the objectivity required of a reliable source.

However, objectivity comes in more than one form. *CCS* is a virtual marketplace in which buyers find out about new products by reading about them. The particular language that the vendor uses to sell his products is objective in the sense that it reflects his judgment about the needs of his customers, about how his products can best satisfy these needs, and about how these products are likely to be used in the client's workplace. In trade magazines such as *CCS*, descriptions of software systems are also sufficiently concrete to include the system's method of use. These descriptions can therefore provide their own verification of what the salesman/writer is saying.

The impact of information technology on the life of a call center agent has three dimensions. First, there is the impact of information technology on the substantive tasks that make up the processes of the industry. Second, there is the impact of technology on the structure of this work: the sequencing of tasks, their division among employees, and their susceptibility to timing. And lastly, there is the impact of technology on relations between managers and employees, whether a technology is used to strengthen or weaken management's powers of surveillance and control.

With two of the call center industry's core processes, sales and marketing, the structure of work and its substantive tasks cannot easily be separated. This is because the shaping of a key element of the sales and marketing process—the telephone or Internet conversation between agent and customer—can itself be a substantive task of the agent. Hammer and Champy's case management or deal-structuring processes are repetitive and predictable: Once a client's credit application reaches IBM, certain things have to happen. But this is not true of a sales encounter between a call center agent and a customer. The call can go wherever the customer and the agent want it to go. Making sure that the call moves in the direction desired by the company can be a substantive skill of the agent.

But the operative word here is "can," because most of the software companies represented in the pages of *CCS* have created an elaborate superstructure of technology designed to "manage" these sales encounters from beginning to end, with the "verbal interaction" between agent and client playing out according to prearranged formulas. The agent loses the power to manage the call and has instead to defer to instructions provided by CRM software, which embodies the detailed preferences of management. A primitive version of this managed call will be familiar to anyone who has been disturbed by the intrusions of a telemarketer trying to sell real estate or Caribbean vacations. But the software systems on offer in the pages of *CCS* vastly strengthen the managed call as a weapon of knowledge management and control. From now on, we will, wherever possible, let the software executives, engineers, and consultants speak for themselves.

Perhaps the best place to begin an analysis of the sales and marketing process is with the stock of information that a company has about a customer, and that can be brought to bear once a customer contacts the company, or vice versa. This "operational customer data repository" has been well described by Greg Stack, senior vice-president and cofounder of Technology Solutions Company of Chicago, a consulting firm specializing in CRM issues: "This data repository stores customer contact events, contact history, preferences, value and current situation across all channels, products and divisions. This provides a single operational view of the customer."[13]

Once a customer makes contact with a call center, whether by telephone or through the Internet, CTI technology delivers this information to the agent's desktop computer. In the words of Lou Volpe, senior vice-president of GeoTel Communications Corporation, also a CRM software specialist:

When the call arrives at the terminating ACD [automatic call distributor] a server process has already obtained the data about the customer and is ready to deliver the information to the agent in the form of a screen pop. Call and data delivery are synchronized once the ACD selects the appropriate agent.[14]

However, by the time this information arrives at the agent's desktop computer, a number of automated decisions have also been made about how the call should be managed. Greg Stack calls these "prescribed action responses" or, in plain English, packaged answers. These are "customized in real-time based on a customer's interaction history, recent events, and perceived present and long-term value to the company." A "soft-data based rules engine," embedded in the CRM software, prescribes exactly which actions must occur. These might include "the script to play, Web page to display, product to cross-sell or pricing plan to offer."[15] Armed with "soft-data-based rules engines" and their "prescribed action responses," companies can, Volpe writes, "have total control over the entire enterprise of networks, disparate equipment and resources"—including "human resources."[16]

Of all the devices used by call centers to manage the interaction between customers and agents, the digital script best evokes the spirit of Taylor and Leffingwell. These scripts are the high-tech equivalents of Leffingwell's experiments with blotters and evaporating ink, and Taylor's investigations about the best way to hold a shovel. Managers reach down to the most basic elements of employee behavior and micromanage them so as to make sure that the one best way is always followed. Thus, once a conversation between agent and customer gets under way at a high-tech call center, the digital script is the principal means by which managers ensure that the call always proceeds according to plan.

In the pages of *CCS*, there are companies specializing in the technology of scripting, just as there are companies specializing in the technology of monitoring and surveilliance. One way in which these scripting specialists draw attention to the sophistication of their products is by reminding readers of how primitive their product was in the recent past. Scripting specialist Rita Dearing, vice president of TeleDirect International of Scottsdale, Arizona, writes of how "traditionally, scripts have been simple paper documents that allowed agents to read a generalized pitch." These were "by their very nature, extremely simplistic," though "certainly an improvement over no scripts."

When there are no scripts, the agent of course has some leeway to decide how a call ought to proceed, and that is the contigency that the entire scripting phenomenon is designed to avoid. Echoing Leffingwell, Dearing writes of the "wrong way" for agents to deal with customers, which is "without scripts, letting agents handle conversations as they see fit."[17] Sharna F. Kahn, a senior project manager at KPMG Consultants defines a deficient CRM software product as one that is so slow that "agents [come] up with their own solutions for the customer."[18] The best way to understand the advanced scripting technologies promoted by Dearing is to go back to the very beginning of the customer-agent interaction process.

As an agent makes or receives a call, the rules engine presents a wealth of data about the relevant customer, and this data includes, in Greg Stack's words "the script to play." Dearing explains that the script may differ according to the customer's "state of residence, gender, age group or income level."[19] At the outset of the call the agent reads the "first off" script that has popped up on his screen. But what happens next? How can managers, supervisors, and software engineers anticipate the multitude of directions in which the call might then proceed and come up with an appropriate script for each and every contingency? Here one has to distinguish between calls that proceed more or less according to plan, and those that do not.

Dearing explains how scriping software can deal with "regular" calls: "While an agent is reading a generalized script to a customer, the customer expresses objection A, then script A is presented, but if objection B is offered, a different script, script B, is displayed on the agent workstation—each of course being tailored to the specific issue at hand." Dearing goes on to explain how the "latest generation of scripting tools" amplifies this "multiple choice" approach with what she calls "branching techniques."[20] With "branching," new script options appear in each phase of the dialogue, depending on how the call is proceeding. But what happens if a call does not proceed according to plan? When reading about these customer-agent interactions in the pages of *CCS*, one sometimes has to remind oneself that although one party to these conversations is bound by the whole apparatus of scripts, screen pops, and "prescribed action responses," the other party, the customer, is not.

The customer is free to take the conversation wherever he wants, whenever he wants. An agent for a financial services conglomerate may therefore be carrying on a perfectly good conversation about the company's mutual funds, following the script to the letter. Then suddenly the customer says he wants to start talking about life insurance. What then? The scripts themselves provide the solution. Scripts can be "attached" to databases about products just as they can be attached to databases about customers. So when an agent is asked about life insurance, the information about the company's life insurance products that the agent summons up from the database carries with it a new opening script geared to that information, along with another tree of branching scripts designed to move the conversation through multiple phases.

As Dearing explains, "All application development tools should be able to define the rules by which any given script is presented to the agent at any given time in the workflow."[21] Moreover, just as items of information from the database will reach the agent's screen with scripts already attached, so managers and engineers can program the scripts themselves to summon selected items of information at appropriate moments in the scripted conversation between agent and customer. Omega Systems of Rancho Cordova, California, has a product, Versa-Com, that allows "agents at a certain point in a script to bring up a Microsoft Access program and at another point, the script could bring up an accounting program or . . . a fax server program."[22] But always it is management, acting through the system, that decides when an agent can or cannot bring up a script or a program.

Sales and marketing are two of the call centers' leading processes. A third is customer service, the handling by telephone or over the Internet of customers' questions about a company's products or services.

The reengineering of this third CRM process comes up against problems of knowledge management and control that are in some ways more demanding than those encountered in the reengineering of sales and marketing. Alan Kessler, a senior vice-president at 3Com Corporation, describes how the techniques of knowledge management used in the reengineering of sales and marketing can also be applied to customer service. At the heart of a "well constructed on line service program," Kessler writes, is to be found an expert system that "incorporates the input of experts in the production, use, functionality and replacement of the products being supported."[23]

Along with this esteem for the "input of experts," Kessler also has the scientific manager's characteristic lack of esteem for the knowledge and expertise of frontline workers. In a "typical pre-KM [knowledge management] technical service call center," Kessler writes, "each team member brings a specific set of skills and expertise to the job—skills that may or may not match the customer's concern." It was also likely that each of these agents "had a distinct manner of addressing issues and explaining solutions. Some approaches will be more appropriate to certain inquiries than others."[24] Reengineering replaces this untidy and unreliable knowledge base with Kessler's "well organized, complete" expert system—just as Taylor's worksheets once displaced the rule-of-thumb notions of the Midvale machinists.[25]

Kessler does not describe in detail how the post-KM customer service call center might work, but it appears from what he does say that the role of the agent is simply to act as a conduit linking customer and expert system. Fortunately, however, we do have a detailed account of how such a post-KM technical service call center operates, and, moreover, one that relies on a detailed analysis of transcripts of conversations between agents and customers. This is Jack Whalen and Erik Vinkhuyzen's 1997 paper "Expert Systems in (Inter) Action: Diagnosis in Document Machine Problems over the Telephone."[26] Whalen and Vinkhuyzen are researchers at Xerox's Palo Alto Research Center (PARC), one of Silicon Valley's most remarkable institutions. In their paper, they describe the realities of customer relations management as few ever have.

In the 1960s, Xerox-PARC became famous for producing seminal technologies that Xerox then somehow allowed to be taken over and developed by competitors.[27] These lost technologies included the personal computer, word processing software, laser printers, the mouse, and the networking software successfully developed by Novell Corporation. Xerox-PARC is also an IT think tank of remarkable radicalism and independence of spirit, considering its corporate affiliations. Here the guiding spirit is John Seely Brown, former director of Xerox-PARC and now chief scientist at Xerox. For thirty years Brown has been among Silicon Valley's most creative thinkers about the use of technology in the workplace. In a September 2002 interview, Brown deplored the "technologically inspired vandalism" corporations had done to their "social fabric over the past decade," and particularly their "myopic focus on business processes, how they can be streamlined and automated using computers."[28]

The subject of Whalen and Vinkhuyzen's paper is an expert system set up by "MMR Corporation," a manufacturer of photocopying machines, and a pseudonym for Xerox. In 1993 MMR began reengineering a call center devoted to the servicing of the company's machines, and the centerpiece of this reengineering was the installation of an expert system that MMR named CasePoint, a system designed to automate the exchanges between customers and customer service agents. Whalen and Vinkhuyzen's connection with Xerox-PARC gave them access to transcripts of conversations between customers and agents, material not usually made available by corporations to researchers. The two authors make extensive use of the MMR transcripts and give a vivid sense of how this interaction between customer, agent, and system actually takes place.

CasePoint was designed to cut MMR's costs of sending out high-wage technicians to repair the company's machines in the offices in which they were installed. The company believed that a significant percentage of these repairs could be handled over the telephone by call center agents, or more accurately, by agents relaying to the customer the recommendations of the expert system. However, in reducing its dependence on one kind of high-cost labor, the company did not want to increase its dependence on another category of high-wage workers.

Whalen and Vinkhuyzen were told that the company "was reluctant to invest in training or support for customer service representatives, that would increase their knowledgeability." Instead, the company believed that "reducing dependency on people knowledge and skills through expert and artificial intelligence systems" offered the best approach. With the expert system containing "most, if not all, of the knowledge required to perform a task or solve a problem," the knowledgeability of the agent could be confined "largely to data entry and information retrieval procedures"—echoes of Hammer and Champy's deal structurers and case managers.[29]

The chief KM problem faced by MMR's software engineers was how to achieve an accurate definition of the problem to be solved by Case-Point. The one thing the expert system could not do was provide for itself an accurate description of the symptoms of machine breakdown. But without such an accurate description to work with, CasePoint could not embark upon its "case reasoning" to come up with the correct solution to the problem. All the cases that reached MMR's call center therefore had three dimensions: the actual fault that was preventing the MMR photocopying machine from working properly, the description of the symptoms of the fault given to the agent over the telephone by the customer, and the account of the fault's symptoms typed up by the agent and fed into CasePoint.

For CasePoint's designers, the more the account fed into the system by the agent reflected the "unconstrained natural language" of the customer, the better. The designers seem to have believed that the raw utterances of the customer were endowed with a native wisdom that the agent at his screen should not attempt to edit or clarify. This meant, very conveniently, that the agents needed to receive only the most rudimentary instruction about the machines they were servicing over the telephone. It did not matter if the customer's language was lacking in fluency and elegance. The system could parse and make sense of any description of a problem "regardless of the spelling of the words" and irrespective of whether the description was "utter gibberish" or "syntactically proper English sentences."[30]

Once the agent had relayed the customer's description of the symptoms to CasePoint, the system could then begin a dialogue with the customer that would end in the prescription of the correct solution to the problem. CasePoint therefore would "not have to depend on [the agent's] understanding of the customer's description of a problem." The agent was only a simple conduit for the passing of information between the customer and CasePoint.[31] The dialogue between the MMR customer and the MMR agent is similar in form to the dialogue between sales and marketing agents and their customers. In both kinds of dialogue, scripts play a central role.

Just as the sales agent had to read out the successive scripts that CRM software came up with at each stage or branch of the conversation, so MMR's agents had to ask questions of the customer in the exact order prescribed by CasePoint, and using the exact script that CasePoint flashed on the screen. Whalen and Vinkhuyzen write that the software's designers expected agents "to ask the questions as they are worded on their computer screen" in keeping with the designer's notion of agents as information conduits.[32] Once CasePoint receives, via the agent, the customer's descriptions of the machine's symptoms, CasePoint summons from its database those past cases that most resemble the case in hand, along with the past remedies prescribed in each case.

The software then lists a number of questions on the screen, and each answer provided by the customer "leads to more points being awarded to some [past] case and the elimination of others, as the system progressively narrows down the search."[33] As the "conversation" moves forward, the wording of the questions "reflects the ranking of cases by CasePoint at that point in the diagnosis," and "questions may be removed from the list with new questions replacing them" as the software awards "points to different cases and eliminates others." Eventually, one case history will receive enough points to be declared "the winner," along with its attached remedy.[34] The remedy is then communicated, via the agent, to the customer. In the next chapter, we will see whether CasePoint has lived up to the hopes of its designers.

In sales, marketing, and customer service, the coming together of reengineering and information technology has given managers unprecedented power to control how employees do their work. Knowledge management prescribes what information is made available to employees, and when. Scripting prescribes the exact wording the employee must use in conveying that information to customers. Rules engines and their "prescribed action responses" determine the exact sequence in which tasks must be performed. But while these techniques of digital control can be used to micromanage an agent's activities, the control of employees and their work has a whole other dimension. There exists a host of software products whose special task is to monitor employees so that managers can be sure that their business rules are being followed.

Whenever agents perform their tasks on the telephone, there is always the possibility that they may not perform the tasks exactly as prescribed by the script, the screen pop, or the rules engine. They may simply deal with customers as they think best. Rita Dearing, as we have seen, describes this as the "wrong way" for agents to behave, and Sharon Kahn of KPMG defines a deficient software product as one that gives agents time to come up "with their own solutions to the customer." Monitoring software detects and records such violations of the rules as soon as they occur. Monitoring software can also detect right away if an agent is not working fast enough and might fail to meet his production quotas.

Companies specializing in monitoring and surveillance software are an all-pervading presence in the pages of *CCS*. One consequence of this crowded field is that the competing companies differentiate themselves by emphasizing the meticulous thoroughness of their monitoring products, along with the power of new technology to open up new fields of monitoring, including the monitoring of agent-customer "conversations" through E-mail and the Internet. There are at least five distinct types of monitoring software. First, there are what might be called "classic" monitoring products, software that embodies the Taylorist preoccupation with timing and measurement: How long do agents take to answer a call? How long does the call last? How long does the agent take to "wrap up" the call by completing clerical tasks that may have arisen in the course of the call?

Second, there are "quality-monitoring" products—software that eases the manager's task of measuring the agent's "soft skills"—his warmth and politeness, and whether his demeanor has strengthened ties of intimacy and loyalty between company and customer. Third, there are what might be called "total monitoring" products, software that simultaneously monitors what is happening on the agent's screen and what the agent is saying on the telephone. With this "total monitoring," it is possible to know whether the agent is following a prescribed script and accurately relaying the information and recommendations provided by product databases. Fourth, there is software that monitors Internet and E-mail "conversations" between agent and customer, and which can, if necessary, integrate this monitoring with the parallel monitoring of telephone conversations. Fifth, there are the digital technologies that are embodied in many of these monitoring products and that have made possible this forward leap in the scope and intensity of monitoring.

As with the scripting specialists, monitoring specialists advertise their successes by reminding customers of a recent and primitive pre-digital past. Garry Shearer of NICE Systems writes of the "silent observation methods" that were in vogue during the 1980s and even the 1990s. With silent observation, "the supervisor listens in on live calls and evaluates the agent's performance by scratching notes on a hard copy survey." Such methods of live listening "resulted in miles of tapes that provided no hint as to where the start and the end of a completed call would be found."[35] As an example of these primitive methods, Shearer cites the case of Electric Insurance Company (EIC) of Boston, which had "taped calls, via cassette recorder using a manual scheduling system."[36]

According to Suzanne Wilson, manager of training and quality at EIC, the drawbacks to this method were "the amount of time and the labor-intensity involved." Furthermore, "agents were generally aware when they were being recorded, and behaved accordingly."[37] Also "calls were difficult to locate; samples were often cluttered with unwanted, unnecessary calls; taped calls were difficult to manage and categorize, and call scoring was paper based, inconsistent, and difficult to summarize at a high level." To reengineer its monitoring processes, EIC purchased a CTI recording system from NICE Systems, which automated "the process of gathering call samples" enabling "the quick retrieval of those calls for review."[38]

The system "concurrently records a representative number of agent's voice and screen sessions, and stores them as highly compressed digital files on network PCs," writes Shearer. Recordings can be scheduled "by agents or groups [of agents] and by time," and managers can "immediately retrieve calls and screen sessions" simply by keystroking the names of agents or groups of agents. Wilson reports that EIC's "supervisors love the multimedia aspects of the system." They are kept busy "listening to the voice, watching the agent's computer screens and grading the performance levels—all at the same time." EIC had seen an "efficiency factor of three times for supervisors' evaluations of calls."[39] In the next chapter, we will explore what it's like to be at the receiving end of all of this multidimensional monitoring.

There are, as we have seen, several varieties of monitoring. Classic monitoring embodies in digital form Taylor's preoccupation with measurement and timing. For example, Teloquent Communications has a product called Desktop Reports for Windows that "displays call activity in an easy to understand graphical manner" and "allows call center managers to quickly evaluate the center's call statistics and share a high-level overview with other business executives." It can illustrate such variables as "time analyses of agent activity, number of calls received, number of calls handled versus those abandoned, delay time of calls, and call volume by agent skill."[40] MicroAge Teleservices has developed an advanced "traditional" monitoring system for itself, which it calls "Big Button."

With the push of the Big Button, managers can "track agent efficiency and view a wealth of information about activity within its call center . . . on one screen managers can view almost any statistical data associated with an individual agent or a whole department." The statistics can include "how long agents talk on each call, how many calls they take and how long they spend closing a file after a call."[41] Stephen Pace of Point Information Systems of Wellesley, Massachusetts, reminds *CCS* readers of the implications of time-centered monitoring for the bottom line: "When your CRM application goes live, you can track activity and use the data to calculate Return On Investment." Thus, "a twenty second time saving on a three minute call means an 11 percent increase in productivity." Pace advises buyers to hire an "experienced consultant or vendor" to help establish "cost saving applications such as time spent per call, problem resolution speed, deal closing rate, contract renewals, customer retention and customer satisfaction."[42]

With a concept such as "customer satisfaction," we are leaving the sphere of classic, time-centered monitoring and entering the new and fashionable field of "quality monitoring." Tony Procops of ASC Telecom lists the aspects of agent behavior that are of particular interest to quality monitors: "how the initial greeting was given, how well the agent probed for further customer needs and how well/whether a given task was completed."[43] In November 1998, CBSI Inc. introduced a newly upgraded "telemonitoring system" that evaluates agents according to such qualitative criteria as "script adherence, smooth transition, enunciation, courtesy, assertiveness and energy."[44]

Don McCormick of Beach Direct Marketing Resources Inc. has described the quality monitor's ideal: "The message is consistently played to the customer universe in the same voice with no degradation of enthusiasm and no deviation from the scripted message as the day wears on. Consistency is the key." However, McCormick's quality ideal is achieved by a digital, not human, agent. McCormick is describing the performance of a "high quality digitally recorded message," developed as part of a "Live-to-IVR software package" by Intelogistics Inc., of Fort Lauderdale, Florida. "IVR" stands for interactive voice response.[45]

With "Live-to-IVR," the agent "pleasantly introduces him/herself and the company" and, "working from a script," asks permission to play a recording. The agent then gets off the line, and with him goes "much of the human error and rejection factor." Then the recorded message is played and there is "no degradation in enthusiasm and no deviating from the scripted message as the day wears on." McCormick looks forward to the day when IVR platforms "will use truly conversant technology," so that "the customer will carry on a dialogue with the machine and in some cases may never know that it was the machine."[46] But when the agent stays on the line and handles the call, it can be said that the ideal of quality monitoring, and indeed the ideal of all forms of monitoring, is to get agents to perform with the consistency and stamina of Intelogistic's digital agent.

While monitoring specialists such as Tony Procops write of "automated quality monitoring," software has not yet reached the point at which it can measure an agent's courtesy and assertiveness in the same way that it can measure how long agents take on each call. Automation in the context of quality means that recorded calls can be classified, retrieved, and then evaluated by supervisors with a minimum of time and effort. Recordings, for example, can include special reserved "spaces" for the supervisors to record their comments. It is this automation that the supervisors of EIC, so love, keeping them "listening to the voice" and "grading the performance levels . . . all at the same time," while tripling their productivity.

Both classic and quality monitoring are "partial" systems in the sense that they do not provide a minute-by-minute account of what the agent is doing both on the telephone and on his screen. Here, CTI has made a decisive contribution, because it can provide parallel recordings of what the agent is doing in both media. By comparing the two recordings, the supervisor can always know whether an agent is fully adhering to a script, and whether he is performing his tasks in the exact sequence prescribed by the software. Funk Software has introduced such a total monitoring product, called Proxy Remote Control Gateway, "a state of the art remote control, screen monitoring system." The system provides supervisors with several monitoring options: "They can view in real-time one or more agents PC's at the click of a button to see how an agent uses the script and if he or she is using the system correctly."[47]

Proxy Remote also has a "cycle mode" so that supervisors can "round-robin among multiple PCs on the network to systematically monitor a group of agents." In addition, Proxy Remote has a "stealth" monitoring capability "that lets supervisors monitor agents undetected."[48] Suzanne Wilson of EIC, gives a user's view of total-monitoring systems: "The screen capture application runs undetected by the agent" and "the playback of both voice and screen is perfectly synchronized." By "re-creating the entire agent session, the monitoring system helps us evaluate the agent's use of the computer system and determine a better means of designing computer application."[49]

The coming of the Internet presents the monitoring community with the new challenge of finding ways of monitoring Internet transactions between agent and customer, and then of integrating this monitoring with the preexisting monitoring of voice and screen. Tony Procops writes of "future logging systems" that will be "technology driven by the Web and e-commerce," in which "automated tools will require more monitoring to allow remote managers to maintain effectiveness and control."[50] Christopher Botting, vice-president for marketing and cofounder of PakNetX, writes of how supervisors "must be able to silently monitor and barge in to Internet multimedia calls just as they would a traditional audio-only call." An Internet-monitoring system "parodies these features and captures the life of the call."[51]

The call center industry fulfills Leffingwell's vision of a white-collar workforce marching to the drumbeat of scientific management. The massed cubicles of the call center are digital assembly lines on which standardization, measurement, and control come together to create a workplace of relentless discipline and pressure. While information technology has been the indispensable agent of such a regime, this use of IT is not an inherent characteristic of technology itself but always reflects management's preferences and choices. Agents do not have to be "simple conduits," their work governed by the digital script. Nor does their talking, walking, eating, and resting have to be measured and controlled to the nearest second. The electronic eye can always be dimmed to allow agents some freedom to deal with customers as they judge best. But for that to happen, managers have to give up some of the enormous power that IT has handed them. So far, they have rarely been willing to do this.

We now need to look at this singular work regime from the perspective of the employees who are living it.

6

ON THE DIGITAL ASSEMBLY LINE

IN THE SUMMER OF 1999, I met with a dozen call center employees who wanted the Communication Workers of America (CWA) to organize their plant, a workplace of about 200 employees located in a small Iowa town. We met in the bland yet reassuring setting of a Baptist meeting-house, but as our meeting progressed it was the call center's physical and psychological aspects were predominant: its cramped geography; the bilious colors of its ceilings, walls, and carpets; the personalities and habits of its managers; its fraught, harassed routines; and above all, the constant efforts of employees to carve out moments of privacy, however modest, for themselves. A CWA organizer was also present, and this was the employees' first meeting with someone from the union. As often happens on such occasions, the accumulated resentments of the years came pouring out.

The first complaints were about the call center's layout. In each of the call center's five departments the employees' cubicles were organized around a central platform at which supervisors presided, surrounded by banks of computer screens. These platforms were slightly elevated so that supervisors could see directly into the agents' cubicles; for the employees, management's ability to keep them under direct observation was particularly burdensome. Rick Hamsen (name changed), a leader of the organizing effort, described the technology at the disposal of the supervisors as "awesome"; the software bundled together all the powers of analysis, surveillance, and control described in the last chapter.

The hyperefficiency of the software encouraged managers to micromanage employees' work. Since the software performed all the substantive tasks of data gathering and analysis, supervisors had to spend much of their time gazing at their screens, waiting for the system to tell them when an employee was falling short in any one of the myriad ways defined by managers themselves and then embedded in the software. Once this happened and the red light flashed, the upbraiding of the employee at the next work break was for managers both a means of exercising their powers and of relieving their boredom. The call center's work regime guaranteed that there would be a steady supply of such incidents and so a steady demand for managerial intervention.

This regime was a service sector variant of what Mike Parker and Jane Slaughter, in their studies of Japanese auto plants, have called "management by stress."[1] Many Japanese plants equip their assembly line workers with a light that flashes green or red according to whether they are performing their tasks within the allotted tac.[2] For scientific managers, counterintuitively, it is not necessarily a positive sign if all the lights along the line are flashing green. It may mean that tacs are too lax and need to be shortened. The ideal situation is one in which a significant minority of workers are operating at the margin of inefficiency, so that supervisors can then bear down on these workers and get them to work faster. Once this is done, and all lights are flashing green, then the next round of speed up can begin.

At the Iowa call center, managers would speed up the line by throwing a digital switch and reprogramming the software, much as Henry Ford had done at his Highland Park plant in 1915. Managers would do this without any prior discussion, let alone negotiation, with employees. The latest tacs would simply be announced at the beginning of the work week. At any given time, between 15 and 20 percent of the workforce would have trouble meeting their target times, and these workers then became the special concern of their supervisors. More than any other workplace issue—pay, benefits, workings hours, shrinking tacs—

it was the arbitrary treatment of these faltering workers by supervisors that had enraged the employees at the CWA meeting and convinced them of the need for a union.

This corrective treatment followed no coherent pattern and varied according to the whims of the supervisor. Some employees were given special coaching so that they could meet their target times. Others were threatened with immediate dismissal unless they improved. Employees supporting the union drive almost invariably found themselves at the receiving end of management's harsh side. The moment an employee wore the union label, management was ready with every manner of harassment, even though such behavior was wholly illegal under the terms of the National Labor Relations Act (NLRA), the toothless federal law that regulates labor-management relations.

The case of Rick Hamsen himself is particularly revealing. Most of those at the CWA meeting saw the relationship between management and employees as inherently adversarial and believed that the best a union could do was to blunt some of management's more egregious practices. Hamsen's view was different and reminded me of a certain kind of Soviet dissident found during the declining years of the Brezhnev regime, who later became a strong supporter of Mikhael Gorbachev. These dissidents, still party members, continued to believe that a store of Leninist idealism remained buried under the corruption and inertia of the Brezhnevian officialdom and that it was the task of party reformers to bring this idealism to the fore before it was too late (which of course it was).

This was Hamsen's approach to the politics of the call center. Hamsen viewed his work as a vocation, and according to coworkers, he was one of the center's best performers. He was very respectful of management and invariably referred to his supervisors as "Mr. Schulz" or "Mr. Kelley," as opposed to his coworkers' usual "that asshole Schulz." Although often disappointed by management's performance, Hamsen viewed their shortcomings as a reflection of their lack of proper training; managers could not understand where their true interests lay. The union would join with the more enlightened managers and persuade their dimmer colleagues that the success of the business depended on a cooperative relationship between management and the workforce, represented by the union.

The Iowa managers should have realized that an employee like Hamsen could be a big asset for any business, whether as head of a union local or of a less formal body representing employee interests. But once the Iowa managers realized that Hamsen was a leader of the union drive, they began to harass him relentlessly. Supervisors started following him into the canteen, staring at him as he had his meals. Hamsen found that his cubicle was being regularly searched. Senior managers interrogated him at length about his pro-union activities. Finally, his supervisor accosted him in the center's parking lot and, falsifying the evidence, warned that Hamsen's performance was unsatisfactory and that he would be fired unless it improved. All these acts were illegal under the terms of the NLRA, but they had the desired effect. Stress took its toll on Hamsen's health, and although he still believes strongly in the need for a union, he has stopped campaigning for one.

The Great Plains states of Iowa, Nebraska, and South Dakota are all strongholds of the call center industry. So, too, are the Sunbelt states of Arizona and New Mexico, which now rank with the Deep South as among the nation's poorest regions. Some of the best reporting on call centers in the Sunbelt has been done by RuthAnn Hogue, a reporter at the Tucson, Arizona, *Daily Star*. In a thirty-part series on Tucson's call center industry that ran in the *Star* in October and November 1998, Hogue showed how the call center industry can play a leading role in the economy of a booming Sunbelt community such as Tucson. Tucson is rated one of the "hot cities" for the industry, along with Phoenix, Arizona; Albuquerque, New Mexico; Omaha, Nebraska; and Sioux Falls, South Dakota. Among the factors that have made these cities "hot" for the call center industry are a plentiful supply of low-wage, predominantly high school–educated workers; the absence of unions; the presence of the phonetically neutral and so "acceptable" midwestern or Rocky Mountain dialect; and, in Hogue's words, "a reduced likelihood that people in a particular region will file law suits."[3]

Hogue comes up with evidence showing that, in the Sunbelt, the treatment of call center employees by their managers is very similar to what I came across in Iowa, and can only be described as harsh. A woman identified only as S. Sullivan worked as a call center agent for Intergroup of Arizona, a company employing 250 workers in Tucson. When Sullivan became pregnant she was criticized by her supervisors because she often had to go to the bathroom to throw up. They told her she should throw up in the trash can at her desk.[4] Paula Dabbart, an employee at an American Airlines reservations center in Tucson, said that she wore a stopwatch on a string around her neck to time each break. She felt that, for her own protection, she had to log all her movements.[5] Chuck Irvin, a fellow employee at the facility, explained Dabbart's precautions: "They tend to treat us like a machine for the eight hours you are plugged in . . . every time your butt leaves the chair you can hear the clock ticking."[6]

Hogue interviewed a middle-aged couple, Vivienne and Douglas Farrow, who were in danger of falling victim to an involuntary nomadism. Neither could satisfy the "average talk time" (ATT) set by their respective supervisors. At American Airlines' Tucson reservations center, Vivienne Farrow could not meet an ATT of two minutes and thirty seconds and was fired. At Greyhound's Tucson call center, Douglas Farrow was struggling to meet an ATT of 1 minute and 30 seconds. Farrow told Hogue that he had got his ATT down from 1 minute 95 seconds to 1 minute and 55 seconds, but the last 25 seconds were a problem: "I don't know how to get it down to one minute thirty. . . . I'm trying, but I can't do it."[7]

One of Hogue's more bizarre findings was that many of Tucson's call centers had drawn up strict dress codes for their employees. This was puzzling since call center employees never come into physical contact with their customers and the dress habits of the Southwest are notably relaxed. But by drawing up and enforcing strict dress codes, call center managers could open up a whole new field of employee activity that they could bring under their control, thus adding to an already draconian regime of regulation and surveillance. Managers at one leading telemarketing company, Teletech, were notable sticklers for sartorial conformity. Carolyn Grogg, a Tucson resident who worked for Teletech for a year, failed to comply with the company's footwear regulations.

Suffering from a swollen toe, Grogg came to work with a closed-toe shoe on her healthy foot, and a matching sock and sandal on her injured foot. Sandals, however, were against regulations, and Teletech's managers were going to send her home, an "occurrence" or demerit that would have been entered onto her employment record. Grogg had to take off her sandal and sock "and show them my toe was black and blue."[8] Hogue also found that managers frequently fired employees for tardiness, even when it was due to illness or a family emergency confirmed in writing by a doctor or teacher.

Kindra Frazier worked at Teletech's Tucson call center, helping United Parcel Service (UPS) customers keep track of their packages.[9] Frazier was highly rated by her supervisors, who described her as a "team player" with a "positive team spirit." In August 1997 her annual employment review described her as "very polite, courteous, and works well with others." She was also "effective and efficient when helping customers track their UPS packages." However, in November 1997 Frazier tripped in the company cafeteria and injured her back. For the next two months, Frazier continued to work, even though she had not fully recovered from her injury and often had to walk on crutches.

In this condition she found it hard to meet the company's draconian punctuality requirements: "It seemed like no matter what I did at work, if I went on crutches, I would get back a minute late." Company memos seen by Hogue reveal that when Frazier tried to take breaks at her desk to avoid being late, she was reprimanded. Despite her injury and her good record, in February 1998 Teletech fired Frazier for tardiness. Her life then went into a downward spiral. She was treated for depression and had to spend time in a mental hospital. In October 1998 she and her husband lost their house when the bank foreclosed, and they went bankrupt.

All the case histories recounted by Hogue were from call centers in which there was no union representation, and in which employees could do little to resist the kind of management practices she describes. But an estimated 7 percent of the call center workforce does belong to a union, mostly in call centers run by AT&T or its offshoots—Lucent Technology, and the now not-so "Baby Bells." Most of this unionized workforce is represented by the Communication Workers of America (CWA). However, the case of Gayle Brown (name changed), a former employee of AT&T's call center at Fairhaven, Massachusetts, shows that, under present labor law, even a relatively strong union like the CWA has limited power to resist the call center industry's harsh employment practices.

Agents at AT&T's Fairhaven call center are direct employees of the corporation, and not of a call center "middleman" such as Teletech or Apac. At the time that Gayle Brown worked there (1997–1998), the chief task of the Fairhaven workforce was to win back AT&T customers who had deserted to other long-distance carriers. Gayle Brown began work as an AT&T trainee early in 1997.[10] On March 7, Brown's mother, with whom she lived, had to undergo surgery for the removal of a malignant tumor in her breast. When Brown told her supervisor that she would have to accompany her mother to the hospital and would miss part of her shift, Brown was told that she should "do what she had to do" but that her absence would count as an "occurrence," or demerit, to be entered into her employment record. At Fairhaven, AT&T's policy on "occurrences" was and is "four strikes and you're out"—fired.

Early in the summer, Brown herself began to experience internal bleeding, and in mid-June this became so bad that she had to see a doctor, who recommended surgery. Once again, she had to take time off from her shift, and once again her supervisor warned "do what you have to do but it'll be occurrence no. 2." At the end of June, Brown underwent surgery, and a number of nonmalignant tumors, cysts, and polyps were discovered behind her ovaries. Brown received her third "occurrence" when, in the opinion of her supervisors, she did not return to work sufficiently soon after her surgery. Then, in July, Brown was injured in a car accident, and although she went to work later that day, she was experiencing the delayed effects of concussion, as well as a loss of reflexes in her right leg.

It was not until January 12, 1998, that she was told by her doctor that she could return to work. But when she contacted AT&T's management at the Fairhaven plant, she was told that she had been fired for her "poor overall attendance record." Gary Johnson, then a steward at the CWA's Fairhaven local, and now president of the local, told me that he had had to deal with many cases of what he regarded as unfair dismissals at Fairhaven, but that the Brown case was the one that troubled him most. He had fought hard for Brown but had failed to get her reinstated. I spoke to Brown soon after her dismissal. She was distraught at her treatment by AT&T, and has not worked since.

There is substantial research showing that these examples of the harshness of working life at call centers are not isolated incidents but form part of a work culture characteristic of the industry as a whole. In 1999 the Radclyffe Group, business consultants whose clients have included CIGNA, Coca-Cola, and New York Life, undertook a survey of the call center industry and identified four factors that drove what it calls a "negative call center culture." With the detached, modular language of the business consultant, Radclyffe describes a work regime very similar to the one that RuthAnn Hogue and I came across in Arizona and Iowa. The first of Radclyffe's four negative factors is the call center industry's "stringent and inflexible rules," particularly the demand that "agents subordinate their psychological, emotional and even physical needs" to the tasks of "consistently handling fluctuating call volumes."[11]

Radclyffe's second negative factor is the "stressful nature of the work": "worried about not meeting their standards . . . representatives can become anxious about going to lunch or sometimes even to the bathroom when they wish. . . . this can lead to their feeling trapped at the phone and out of control."[12] Radclyffe's third and fourth "negative factors" are both bound up with management's focus on "quantitive measurement." In almost all call centers," Radclyffe reports, "the availability of representatives is monitored on a real time basis, and reports can be reviewed in half hour intervals." A drop in performance levels can lead to a "concerned reaction from managers who are held accountable for a specific service level." This "adds fear to an environment already laden with negative emotion." This management approach, along with the relentless demand for call volume, "means representatives often become entrenched in feelings of victimization, hostility and resentment."[13]

Of all the ingredients that make up Radclyffe's "negative call center culture," it is perhaps the monitoring of employees by their managers that has most contributed to the employees' feelings of "victimization, hostility and resentment." In 1989 the Massachusetts Coalition on New Office Technology carried out a survey on employee attitudes toward monitoring, based on interviews with seven hundred employees, working for forty-nine companies, in a dozen different industries. Although the report is now fourteen years old, monitoring technology has grown ever more detailed and intrusive during these years and is today more burdensome for employees than it was in 1989. In 1989, 80 percent of those interviewed said that monitoring made their job more stressful, 65 percent said that they could not do a quality job because monitoring and the quotas it enforced obliged them to work too fast, and 68 percent said that employers used the results of monitoring as grounds for disciplinary measures. Sixty-four percent said that monitoring made it hard to get up for a break, even to go to the bathroom.[14]

Still another telling category of evidence supports the Radclyffe Group's findings about the "negative call center culture." Job turnover at call centers is exceptionally high as employees vote with their feet and leave the digital assembly lines in droves. At the sixty-two call centers surveyed in 1998 by the consultants Omnitech, the mean annual rate of employee turnover was 24 percent.[15] Dina Vance of the consultancy FTR Inc., and a leading expert on the call center operations of the financial services industry, estimated the annual turnover rates at her industry's call centers to be around 39 percent.[16] Mike McGrath, chief organizer for Local 1026 of the CWA in Tucson, puts annual turnover at some of the city's call centers even higher, at between 50 and 60 percent.[17] Contributors to *CCS* often remind readers about the industry's very high rates of employee turnover. In 1999 Rodney Kuh, president of Envision Telephony of Seattle, told *CCS* readers that "more than 25 percent of your call center staff could seek employment elsewhere this year."[18]

The call center industry and its work practices provide near-textbook examples of what I have called the new ruthless economy. Possessed of overwhelming power, unconstrained by organized labor or by effective workplace regulation, management drive their employees as hard as they can, and usually get away with it. This is exploitation in the classic manner of the nineteenth and early twentieth centuries, but there is also a basic difference between these contemporary practices and those of a century ago. Ford and Taylor were mostly intent on controlling the bodily movements of workers tied to machine shops and assembly lines. But today's scientific managers are trying also to control the minds of their white-collar employees. That is what the whole superstructure of control, scripting, and surveillance along the digital assembly lines is designed to achieve.

Here are the outlines of a project truly Orwellian in its ambitions. The project is to develop technologies that are essentially human-proof in their operation, technologies whose control over employee behavior is so powerful that, no matter how ill trained, alienated, or transient a workforce may be, technology can still be relied upon to deliver strong and improving levels of employee productivity. No other hypothesis can account for the call center industry's surreal and chilling combination of employee exploitation combined with hyperimmersion in information technology. With this technology the employee's managers apparently believe that they can keep employees working flat out, pushing aside the employee's knowledge in favor of scripts and databases, and relying on technology's all-seeing eye to detect and contain manifestations of employee discontent.

But can this project really work? Can technology be relied upon to neutralize the effects of an employee's alienation and lack of training? In their paper, "Diagnosis Document Machine Problems over the Telephone," Jack Whalen and Erik Vinkhuyzen show in detail what happens when a corporation uses undertrained workers to perform complex tasks, while relying on information technology to make up for the em-

ployee's deficiencies.[19] In the last chapter, we saw what MMR Corporation, a thinly disguised Xerox, hoped to achieve with CasePoint, an
expert system that provides solutions for customers whose copying machines are malfunctioning. MMR Corporation wanted customer service agents to become passive conduits relaying the customer's testimony
to CasePoint, and then CasePoint's recommendations back to the customer. Whalen and Vinkhuyzen stayed around to see how the system
actually worked. Their findings are based on transcripts of recorded
conversations between agents and customers.

Whalen and Vinkhuyzen found that CasePoint did not deliver. The
system's deficiencies were bound up with the difficulties of reconciling
the two languages used in the transactions between customer, agent,
and system: the language used by customers to describe the symptoms
of their faulty machines, and the language that the expert system was
programmed to understand. CasePoint's designers assumed that no
such problem of reconciliation existed, which is why agents could simply pass along the customers' descriptions to the system. But the MMR
tapes show that problems of reconciling the two languages permeate
the interactions between customer, agent, and system. These problems
arose for three reasons.

CasePoint's designers had programmed the system to recognize a
vocabulary of machine error that they and their management colleagues
used, and that they assumed the customer would use as well. But customers frequently used "unauthorized" words of their own. When this
happened, it was the inescapable task of the agent to try to establish
which of the designer's authorized words best corresponded to the
customer's rogue word. But agents were not trained to carry out this
kind of interrogation and had to do the translations on a hit-or-miss
basis. When agents got the translation wrong, CasePoint would take off
on an irrelevant line of questioning and end up making a faulty diagnosis.[20]

A second and even less realistic assumption of the software designers was that customers would provide a description of a faulty machine's
symptoms which, in its logical structure, would conform naturally to
the structure the system was programmed to understand. But cus-

tomers often came up with rambling, incoherent descriptions that Case-Point could not possibly digest, and agents then had to make sense of the customer's raw utterances. The transcripts show agents trying to perform this editorial task but finding themselves severely handicapped by a lack of training, a lack of confidence, and the pressure of time. More often than not, agents would abandon the struggle and arrange for a technician to visit the customer's offices—the very outcome the expert system was designed to head off.

A third error of the software engineers was their assumption that a digestible account of a machine's symptoms could be put together at the very outset of a conversation between agent and customer. But customers had the inconvenient habit of failing to provide all the relevant information up front, with vital bits of information instead dribbling out when a conversation was already under way. But for a new description of a problem to be considered by CasePoint, the system had to be reset and questioning started anew. There were strong pressures on the agent not to do this. Coming up with a new problem description took time, and agents were always under pressure to fulfill their quota of calls per day. With more than one problem description now on offer, agents also had to choose between them, again something the agents were not trained to do.

After observing CasePoint for twenty months, Whalen and Vinkhuyzen found the systems deeply flawed. Less a substitute for skill, CasePoint created a demand for new skills, those needed to cope with CasePoint itself. The system ran like an aging machine tool whose eccentricities had to be offset by expert handling, an expertise its handlers did not possess. Whalen and Vinkhuyzen do not try to estimate Case-Point's effect on the productivity of MMR Corporation's customer service workforce. But in their paper, they do not come up with a single example in which CasePoint worked as it should have, with the system providing a correct solution to a customer's problem based on information relayed by the agent.

CasePoint is just one expert system and MMR/Xerox just one corporation. But there is also major research evidence showing that the call center industry, and indeed service industries generally, pay a high price in increased costs and lost output for their reliance on an underskilled and transient workforce, and despite an ever greater reliance on information technology. Frederick Reichheld of Bain and Company, the Boston consultancy, has broken new ground in estimating these costs. A maverick thinker in the world of business consultants, Reichheld sees the industrialization of service industries as a ubiquitous phenomenon: "Most business people," he wrote in 1990, "without knowing it, see the service world through the lenses of manufacturing goggles. . . . They are influenced by historical traditions in business training, strategy techniques and organizational theory, all rooted in manufacturing."[21]

Symptomatic of this industrial mindset has been the way in which most service companies "focus their cost reduction efforts on process reengineering and layoffs," which appear to lower costs "but in fact lower employee motivation and retention, leading to lower customer retention, which increases costs."[22] Much of Reichheld's research has been about the impact of customer loyalty on company revenues and profits. But he also shows how the loyalties of customers and employees are closely linked, and so extends his analysis to include the revenue and profit effects of differing levels of employee turnover. His research is focused on service industries such as banking and insurance, and while he does not single out call center agents as special subjects of research, nonetheless, as the company's front line in the battle for customers, call center agents clearly have a major role to play in his scheme.

Reichheld describes the many ways in which loyal, long-term customers are good for company profits: such customers spend more, they tolerate higher prices, they do not have to be paid for with special discounts and offers, and they bring in new customers. Pulling all these factors together, Reichheld shows how even marginal changes in customer retention rates can have a spectacular impact on the value of a customer to a business. In the case of a credit card company that was also a Bain client, Reichheld found that an increase in its annual rate of customer retention, from 80 to 90 percent, increased the value of each new customer from $134 to $300.[23] However, Reichheld also found that customer loyalty and employee loyalty were inextricably bound, so that these rewards could not be harvested unless companies found ways of reducing their rates of employee turnover, and here Reichheld does mention the call center agent:

> Those employees who deal directly with customers day after day have a powerful effect on customer loyalty. Long-term employees can serve customers better than newcomers; after all a customer's contact with a company is through employees, not the top executives. It is with employees that the customer builds a bond of trust and expectations, and when those people leave, the bond is broken.[24]

Reichheld has found that a strengthening of employee loyalty, and the accompanying reduction of employee turnover, can have as positive an impact on company earnings as a reduction of customer turnover. In his book *The Loyalty Effect* (1996) Reichheld describes in detail how reduction in employee defection rates can benefit company revenues and profits.[25] When an employee stays with a company years rather than months, recruitment and training costs are not wasted and can instead be amortized over the entire period of an employee's stay with the company. Longer-term employees are also more efficient.

"As a general rule," Reichheld writes, "employees who stay with the company because they're proud of the value they create for themselves, are more motivated and work harder." Experienced employees cement higher customer loyalty and are skilled at finding and recruiting the best customer. They can also generate the "best flow of high caliber job applicants," which not only raises the quality of new employees but also reduces a company's recruitment costs. Reichheld notes that companies with the highest level of employee retention "consistently hire the vast majority of their recruits through employee referrals."[26]

As with his analysis of customer loyalty, Reichheld pulls these factors together and shows how an employee's value to a company increases dramatically with his tenure.[27] Bain has developed a model showing the results over time of seven economic effects of employee loyalty. The model is based on a ten-year study of a range of service industries. Bain found that the per-annum value of an employee who stays with a company seven years is three times the value of one who stays for only three years; the annual value contributed by this three-year employee is in turn double the value contributed by an employee who stays only a year. The value of an employee who stays less than a year is negative. His recruitment and training are not offset by any gains in efficiency, customer retention, or customer referral.

In their paper, Whalen and Vinkhuyzen show what can be achieved with the kind of experienced and committed employee whom Reichheld writes about. In one of the MMR transcripts, an agent pushes aside the expert system and decides to solve the customer's problem himself.[28] The agent begins by listening to the customer's rambling account of the faulty machine. The agent then starts his own line of questioning, which elicits a fuller and more complex description of the machine's symptoms. The agent makes a number of deductive leaps from one symptom to another and finally comes up with a description that CasePoint can digest and understand. But in this case the agent would not need to give CasePoint his description, for the obvious reason that the expertise that is advanced enough for the agent to formulate his description is also advanced enough for the agent to bypass CasePoint altogether.

Drawing on this example, Whalen and Vinkhuyzen come up with a bold suggestion about how the productivity of a system such as CasePoint could be improved, and in a way that enhances rather than diminishes the role of employee skills. They propose that this expert system and others like it become "systems for experts."[29] At the heart of a conventional expert system such as CasePoint are the judgments of senior engineers and managers about all the possible ways in which a machine can go wrong, with an appropriate remedy attached to each problem. Both kinds of judgment then become embedded in the software. But with a system for an expert, the expertise of the agent is equal in importance to the engineer's and manager's expertise that is already built into the system.

With a system for experts, whenever an agent comes across an unusual case of machine failure, or whenever the agent himself finds a new way of dealing with a faulty machine, this knowledge is entered into the database, alongside the knowledge of managers and engineers. The system's database therefore loses its closed, canonical status and becomes instead an open, expanding resource that any agent can use and renew. When such a system for experts was introduced for MMR-Xerox's field technicians, their productivity quickly rose by between 10 and 15 percent. However, with the field technicians the introduction of a system for experts did not require a major change in their status and pay. They were already skilled workers, and the new system simply required them to exercise their skills in a somewhat different way.

But for call center agents a system for experts would change significantly both their status and their methods of work. Agents would have to be properly trained in the operations of copying machines and, as newly skilled workers, they would have to be better paid. Reform would therefore come with a price tag. These bottom-line issues may explain why senior managers' tolerance of a system for experts did not extend from the field technician in the pickup truck to the call center agent in the cubicle. When Whalen and Vinkhuyzen presented their diagnoses and remedies to MMR-Xerox's senior management, they came up against managers' "unshakable commitment" to the status quo. Managers did not "want to invest in any modification in the design and deployment of the system." They were backed up by CasePoint's software designers, who were still interested in seeing how far they could go in relying "exclusively on machine expertise as a substitute for agent knowledge."[30]

A technical support center such as Xerox's stands at the higher end of the call center industry, but the high-performance model can be extended to the entire industry, even to the present-day wastelands of sales and marketing that are so heavily represented in the pages of *Call Center Solutions*. But this cannot happen until the call center industry rids itself of its whole oppressive superstructure of digital surveillance and control. Employees cannot exercise skills in a workplace heavy with scripts and prescribed action responses. Nor can they do so in a workplace ruled by the grim vehicles of classic Taylorism: active talk time, time between calls, calls per half hour, length of calls, time unplugged, time spent going to the bathroom.

The unwillingness of managers to dismantle this apparatus testifies to the still-dominant influence of scientific management and its industrial model. Moreover, the constant flow of new and upgraded software products encourages managers to believe that the faults of a system such as CasePoint can always be patched with the latest high-tech fix. MMR/Xerox's software designers had the spirit of the times on their side when they opposed Whalen and Vinkhuyzen's plans for a high-performance call center, urging management to continue "relying exclusively on machine expertise as a substitute for agent knowledge." This the corporation has been doing, employing more and more temporary workers in its call centers and tolerating high rates of employee turnover.[31]

The call center industry is in need of renewal because it is, despite its present condition, an industry emblematic of the digital economy. It is fast-growing and intensive in its use of technology, the chief means by which a company reaches its customers, as Bill Gates, Tom Peters, and the reengineers have all pointed out. With its huge workforce, the industry is also an important employer of Americans who have not been to college, and with the decline of the blue-collar middle class of unionized factory workers, there is a need to create good jobs for the non-college educated—jobs that are skilled, pay well, and offer the prospects of a career. High-performance call centers can provide such opportunities. But the industry has first to rid itself of the all-pervading legacy of Fredrick Winslow Taylor and William Henry Leffingwell.

7

THE SCIENTIFIC MANAGEMENT OF LIFE—

AND DEATH: PART I

THE CALL CENTER WORKFORCE is one of the first proletariats of the digital age, with the empowered computer and its software imposing the discipline and control that, in the mass production plant, has always been the task of the assembly line and the automatic machine. But this transfer of industrial methods from manufacturing to services is not confined to a lower-income, lower-skilled workplace like the call center. With the coming of "managed care," medicine has become the latest service industry to find itself the target of this industrial reengineering. However, the lead employee in health care, the physician, is a high-wage, highly skilled worker, and the attempts of the managed care industry during the past fifteen years to subject the physician to the disciplines of "process" represent perhaps the most dramatic example of reengineering's vertical mobility in the new economy.

The decline of the old fee-for-service system of health insurance in the United States sets the scene for the rise of managed care in the late 1980s and early 1990s. The weakness of the old system was its failure to control health care costs, a failure that had a long history. Between 1965 and 1983, per-capita health care expenditures in the United States rose at a rate of 12.5 percent per year, nearly 5 percent greater than the underlying rate of inflation.[1] Early in his first term, President Nixon told a news conference that rising health care costs in the United States constituted a "massive crisis" that, unless acted upon, would lead to a "breakdown in our medical system."[2] The crisis became acute in the late 1980s when yearly increases in health insurance premiums of 15 to 20 percent became commonplace.[3]

A triangular relationship between insurers, employers, and physicians fueled health care cost inflation. The monthly premiums that insurers charged to businesses on behalf of their employees were calculated on a cost-plus basis: The premiums reflected the existing costs of health care plus a markup for profits. As long as the insurer could pass on the higher costs of health care in the form of higher monthly premiums to be paid by the employer, physicians could err on the side of caution in ordering up multiple tests, drugs, or surgical procedures for their patients. The acceleration of health care inflation in the late 1980s led employes to cast around for ways of controlling their health care costs. Managed care seemed to offer a means of breaking these links between higher medical costs and rising insurance premiums.

With the coming of managed care, large employers such as General Motors would contract with selected managed care organizations (MCOs) such as Aetna or Humana for the insurance of all or part of their workforce. The MCO offered the corporation comprehensive coverage of its employees for a fixed payment per insured employee. Employees of companies that enrolled with MCOs then faced restrictions on their choice of physicians. The most restrictive of the MCOs, the health maintenance organization (HMO), limited the employee's choice of physicians to a panel approved by the HMO. The preferred provider organization, or PPO, allowed employees to pay a higher fee and select a physician "out of network."[4] The critical difference between the managed care and fee-for-service models of health insurance was the promise of MCOs, whether of the HMO or PPO variety, to keep insurance premiums rising in line with the economy's overall rate of inflation.

MCOs believed they could make this promise because, unlike the old fee-for-service insurer, they took on the power to control medical costs. This control was greatest for those MCOs that owned their own network of hospitals and directly employed their own medical workforce of doctors, nurses, and administrators. But even when MCOs had to negotiate with independent hospitals, physicians, or groups of physicians,

MCOs could use their control of what they call "covered lives" to beat down the prices they would pay for surgical procedures, doctor's consulting fees, and hospital stays. MCOs also relied on bureaucracies of case managers, often medically untrained, to contain medical costs. Working on the telephone, and with the MCO's rule book at hand, case managers subjected the decisions of physicians to "utilization review," telling them which drugs, procedures, tests, and treatments they could and could not prescribe for their patients.

The early success of the managed care model can be measured in two sets of statistics: the falling rates of health care inflation in the early and mid-1990s, and the rising percentage of the employed population insured through MCOs. Measured by the rise in the average premium paid by employers with a workforce of two hundred or more, the inflation of medical premiums fell from 11.5 percent in 1991 to 8 percent in 1993, and to 2.1 percent in 1995.[5] Employers rewarded MCOs for their success in controlling health care costs with a spectacular increase in the percentage of employed private sector workers enrolled with managed care companies, from 25 percent in 1988 to 80 percent in 1997.[6] But the employees entrusted to the care of MCOs by their employers have never shared the employers' enthusiasm for the managed care model.

A September 2000 poll in *Business Week* showed MCOs to be running level with the tobacco companies in their unpopularity with the American public.[7] Seventy-one percent of those polled judged MCOs "poor" or "fair" in the service they provided their customers, while only 18 percent judged their service to be "good" or "excellent." By comparison, 34 percent thought the computer industry was providing poor to fair service, and 50 percent thought its service good to excellent. In the summer of 2002, a Harris poll found that only 17 percent of the public believed that a health care system dominated by managed care "works pretty well and only minor changes are necessary."[8]

The growing unpopularity of managed care has meant that the U.S. patient population has been less and less willing to accept the denials of care handed down by MCO case managers, decisions that it regards as often arbitrary and unfair, and dictated by the MCOs' own drive for revenues and profits. Responding to this sentiment, legislators in forty-three states (as of January 2003) have passed laws providing for independent review of MCO decisions denying care.[9] With this loosening of MCO controls, the health care consumption of the U.S. population has been rising, and in both 2001 and 2002, health care costs rose at double-digit rates not seen since the early 1990s.[10] In a May 2002 survey the consultants Hewitt Associates found that MCOs had increased their premiums charged to employers by 10.2 percent in 2001, by an estimated 15.6 percent in 2002, and with increases for 2003 running at 22 percent.[11] Whatever the early successes of managed care, it is now failing to deliver on its promise to contain health care costs, and an overwhelming majority of the U.S. public also believes that it falls short as a system of health care. A successor to the old fee-for-service model of health insurance has yet to be found, and the search for one continues.

The adversarial relationship between the managed care industry and the U.S. patient population can be traced to a basic feature of the industry's economics. For-profit MCOs overwhelmingly dominate the managed care industry, and these MCOs make money when their average spending per enrolled patient falls below the average value of the premiums they receive from employers. The less an MCO spends on its patients, the greater its profits, and the greater the shareholder value it contributes to its investors. The industry uses the phrase "medical losses" to describe the payments it has to make on behalf of its sick customers, and this choice of words reveals much about how the industry regards such payments. An MCO's "medical loss ratio" calculates the payments to MCO customers as a percentage of total revenues, and is an amount that MCO managers try to keep as low as possible. But an MCO's "medical loss" may be a patient's lifeblood, literally. The case of Aetna Inc., one of the largest MCOs, shows how this perverse economics distorts the performance of MCOs and harms their patients.

On April 25, 2002, Aetna announced results for the first quarter of 2002 that impressed Wall Street and raised Aetna's stock price by 13 percent in a single day. Excluding special charges, Aetna's operating profits rose to $64.9 million from $15 million in the first quarter of

2001, and earnings per share jumped from 10 cents to 44 cents over the same period. Wall Street analysts applauded Aetna's results along with the methods the corporation used to achieve them. Josh Raskin of Lehman Brothers praised Aetna as "a different company. . . . we have tangible signs of improvement with the medical loss ratio considerably lower." Aetna had improved the medical loss ratio in part by shedding "unprofitable clients"—that is, clients who got sick too often and so pushed the medical loss ratio in the wrong direction.[12]

The patient population and the medical profession have increasingly come to view the managed care industry as their opponent in the numberless disputes that arise when the industry's drive to minimize "medical losses" runs up against the patient's and the physician's determination to receive or deliver care that they consider medically necessary. These disputes encompass every conceivable aspect of medical practice: whether a certain drug should or should not be prescribed; whether a surgical procedure should or should not be performed; how long a stay in hospital should last; whether a patient with advanced cancer should or should not receive a course of chemotherapy; and whether a patient with a chronic illness such as congestive heart failure should be treated in a hospital, a clinic, or at home.

At their worst, these disputes escalate to become MCO horror stories: gravely ill patients turned away from emergency rooms, women with mastectomies sent home from hospitals with their saline drips still attached, a child with cerebral palsy denied coverage by Humana in mid-treatment—an actual case covered by Hedrick Smith in his fine three-hour documentary on U.S. health care shown on PBS in October 2000. In July 1999, the *Journal of the American Medical Association (JAMA)* carried a study that quantified the medical cost to the U.S. population of the for-profit MCOs' drive to keep down "medical loss ratios."[13] The study relied on MCO accreditation surveys and on a data series known as the "health plan employer data and information set," or HEDIS.[14]

The study found strong evidence of inferior performance by "investor-led" health plans when compared with their not-for-profit counterparts. The authors looked at fourteen "quality-of-care variables" included under the National Committee for Quality Assurance's (NCQA) rubric "effectiveness of care." The investor-led plans had lower performance ratings for all fourteen indicators, but their underperformance was greatest for the two indicators that involved serious illness. Among heart attack victims for whom treatment with beta-blocker drugs was recommended, the study found that 70.6 percent of patients in not-for-profit plans filled a prescription for beta-blockers, compared with 59.2 percent of patients in investor-led plans.[15]

The same performance gap was present for another recommended treatment, the use of eye examinations for patients with diabetes. As of 1996, a total of 47.9 percent of diabetic patients in not-for-profit plans had received an eye examination in the past year, compared to 35.1 percent of patients in investor-led plans. The not-for-profits also led in the performance of other preventive treatments. The completion rate of immunization for two-year-olds averaged 72.3 percent in not-for-profit plans, versus 63.9 percent in investor-led plans. Similarly, the proportion of women aged 52 to 69 who had had a mammogram within the past two years averaged 75.1 percent in not-for-profit plans, compared to 69.4 percent in investor-led plans.[16]

The for-profit MCOs' lower rates of treatment are built upon countless omissions or denials of treatment to the U.S. patient population. These denials, in turn, largely account for the public's negative view of the managed care industry. The industry has become the accumulation of all of the unappealing traits it exhibits in the course of the skirmishes: meanness, heartlessness, putting the bottom line ahead of the patient's welfare. This image may be accurate as far as it goes, but it ignores a whole body of ideas and ambitions that drives the managed care industry and accounts for its behavior. No less than Coca-Cola, GE, or Microsoft, MCOs have their own operating philosophies, and these provide MCO executives and their lobbyists with elaborate justifications for what they do.

Thus, MCOs and their lobbyists insist that they can both earn good profits and provide "quality affordable health care" for their customers. The reasoning that underlies such claims may be flawed, but it must be taken into account if the behavior of the managed care industry is to be understood. The ideas that drive the industry are rooted as much in management theory as in medicine, and so management consultants have written many of the chief texts of managed care. Books such as Andersen Consulting's *Changing Health Care* are, therefore, important guides to what is now happening in health care.[17] Much can be learned about such books by simply looking at the credentials of their authors.

One author of *Changing Health Care* was a director of Andersen Consulting's "healthcare merger and acquisition practice," and his areas of focus were "leadership development and organizational design." A second author was a partner in charge of Andersen's "global care delivery and medical management solutions teams." His work focused on "creating strategies to reduce medical costs." A third author was the author of *Zap! Empowerment in Health Care,* and her expertise was "in the areas of health care management and organization."[18] Common to all three authors is their complete absence of any medical qualification. The three authors set out to transform the practice of medicine, but none has been to medical school, none has practiced medicine, and so none has ever examined or diagnosed a single patient.

Consultants such as the Andersen authors typically believe that they can dispense with such credentials because, as recipients of their advice, MCOs are no different from any other kind of business. Knowledge of medicine is no more required of the health care consultant than knowledge of meatpacking is required of those having to sort out Burger King. But one kind of specialized knowledge is required for tasks such as "organizational design," and that is a knowledge of reengineering. The hospital and the doctor's office, no less than the machine shop and the call center, are places to be reengineered. For this task, the three Andersen authors are well qualified.

The language of reengineering, therefore, pervades the manuals of managed care, just as it does the texts of call centers, machine shops, and auto assembly lines. In *Changing Health Care* the three Andersen authors speak of "processes, reengineered to reflect the longitudinal maintenance of health—physical, mental and spiritual" and of the "step by step performance measures that [trace] the process from the time the

consumer placed the initial call to the checkout"—when the checkout
in question is from a hospital, not a supermarket.[19] In its study of managed care, the consultants Ernst and Young describes the "reengineering of existing [health care] processes" as a "multistep effort" that
involves "building a business case, documenting existing processes with
cycle times and volumes, indentifying opportunities for improvement."[20]

The "process reengineering" of health care works in familiar ways.
Medical reengineers simplify existing processes and speeds them up.
Patients get to spend fewer days in the hospital. Patients are allowed
fewer visits to the doctor, and those visits that do occur are rigorously
timed and shortened. Medical reengineering also creates new proceses
where none existed before. Patients with routine symptoms find themselves diagnosed over the telephone. As in the call center, automated expert systems pose scripted questions that are then relayed, via a "call
taker," to the patient. Treatment of the chronically ill, too, can be
reengineered, as patients with cancer or heart disease can become objects of "disease management." With this reengineering, care consists of
a uninterrupted flow of preplanned events and interventions put together by automated expert systems.

But while "process" is common to the managed care organization,
the machine shop, and the call center, the processes of managed care
differ from these others in several critical respects. ERP excepted, all the
processes we have so far examined have belonged to what Thomas Davenport has called the operational side of a business, the mostly routine
activities that are performed by semi- or unskilled workers. There are
many such operational processes in managed care: the ordering of medical supplies, the billing of patients, the procedures of an MCO's own
call centers. Ernst and Young warns its clients to take "a very close look
at the operational processes in place at the enterprise and entity-specific
level."[21]

But the managed care industry is also deeply engaged in reengineering what are, in the context of Davenport's distinctions, "higher"
processes, and these are the core professional activities of the physician:
his or her screening, diagnosis, and treatment of patients. As we shall
see, the great ambition of the managed care industry is to incorporate

the physician within a regime of process whose rigor and discipline resembles those governing the activities of machinists and call center agents. A second critical difference between managed care and all other industries concerns the unique, dual relationship that patients have with the health care industry, and particularly with managed care.

For the patient is not only a consumer of health care products, he or she is also the product itself. The object traveling down the medical assembly lines is not a chassis or an engine, it is ourselves; and as more and more physicians become links in the chains of medical process, so also does the treatment that we as patients receive from physicians. As patients, we are not well equipped to deal with this industrialized medicine. In the workplace our public selves can give us some protection against the often cold, mechanical workings of process. But in the clinics of managed care, illness and disease expose our vulnerable, private selves, and it is in this naked condition that we are processed, as fast and cheaply as possible, along the waystations of business medicine. A belief that this industrialization of medicine is morally as well as medically inappropriate has fueled the public backlash against managed care.

Subjecting the physician to the disciplines of process is the most ambitious project of managed care, but the reengineering of this higher process is perhaps best approached by looking first at the reengineering of health care's lower, operational processes. Managed care's record in tackling these simpler reengineering tasks can then set the scene for the industry's more complex dealings with the physician. At this lower level of process, a good place to start is with a project called the Idealized Design of Clinical Office Practices, or ID-COP. ID-COP is the brainchild of Donald Berwick and Chuck Kilo, both of the Institute for Health care Improvement, and both noted experts in health care efficiency.

For Berwick, the ideal clinical office best resembles a Japanese automobile plant: "Tenets of lean production that emanated from Toyota are central to the ID-COP design. . . . We need to create some health care Toyotas, and we need to understand the path to get there." Berwick lauds Taiichi Ohno, cofounder of the Toyota system, as a "ferocious foe of wasted human effort" and, as with the engines and chassis on the Toyota line, patients visiting an ID-COP must be processed in and out of the doctor's office at the maximum possible speed.[22] In Kilo's words: "We strive to create offices that function at unprecedented levels of ambulatory performance."

In her book *Strategies for Integrated Health Care,* the managed care consultant Jane Metzger provides a revealing account of how health care reengineers go about measuring a particularly important sub-process: the amount of time patients spend with the physician. In Metzger's words: "Capturing the start and end times of the clinical interaction is critical to managing the patient flow." This information is required as an "input to reengineering visit times to correspond with the amount of time actually required for the type of encounter."[23] Some organizations had considered using "sensing or card-swipe technology" to detect when providers (i.e., physicians) "enter and leave examination rooms." But in Metzger's view, "the most natural way to capture information on clinician-patient interaction time" is "as a by-product of the provider signing on to, and then signing off from a patient care system in the exam room." By "patient care system," Metzger means a computer terminal.[24]

Another revealing example of managed care's reengineering of a lower-level process is the use of "telephone triage" systems to deal with the supposedly routine complaints of patients. Here, managed care has borrowed heavily from the processes of the call center industry. Ernst and Young explain that "triage systems are generally used at a call-in desk for a health plan." As at a call center devoted to sales or marketing, the "call taker" need have no expertise in the subject to be discussed with the caller: "The software guides the call taker through a list of queries and responses based on the caller's supplied information." It is again the software that "helps in determining the urgency as well as the directing of care."[25] J. D. Kleinke, an influential health care economist and consultant, and a particularly aggressive proponent of managed care, commends this "rational, low-cost mechanism at the very front end of the treatment system," along with the "sophisticated decision tree analysis" that, as in the call center, guides the call taker in the right direction.[26]

In 2000–2001 Kaiser Permanente of California operated a triage system that shows how such systems can be used to contain "medical losses." At its three call centers in Northern California Kaiser's phone clerks could earn bonuses of up to 10 percent of their salaries if they hit various targets set by the company: limiting patient access to appointments to less than 35 percent of callers; keeping average call time to less than 3 minutes and 45 seconds; and transferring fewer than 50 percent of callers to nurses for help. The nurses themselves were, according to a union representative "under tremendous pressure to cut off the calls. . . . to quickly deal with these people, write it up and move on to the next one or else they're disciplined." Kaiser monitored the nurses' "average handling time" and included the data in each nurse's annual evaluation.[27]

The goal of all these activities is to speed up, the primordial goal of scientific management throughout its history. In his seminal work on medical education, *Time to Heal,* Dr. Kenneth Ludmerer describes the impact of medical speed up on the education and training of physicians. Ludmerer sets the scene by citing some of the leading statistics on "clinical productivity." In the late 1980s most physicians felt that examining 30 patients a day was "pushing the limit." But by the mid-1990s, 25 to 30 patients a day was common at many MCOs, and stories circulated about "primary care physicians treating as many as 70 patients a day."[28]

In 1997 doctors spent an average of eight minutes talking to each patient, less than half as much time as a decade earlier. In the relentless drive for "clinical productivity," even teaching hospitals have begun avoiding "unproductive" patients—sick patients whose treatment is costly and whose prognosis is poor. Ludmerer describes what happened at the University of California at Irvine's Medical Center when the chief administrator saw that productivity suffered "from caring for too many patients with serious illnesses." The chief administrator told his staff [that the center could] "no longer tolerate patients with complex and expensive-to-treat conditions being encouraged to transfer to our [medical] group."[29]

Ludmerer shows how managed care's relentless pursuit of clinical productivity has eaten away at the time needed for medical students to learn their craft, and for faculty members to teach them. With the acceleration of the patient flow, even senior physicians on the faculty of leading medical schools become "work up machines and disposition arrangers: admitting patients and planning their discharge, one after another, with much less time than before to examine them, confer with attending physicians, teach medical students." At Johns Hopkins School of Medicine, among the most prestigious medical schools in the nation, senior physicians found themselves becoming "just pairs of hands" with students "just observers."[30]

At the University of Iowa College of Medicine, faculty members described how, under pressure of time, residents were becoming "too quick to accept admitting diagnoses from referring physicians" and too ready to "pursue the evaluation of the most likely diagnoses to the exclusion of other pertinent diagnoses."[31] Some medical educators have looked to the outpatient clinic as a place where the time lost to education at the teaching hospital might be made good. With the coming of managed care, much diagnosis and treatment of patients is being shifted from the hospital to the outpatient or "ambulatory" clinic. Gordon T. Moore, an educator at the nonprofit Harvard Pilgrim Health Care, advanced the concept of the "teaching HMO" which, centered upon the outpatient clinic, had the "potential to transform academic medicine in the next century."[32] However, time has become as scarce a commodity at outpatient clinics as it has at the teaching hospital, and for the same reasons.

Those trying to find time for teaching at the outpatient clinics soon came up against obstacles such as Chuck Kilo's drive "to create offices that function at unprecedented levels of ambulatory performance," and Donald Berwick's "need to create some health care Toyotas." The essence of the Toyota system, as we have seen, is to hoard every single second saved on the line, so that eventually one less assembler, or in this case doctor, need be employed there. At the ambulatory clinics, therefore, the pressures for "clinical productivity" were no less ferocious than they had been at the teaching hospital, and Ludmerer found that administrators of medical schools and teaching hospitals were as zealous as any health care consultant to make sure that students and faculty not obstruct the patient flow.

Officials at Johns Hopkins School of Medicine, for example, told students and teachers that they could work in a new outpatient clinic "only with careful orchestration by the clinical chiefs who would be charged to make sure that such education did not interfere with efficient patient care."[33] An unnamed southern medical school had set up a program allowing third-year students to rotate through physicians' private offices. Administrators were unconcerned when the physician's daily load of up to sixty patients limited the opportunities for teaching and learning.[34] Indeed, Ludmerer found that top administrators at teaching hospitals were inclined to identify themselves more with a corporate, than an academic, culture. These administrators started calling themselves "presidents" and "chief executives," demanded corporate-level compensation, and brought in hordes of management consultants. They talked of "rightsizing," "downsizing," "total quality improvement," and of course, "reengineering."[35]

Beyond the familiar reengineering worlds of process and speed up, managed care's most ambitious claim is that it has pioneered methods of medical decision making that are superior to the methods habitually used by physicians. J. D. Kleinke writes of the "industrialization of the physician and his practice of medicine," of achieving "predictability of operations, costs and outputs," and of "standardizing how we measure and compare patient care processes, with the goal of quantification."[36] On the face of it, MCOs are not well placed to impose such medical standardization on the work of practicing physicians. Medical reengineers such as the Andersen authors have no medical qualifications at all, nor can they make up for this deficiency by pointing to the presence within MCOs of high-caliber physicians who might provide medical judgments superior to those of front-line physicians.

With few exceptions, MCO "medical directors" are no longer practicing physicians who actually take care of patients. Even fewer are engaged in advanced medical research. Rather, they have become medical administrators who pass judgment on the medical decisions of others, though they themselves often lack the relevant specialized knowledge. In February 1994, the *New England Journal of Medicine* carried a piece by an MCO medical director in which the author describes a day in his professional life. He describes himself handing down life-and-death judgments on the treatments that patients with advanced cancer should or should not receive. The MCO medical director himself was not a cancer specialist, but this lack of specialized knowledge did not seem to bother him.[37]

If the claims of MCOs to have privileged knowledge of the "best ways" of medicine are not based on superior medical training and knowledge, what are they based on? Information technology is the philosopher's stone of managed care, and with the ambitions of industry so firmly hitched to the star of IT, there is in the literature of managed care a celebration of IT giganticism, a belief that the greater the size of the medical databases in the hands of MCOs, the more likely it is that they will come upon their "best ways" of treating patients.

The Andersen authors describe how "most health care organizations" are "treasure troves of both clinical and nonclinical data," which is "scattered in patient records, physicians summaries, financial records, family histories, and innumerable other sources." The Andersen study singles out Aetna, one of the largest managed care organizations, for the data collected from its millions of members that provides "extraordinary useful information on specific outcomes."[38] *Healthplan Magazine* praises Humana's "integrated data base that incorporates information on more than 6 million members and 24 Humana affiliated health plans across the country."

The database, which Humana uses to "target and track disease management programs for more than 30 chronic conditions," was "amassed as the company grew, with each acquired plan adopting Humana's data platform."[39] Similarly, Cornelia Tilney, vice president for business development at the disease-management company Cardiac Solutions Inc., boasts of the ten thousand "complex patients with huge medical records that we are managing right now." Managing these databases required "a big investment" in IT, and the willingness of companies to make such an investment "is one of the ways you can differentiate the thorough-breds from the Shetland ponies" in the disease-management business.[40]

Once MCOs have accumulated these vast quantities of data, the MCOs' own version of "population-based medicine" comes into play, creating for the managed care industry its own brand of medicine. This closely mimics established medicine while quietly abandoning practices that have been at the heart of medicine since ancient times. The physician who has given perhaps the clearest account of this new medicine is Edward Wagner of the Group Health Cooperative and the W. A. (Sandy) MacColl Institute for Health care Innovation, both of Seattle, Washington. Wagner's ideas are set out in a piece he and two colleagues wrote in 1996 for *Managed Care Quarterly*, and also in an interview he gave to the *Journal of the American Medical Association* in May 1994.[41]

In his 1996 piece, Wagner draws a distinction between what he calls "usual" and "planned" medicine. "Usual medicine" turns out to be the kind of medicine that physicians have been practicing since the time of Hippocrates. The physicians of usual medicine are taught that "patients are unique, their problems are idiosyncratic, and good care is highly individualized." "Planned care," by contrast, "required an intellectual leap for the doctor from constantly thinking and worrying about specific patients, to considering all patients with specific clinical features or needs and how these needs might be met."[42] The lead role in working out how patients with "specific clinical features" should be treated is not played by physicians but by information systems.

It is here that the MCOs' vast databases come into their own. Wagner explains in detail how information systems can assume more and more of the responsibility for medical decision making. Using computer algorithms that analyze the "patient base," planned care begins with "the definition of the sub population of interest," which may consist of "patients with diabetes, or elderly patients no longer able to ambulate."[43] The greater the size of the MCO's patient database, and the more powerful the software attached to it, the more elaborate this segmentation of the patient population can be.

With the establishment of these patient groupings, computer algorithms are also used to identify a "special set of services" that distinguish the "clinically significant subgroups" and that each subgroup must receive. These treatments take the form of "a protocol or plan which provides an explicit statement of what needs to be done for patients, at what intervals and by whom." "Usual medical care," Wagner comments, "generally does not operate by protocol," and "many practitioners resent the notion that care should be homogenized." Wagner clearly regards these usual practitioners as medical Luddites, and we can now see why he believes that physicians practicing planned medicine should "stop worrying about specific patients" and start considering "all patients with specific clinical features."[44]

In planned medicine, the most important decisions physicians have to make concern the broad classification of their patients, and what counts in this classification is not the patient's "individualized" or "idiosyncratic" profile and symptoms, but those characteristics and symptoms that the patient may share in common with a "clinically significant subgroup." This will determine to which subgroup he or she will be assigned. Once the physician has slotted the patient into a particular subgroup, he has already made his most important decision, because the patient's further treatment has already been decided. Algorithms have already "analyzed the patient base" to which the patient now belongs, and also determined "which patients need specific services."[45] The physician now becomes a provider of these services but, as we shall see, this is not to be his task alone.

For the most part, Wagner discusses his automated medicine in the context of chronic illnesses such as stroke, heart disease, cancer, and diseases of the kidney, liver, and lung. But a crude version of this managerial medicine comes into play every time a physician crosses swords with an MCO case manager or medical director. With "clinical productivity," the ever-present concern of the MCO, there is usually, in these telephone conversations, only enough time for a physician to describe the patient's leading symptoms. But that is time enough for the MCO case manager or medical director to allocate the patient to a subgroup, look up the MCO's treatment guidelines in a manual or database, and tell the physician what can and cannot be done.

The practice of this managerial medicine has profound implications for the relations between physicians and their coworkers. As MCOs try to diminish the responsibilities that have always set physicians apart from nurses or social workers, administrators can go about integrating the physician within medical processes that are standardized, repetitive, and subject to rigorous timing and monitoring in the manner of Kilo and Berwick's Toyota-style clinic. The Andersen authors flatly state that "the new team structure removes doctors as the essential link in the chain of every consumer's care," while the Ernst and Young study claims that "the health care system as a whole is shifting away from encounter-based care" between doctors and patients.[46]

Thus the private consultation between patient and physician, the indispensable event of usual medicine, is destined to fade away. Writing in *Health care Business,* Dennis J. Streveler, Ph.D., a health care IT consultant, explained how

> just as the American notion of the medical house call is now only a pleasant memory, so too will today's medical consultation become an anachronism as the skills of the physician are fundamentally refocused and reshaped to better interface with a technologically advanced world.[47]

Karen Niemi, a medical reengineer from North Carolina, gives a sense of the physician's submersion within the elaborate and proliferating team structures of managerial medicine:

> The role of the clinical design team is to create a clinical algorithm or service sequence for the target condition or illness. Team members will typically include physicians, nurses, educators, health department members, social workers and payer representatives. In many instances the members of the clinical design team will remain to form the support process design team and implementation team.[48]

Dr. William D. Schumacher, CEO of an "emergency medicine management firm" in Indiana, shows how this remarkably bureaucratic approach to medicine can work in dealing with a simple ailment such as a sore throat:

> There is no more physician/patient relationship, at least not in the one-on-one sense. Patient care is now a team concept in which a simple sore throat can involve a dozen people, by the time coding and lab work are completed. The art of administering this process and ensuring that the patient has a positive experience is almost as delicate as providing patient care.[49]

The Andersen authors consistently use the word "provider" to describe the physician, as does J. D. Kleinke, and such a choice of vocabulary is itself subtle evidence of the diminished role of the physician in managerial medicine. This linguistic sleight of hand, very common in the literature of managed care, is an example of George Orwell's famous dictum that changes in vocabulary are often used to confirm or conceal important changes in political or bureaucratic life. In July 1999, *Health care Business* reported that the Oregon Medical Association had passed a resolution urging "health insurers, hospital systems, government entities and others to stop using the term 'provider' and stick to physician or doctor" when referring to the medical profession in government regulations and medical histories.

The American Medical Association told *Health care Business* "people understand that doctors are the most highly trained health care professionals in the world, and we don't want to be lumped in with everyone else."[50] Jim Kronenberg, associate director of the Oregon Medical Association, told *Health care Business* that the response in Oregon to the association's request had been "good."[51] However, a reading of recent managed care literature reveals scant reduction in the industry's description of the physician as provider, and with good reason. Lumping the physician in with everybody else reflects the determination of MCOs to integrate the physician ever deeper within the processes of managerial medicine.

Thirty years ago Minnesota neurologist Paul Ellwood coined the term "health maintenance organization" and persuaded President Richard

Nixon to promote HMOs as part of his administration's health care policy. Ellwood saw the HMO as a business model that could bring the methods of the industrial revolution to health care: "conversion to larger units of production, technological innovation, division of labor, substitution of capital for labor, vigorous competition, and profitability as the mandatory condition of survival."[52] Ellwood speaks in the broad, detached language of economics, but there has been nothing detached about the industrialism that has gripped health care for the last fifteen years. Medical reengineers have set out to transform the doctor's office and the hospital ward into workshops of medical production, with the speed, standardization, and control of the industrial plant and with the physician becoming "a highly paid foreman in a medical factory."[53]

In most sectors of the manufacturing and service economies, managers and reengineers have been able to introduce the new forms of mass production and scientific management without serious opposition from the workforce. This has been true of machine shops and assembly lines, of offices and call centers, and along the obscure corridors where ERP is transforming the practices of corporate management. But in health care, medical reengineers have come up against the fierce resistance of both the medical profession and the U.S. patient population. This coalition has been strong enough to win the support of most state legislatures, and so also strong enough to have had laws passed that blunt some of the core practices of managerial medicine. It is now time to visit this medical battleground.

8

THE SCIENTIFIC MANAGEMENT OF LIFE—

AND DEATH: PART II

MANAGERIAL MEDICINE TRIES TO GRAFT the standardization of industrial engineering onto the hospital, the clinic, and the doctor's office. It looks for standard medical remedies for standard medical problems, all with known, standard outcomes. It also looks for the efficiencies of mass production: faster medical output with lower costs and lower prices per unit of output, and higher profits earned on increased market share and higher volume of sales. In this mass production regime, the physician is slated to become a link in the chain of medical process, and an object of scientific management. The physician's activities have to be monitored, controlled, and judged according to the dictates of the "one best way." The exercise of judgment and skill by the physician, and, in the words of Dr. Jerome Kassirer, former editor of the *New England Journal of Medicine,* "his unstructured problem solving," his need to "formulate unique solutions for each patient"—these ancient attributes of the physician's craft—are designed to fade away.[1]

In its fight to escape such professional demotion, the medical profession has a powerful weapon of its own: the credibility and rigor of its own research. This can just as easily be used to investigate the scientific claims of managerial medicine as it can to investigate cancer, strokes, and heart disease. Managerial medicine provides a long agenda for investigation: the validity of its version of automated medicine; the reliability of the databases upon which this automated medicine so heavily depends; the degree of variation in the medical decision making of different managed care companies; and finally, at the level of "process," the record of medical reengineering in making the health care industry more productive and efficient.

In February 1994 the *New England Journal of Medicine* published a research paper that sheds light on this last claim. The paper looks at variations in insurance coverage for a trial of an experimental treatment of breast cancer, autologous bone marrow transplant.[2] Tucked away in the study was a remarkable statistic: The physicians running the trial had to deal with 187 insurance companies providing coverage for the 533 participating patients. Each company had its own database, expert panel, treatment guidelines, and bureaucracies of medical monitoring and control. Similarly, in a November 1999 interview, Alan Enthoven, the former Pentagon official and leading advocate of managed care, admitted that in California the average group of physicians work with fifteen different MCOs, which was "just too many" and "confusing to everybody."[3]

Such anecdotes point to the spectacular proliferation of health care bureaucracy that has taken place over the past thirty years and that can be directly attributed to the coming of managed care. In the last chapter, I described the role of MCO case managers who set out to micromanage the decision making of physicians and who also deal with the numberless billing disputes that arise between MCOs, patients, and physicians. The existence of this MCO bureaucracy has given rise to two counter-bureaucracies: one within doctors' offices as physicians hire administrators to deal with MCO case managers, and another in hospitals as managements hire administrators for the same purpose.

Moreover, each of the three medical actors—MCO, physician, hospital—has to deal with the other two, each fighting their health care battles simultaneously on two fronts, and this calls for still more administrators and case managers. Hospital administrators are dealing with the pressure from MCO case managers to cut hospital stays and curtail surgical procedures, while carrying out their own "utilization review" of what physicians and surgeons are doing within the hospital walls. Similarly, physicians and their staff are having to argue both with

MCO case managers about the treatment of patients, and then argue with another tier of case managers once their patients enter the hospital. Managed care has also nurtured a fourth bureaucratic universe comprising businesses that advise MCOs, mediate their disputes with physicians, and perform various outsourced tasks for them—yet which contribute marginally, if at all, to the care of sick patients.

But each of these businesses contributes its own layers of administrators and case managers. The health care departments of large corporations monitor the performance of MCOs and negotiate contracts. Disease-management companies, contracted by MCOs to "manage" the treatment of patients with chronic illnesses such as diabetes and heart disease, add a whole new layer of administration to an industry already saturated with administrators. Health care consultants, such as Andersen Consulting (now Accenture) and Ernst and Young, advise MCOs about reengineering and cost containment; auditing companies carry out the independent reviews of MCO decisions, as mandated by state legislatures; billing companies handle one of the most time-consuming of MCO activities; and marketing and advertising companies help MCOs find new and profitable groups of clients.

In their research, Drs. David Himmelstein and Steffie Woolhandler of the Harvard Medical School provide detailed statistical evidence of this administrative bloat and show how the cost of bureaucracies created to contain costs can overwhelm whatever savings these bureaucracies might achieve. Himmelstein and Woolhandler's research begins in the 1960s, and so goes back far enough to take in the entire history of managed care in the United States. Their statistics are compelling, and challenge all those free-market conservatives who claim, along with the Bush administration, that health care reform in the United States should defer to the efficiencies of the private sector.

Between 1968 and 1993, the number of managers and administrators in U.S. health care rose fourfold from 719,000 to 2,792,000, outstripping the growth in the number of physicians, which less than doubled from 430,000 to 761,000.[4] The very high growth in of administrators changed the structure of employment in the health care industry significantly. Between 1969 and 1993, the percentage of the total health care workforce employed in administration rose from 18 percent to 27 percent, while the percentage of physicians in the total health care workforce declined from 10.8 percent to 7.4 percent, and the total percentage of nurses fell from 40.6 percent to 36.3 percent. In U.S. hospitals, employment of administrators rose sharply, even as the number of patients declined.[5] On an average day in 1968, U.S. hospitals employed 435,100 managers, administrators, and clerks to support the care of 1,378,000 inpatients. By 1990, the average daily number of patients had fallen by 39 percent to 853,000, but the number of administrators serving them had risen by 280 percent to 1,221,600. In 1968, there was one administrator for every three patients, in 1990, 4.3 administrators for every three patients.[6]

Himmelstein and Woolhandler cite evidence of what is perhaps the chief folly of health care policy in the era of managed care: how the high administrative costs of the system can overwhelm the savings that the system is designed to achieve. In 1999, the two authors compared the cost of for-profit and not-for-profit hospitals in the United States—the latter includes all public, charitable, and veterans' hospitals. Of the two groups, it was the for-profits that led in such cost-cutting measures as the avoidance of charity care, the shortening of patient's hospital stays, the reduction of medical staffing levels, and the carrying out of detailed "utilization review" of the hospital's dealings with physicians and MCOs. But administrators were needed for all these tasks, and once these costs of administration were added to the for-profit hospitals' higher spending on consultants, marketing, and advertising, the for-profit hospitals were between 3 and 11 percent *more* expensive than their not-for-profit counterparts.[7]

Himmelstein and Woolhandler also compare administrative costs in U.S. and Canadian health care, the latter having a single-payer system. They show that the proliferation of bureaucracy in the United States is not an inescapable characteristic of contemporary health care but a characteristic of the particular system operating in the United States. In 1990, Blue Cross/Blue Shield of Massachusetts covered 2.7 million subscribers and employed 6,682 managers and administrators, more than the total number of administrators employed by all of the Canadian provincial health plans, covering the entire Canadian population of 25 million.[8]

In 1987, a year in which the growth of managed care in the United States was taking off, U.S. administrative costs per patient in various sectors of health care exceeded Canadian costs by spectacular ratios: 6:1 in insurance administration, 3:1 in hospital administration, 3:1 in nursing home administration, and 2.5:1 in the administration of physician's offices.[9] In the last thirteen years, the reengineering of U.S. health care has, as we have seen, been directed toward reducing care, not administration, so there is no reason to believe that these ratios are any different today. In 1997, the General Accounting Office calculated that if the United States adopted a system of national health insurance, the savings achieved through the elimination of health care bureaucracies in the private sector would fund the coverage of the uninsured U.S. population.[10]

Managed care's record of waste and inefficiency puts a fresh perspective on the issue of rising costs in U.S. health care. For the past fifteen years, the burden of cost containment in health care has fallen heavily on working Americans, and particularly on older Americans. They are the losers when MCOs and Medicare MCOs rely on "utilization review" to turn down their requests for care. They are also the losers when employers trim their health care costs by raising employees' and retirees' co-payments and deductibles. However, the MCOs' own inflated bureaucracies have been given a free ride by the cost cutters and tolerated by both the Bush administration and the leaders of both political parties. But it is hard to see why older Americans should go without prescription drugs while MCOs and their satellites continue to squander very large sums of money on utilization reviewers, disease managers, billing specialists, marketers, and medical reengineers.

The promise to contain health care costs has been a pillar of managed care. So has its claim to place medical decision making on a more rational footing, with MCO case managers relying on the medical evidence to eliminate unnecessary and wasteful treatments. This project has been strongly resisted by the bulk of the medical profession, but confusion surrounds this conflict because there are legitimate issues of health care reform that concern the performance of physicians themselves. MCOs have been able to exploit these concerns by arguing that, with the coming of their planned, managerial medicine, the fallible, human judgment of the physician is replaced by the objective, scientific judgment of case managers relying on databases, practice guidelines, and expert systems.

In a 1999 report, the Institute of Medicine (IOM) estimated that between 44,000 and 98,000 hospital deaths can be attributed to medical error every year.[11] The IOM found that the chief cause of death was not major surgical error but rather a variety of more commonplace mistakes: patients given the wrong drug because the pharmacist could not read the physician's handwriting, and patients given the wrong dosage of a drug because the physician had not thoroughly examined the patient or had failed to allow for a drug that the patient was already taking. With its retinue of malpractice lawsuits, punitive jury awards, and ever costlier malpractice insurance, medical error goes hand in hand with the inflation of health care costs. Physicians also protect themselves against lawsuits—and add to health care costs—by ordering up unnecessary tests and treatments. In an April 2002 poll, Harris found that fear of malpractice suits led 91 percent of physicians to order "more tests than they would based only on professional judgment of what is medically needed."[12]

Doubts about the professional competence of physicians add another dimension to an already formidable list of health care failings: the rising number of the uninsured; the failure of Medicare to cover the cost of prescription drugs for many older Americans; and the impact of rising health care costs on the incomes of working Americans, as higher co-payments and deductibles erode the value of already meager pay raises. But the problem of physician competence raises issues that go beyond the day-to-day difficulties of health care and concern the nature of medicine itself. It is impossible to discuss the professional standards of physicians without first asking what these standards should be—

those of the old medicine or the new? As we saw in the last chapter, the role of the physician in planned, managerial medicine is very different from the role that Americans have become used to in their two-hundred-year history, and indeed different from the physician's role in over two millennia of Western civilization. In the new, planned medicine, the physician's chief task is to place the patient in the correct subgroup so that the appropriate "protocol or plan" for that group can then be put into operation.[13]

This significant de-skilling of the physician makes him increasingly a cog in the wheel of the medical process, and so vulnerable to the disciplines of scientific management. With the declining popularity of managed care and the loosening of its control over medical decision making, it is tempting to write off this vision of the physician's diminished role as a passing aberration that will go the way of the dot-coms. But the managed care industry harnesses two extremely powerful forces at work throughout the economy: the drive of corporations to raise productivity and profits by applying the methods of industrialization to service industries, and their belief that information technology gives them the means to do it. In health care, this project has run up against some major obstacles, but that does not mean that the project will soon be abandoned. By the standards of past eras of technology, the project is still in its infancy, and the project is also sustained by our present-day belief that technology can indeed overcome all obstacles. There is still a need therefore to explain why this project is so deeply misconceived and why both the medical profession and the U.S. patient population have been right to resist it.

In January 1992 the *New England Journal of Medicine* began a series, "Clinical Problem Solving," that showed in detail how physicians go about making decisions under conditions of what the journal calls "clinical uncertainty."[14] In each installment of the journal's series, physicians are asked to put themselves in the position of a patient's original treating physician. Information about the patient's condition is made available to these physicians in stages, just as it had become available to the treating physician. The journal's physicians are asked to make diagnoses and to recommend treatments in light of the information available to them at each stage. The patients and problems selected for the series are similar to those "that clinicians might be expected to encounter in the course of a busy practice." In introducing the series, Dr. Jerome Kassirer, then editor of the journal, wrote "simple rules frequently fail us and we are forced to formulate unique solutions for each patient."[15]

The cases described in the journal series play havoc with the medical reengineer's ordered vision of medical practice as a series of standard processes, all susceptible to external timing, monitoring, and control. In the journal's case histories, the reengineer's world vanishes in a tumult of uncertainty and disorder. Diseases often play the wrecker because they do not behave in ways compatible with the tidy processes of managerial medicine. Grave illnesses such as cancer and heart disease mutate without warning "as the malfunction of one body system disrupts neighboring systems which fall like dominos."[16] Diseases combine with one another in unexpected ways, give misleading symptoms, and dispatch the treating physician on a wild goose chase of misdiagnosis, revealing their identities only when the physician may have traveled some way down the road of medical error.

The difficulty of diagnosis is a theme running through virtually all the case histories examined in the journal. Patients come forward with vague symptoms: headache, abdominal pain, back pain, breathlessness, fever, cough, vomiting, depression, forgetfulness, and confusion. At the outset of diagnosis, the physician must often reckon with a long list of possible causes. In his book *The Nature of Suffering and the Goals of Medicine*, Eric Cassell lists the possible causes of a patient's shortness of breath: "congestive heart failure, emphysema, asthma, a collapsed lung, fluid in the chest, fluid in the abdomen, pregnancy, clots in the lung, or anxiety attacks."[17] One reason that computers have a mixed record as diagnostic tools is that at the outset of the diagnostic process they too often overwhelm the physician with an endless list of diagnostic possibilities.[18]

The journal series provides many insights into the nature of diagnostic skill. The diagnostic process can be formally defined as the discovery of causal links in a patient's symptoms that support a diagnostic hypothesis about the nature of the patient's illness. The hypothesis is confirmed or rejected through further testing and investigation. Advanced skills of diagnosis are most needed when a wealth of symptoms suggests a multiplicity of hypotheses, and the physician needs the intellectual stamina to keep several hypotheses in play at the same time, shifting the weight accorded to each of them as new information about the patient becomes available.

In the search for diagnoses patterns of symptoms and the connections between them, become visible to an experienced physician that a novice may overlook. Once a diagnosis is hypothesized and treatment begun, the medical reengineer's division of medical reality into discrete, measurable events—diagnosis, treatment, outcome—crumbles away. Decisions have to be made and re-made in the light of a patient's evolving condition. The more serious the condition of the patient, the more rapidly these decisions must succeed one another.

In such conditions, decisions become complex entities in which judgments about diagnosis, treatments, and outcomes are inextricably bound up. A decision may contain elements of a diagnosis, because the physician must make a judgment about the patient's condition in light of the treatment the patient is receiving. A decision may comprise judgments about outcomes, because physicians have to judge whether their diagnosis is bringing the patient any nearer the desired outcomes of the treatment. A decision may also comprise judgment about treatments: whether an existing treatment should be continued or discontinued; and if continued, whether at a dosage or intensity that is higher, lower, or unchanged.

In his book, Cassell provides an illuminating account of the reasoning that can accompany this decision making and that helps define the concept of "good clinical judgment." Ironically, it is that ubiquitous conceptual workhorse of contemporary scientific management, "process," that gets to play a leading role in Cassell's account of clinical reasoning. But the processes in question are unique to the lives of particular patients and cannot be objects of the automated, preplanned treatments of managerial medicine.

Cassell's "processes" are artifacts of pathophysiological reasoning and[19] they are the physician's best defense against the anarchy of disease. Just as physiology maps the processes of the human body under conditions of normality, so pathophysiology maps them under conditions of abnormality. Thus, in the familiar language of reengineering, arteriosclerosis is a process, the hardening of the arteries, often marked by a characteristic event—coronary infarction or heart attack—that defines the progress of the disease. Pathophysiological reasoning enables the physician to construct a mental, virtual model of the patient's disease as a process, which includes a prognosis of its future course. Such reasoning also enables the physician to conceive of treatment as an intervention that affects these processes in ways beneficial to the patient. But as Cassell develops the concept of pathophysiological reasoning, the processes of disease get to look less and less like those of the office or the factory.

Successful pathophysiological reasoning consists of relying on "standard" processes characteristic of diseases such as coronary artery disease or pulmonary failure, amended or supplemented by processes reflecting the medical condition of the particular patient. The greater the physician's knowledge of the patient, the more complete the charting of his or her pathophysiology, and the less the physician is likely to be thrown off by the erratic progress of a disease. Cassell provides a revealing example of such advanced pathophysiological reasoning. The patient was a young woman named Caroline Preskauer who had a congenital deformity of the heart, due to her heart's being located on the right, rather than the left, side of her body.[20]

Cassell enumerates Preskauer's complex pathophysiology: an uneven flow of blood to the lungs; the thickening of blood vessels in areas of the lung in which the blood flow was concentrated; a strain on the heart as it pumped harder to force a passage through the constricted blood vessels; the weakening of the lungs as the heart became enlarged, crowding out the lungs in the patient's chest cavity; and the disruption of the heart's rhythm as the patient's blood carried abormally high levels of carbon dioxide and abnormally low levels of oxygen. With some candor, Cassell admits that there were two aspects of this pathophysiology to which he, as the patient's treating physician, did not give sufficient weight: the enlargement of the heart and its effect on the lungs, and the vulnerability of the heart rhythm to the abnormal levels of oxygen and carbon dioxide.

Cassell mentions his own omissions to drive home an essential point about good medical practice, and one that runs counter to the entire spirit of managerial medicine, with its subordination of the patient to the group:

> Doctors, whether they are aware of it or not, prognosticate by construct- ing a whole picture of the patient out of every bit of knowledge they have about that person, and then base their predictions on the whole picture. To the extent that their picture-in-the-round accurately represents the sick person. . . . their predictions have a chance of accuracy.[21]

Both Cassell and the *New England Journal of Medicine* series give a strong sense of what the treatment of sick patients should be like, with full consideration given to the uniqueness of the patient; the uncer- tainties surrounding his or her diagnosis and treatment; and, at every stage, the need for the physician to make judgments that are complex and difficult. But underlying this shared approach to the care of sick pa- tients is a basic truth of medicine: The discipline does not yield a body of unequivocal rules and guidelines that can then be used to surround the physician with the regulation and control of managerial medicine. Even the randomized clinical trial (RCT), the acknowledged gold stan- dard of medical evidence, is an uncertain source for MCOs looking to fill their instruction manuals.

A surprisingly small percentage of medical procedures are unequiv- ocally validated by the results of RCTs. One study in the *New England Journal of Medicine* found that only 15 to 20 percent of medical prac- tices could be justified on the basis of "rigorous data estimating their ef- fectiveness," and this figure reflects some well-known difficulties in conducting RCTs: the need to enroll very large numbers of patients in a trial, the need to sustain the trial over long periods of time, and the fact that trials often yield inconclusive results.[22] But trials can also be an uncertain guide to medical decision making even when there is wide agreement that the trials themselves have been properly carried out and are free of bias. In a landmark article "Complexity and Contradiction in Clinical Trial Research," Dr. Ralph Horwitz of the Yale Medical School looked at two hundred RCTs in the fields of cardiology and gastroenterology.[23]

For all thirty-six topics covered, the trials yielded differing results, and Horwitz found nine sources for the variations: Six were concerned with the design of the trials and three with the interpretation of their outcomes. However, Horwitz's key finding was that variations in the results of similar trials did not arise because there had been errors in the conduct of the trials themselves. Rather, it was the very rigor of the different trials on the same topic that gave rise to variations in their results. Horwitz often uses the words "contradictory" and "conflicting" to describe these multiple results. But this is a misleading use of words, implying that the trials that yielded "contradictory" or "conflicting" results were the "same" trials.

What Horwitz really shows is that these were not, strictly speaking, the same trials at all. Trials of the same drug or procedure differed according to the characteristics of the patient population participating in the trial, the exact treatments administered, and the outcomes studied. The results of each trial turned out to be highly sensitive to these differing characteristics. Physicians are therefore left with a patchwork of evidence related to narrowly defined groups of patients treated in controlled, near-laboratory conditions. Horwitz lists and describes some of the factors that led the same trials to yield different results. Six trials of a treatment of hypertension yielded varying results because the trials had different eligibility criteria for patients participating in the trials. Some groups of patients had preexisting illnesses, whereas others did not.

Two trials of a drug for heart attack victims, discussed in the same edition of the *New England Journal of Medicine,* had varying results because each trial had its own rules governing the treatments that could or could not accompany the administration of the trial's drug. With trials of drugs to treat liver disease and septic shock, the results differed because the drugs were administered according to different timetables.[24]

Horwitz shows that, even when trials have been properly conducted and provide evidence for or against a treatment, the physicians must still consider whether the profile of his or her particular patient matches the profile of the trial's patient population, and whether therefore the outcomes of the trial are in fact relevant to an estimate of outcomes in particular case.

Horwitz's research, along with Casell's and the journal's case histories, help define medicine's sprawling gray areas, within which physicians must exercise their judgment. Physicians constantly have to make decisions based on incomplete or ambiguous evidence, decisions they must be ready to reverse in the light of the patient's changing condition, and these decisions cannot be confined within the rigid straightjacket of process. Since the managed care industry itself justifies its participation in medical decision making with reference to a canon of unequivocal evidence, it is worth asking what the industry itself makes of a body of evidence which is in fact uneven and fraught with ambiguity.

In 1996 a team of doctors from the Johns Hopkins School of Medicine carried out an extensive survey of how MCOs go about making coverage decisions for emerging medical technologies.[25] The 231 MCO physicians, mostly medical directors, who responded to the survey represented MCOs covering approximately 70 percent of the U.S. insured population. The Johns Hopkins researchers were mindful of patient concerns that "final coverage decisions of medical technologies are not uniform from plan to plan, are difficult to predict and differ from assessments done by the medical scientific community."[26] The Johns Hopkins researchers came up with substantial evidence that these concerns were well founded.

There was wide variation in the sources used by medical directors in making their decisions. No one source was used by more than half the directors. Medical journals, widely viewed by the scientific community as providing the most rigorous sources of data on the use of new technologies, were not listed as a source by half the directors. The Johns Hopkins researchers had an explanation for this neglect which should not reassure the U.S. patient population: "interpreting these articles takes time and experience and also may explain why they were not the principal source of information." Some of the other sources listed by the medical directors also looked decidedly shaky: "opinions of local experts" (45 percent of the directors); "information provided by trade associations" (40 percent); and unidentified "practice guidelines" (35 percent).[27]

Clearly MCO medical directors need to be better educated, but so also do practicing physicians. The first line of defense against the kind of medical error described in the Institute of Medicine's 1999 report is the quality of medical education. The vandalizing of medical schools and teaching hospitals by medical reengineers, as described by Kenneth Ludmerer in *Time to Heal*, is therefore a major act of desecration and one that risks producing future generations of error-prone physicians. Protecting the integrity of medical education is an urgent task of health care policy. Information technology can also help eliminate the kind of administrative errors chronicled in the IOM report. With many deaths resulting from faulty drug prescriptions, IT has a role to play in ensuring that physicians know about a patient's complicating condition or pre-existing drug regime. But the use of IT for these targeted, specific purposes is very different from its use to create a whole superstructure of medical control manned by untrained MCO case managers.

So what can happen when something so deeply misconceived as managerial medicine comes up against the kind of serious illness described by Cassell and the *New England Journal of Medicine*? Dr. Jerome Groopman describes such a case in his book *Second Opinions*.[28] Groopman's patient was Isabella Montero, a thirty-six-year-old Hispanic woman who worked as a cleaner at the Hyannis office of a Cape Cod, Massachusetts, bank.[29] Montero became Groopman's patient when she was admitted to Beth Israel Deaconess Medical Center in Boston in the fall of 1996 with a high fever and labored breathing. Montero's primary care physician, a doctor under contract to her local MCO, had diagnosed Montero as a routine case of asthma, but Groopman soon realized that this was almost certainly a misdiagnosis. The standard treatments for asthma had been given to Montero on admission to

Beth Israel and had not worked. Groopman also knew that asthma was unlikely to develop for the first time in someone of Montero's age. But, as with the many cases in the journal's problem-solving series, a detailed examination of Montero yielded diffuse signs and symptoms not immediately suggestive of a single diagnosis: weakness of the right hand and arm, loss of the use of the right eye, and the appearance of infection on the roof of the mouth.[30]

Once Groopman received the results of Montero's blood test, it became clear that she had acute leukemia, with a wild profileration of immature white blood cells known as blasts. A side effect of the disease was Montero's low count of platelets, the blood cells that form clots. Montero's treatment at Beth Israel consisted of plasmapheresis, a kind of dialysis that reduces the level of blast cells, blood transfusions to restore her platelet count and chemotherapy to eradicate her cancer cells. The plasmapheresis and blood transfusions were somewhat successful in lowering Montero's white blood count and raising her platelet levels, but the chemotherapy did not eradicate the diseased white blood cells, and after refusing experimental treatment, Montero died at home, looked after by a hospice nurse.[31]

After Montero's death, Groopman was haunted by the thought that had her leukemia been diagnosed when she first made contact with her MCO doctor in October 1996, she might have survived. Groopman's account of the treatment Montero received from her MCO doctor provides an illuminating example of how the industrialization of medicine can fail the sick. Montero came up against one of the flaws of managerial medicine the very first time she visited her doctor's office on October 6, 1996. She did not get to see the doctor, who was too busy to see her, and instead she saw a nurse. The nurse diagnosed a routine case of asthma and prescribed a standard treatment, the use of a Ventolin inhaler.[32]

Nearly two weeks went by, and the inhaler had had no effect, so Montero's daughter arranged another visit to the doctor's office for her mother. Again the visit was slated to be with a nurse, and it was only after her daughter complained that Montero got to see the doctor as his last appointment of the day. This took place on October 24, fifteen days after Montero's first visit. Once again the doctor diagnosed a routine case of asthma, again prescribed Ventolin, and added an antiasthmatic drug, aminophylline.

In a tense telephone interview that followed Montero's admission to Beth Israel, Groopman asked the MCO doctor why, following the failure of the initial treatment, he had not widened his diagnostic search by ordering tests such as a blood count, a chest X-ray, or a sputum culture. Groopman added, "We usually do that when symptoms don't respond to empiric therapy."[33] The doctor's defense was that the MCO had "proven guidelines for what tests to order and what treatment" to give in cases such as Montero's. These guidelines were based on clinical algorithms that showed that it was not efficient or cost-effective to order tests for cases such as Montero's. In the doctor's own words: "It's not cost-effective to do more than what I did for a routine case of asthma."[34] Groopman was shocked by the MCO doctor's continued willingness to subordinate his own medical judgment to an automated system, particularly one that had just failed with such disastrous consequences. There was also the doctor's cynicism, his lack of feeling for his many low-income patients, including Montero. "Come down here from your ivory tower and start working in the trenches," was the MCO doctor's reproach when Groopman mentioned Beth Israel's diagnostic policies.[35]

Groopman acknowledges that for primary case physicians such as the MCO doctor, "working in the trenches" means having to see more and more patients "per unit hour," and being ever more parsimonious with their care. He is also honest in acknowledging that he himself, as someone ensconced in the Boston-Harvard medical athenaeum, is largely spared the afflictions of managerial medicine. But down in the medical trenches, the relations between doctors and patients are the first casualties of this assembly line medicine. "I vaguely remember her," the HMO doctor said of Montero. "I'm assigning everyone from the bank's four branches. . . . spend a week with me here. I have ten Isabella Monteros a day in the waiting room, complaining in broken English they need time off from work because they're tired or can't breathe."[36] Groopman found the HMO doctor's lack of feeling for Montero, his lack of remorse for the treatment he gave her, hard to forgive. One also has to ask whether such summary treatment would have been meted out if the patient in question had been the CEO of the Cape Cod bank and not a low-level, low-wage employee. But Groopman also sees such MCO doctors as prisoners of the system of managed care, this "monstrous creation" that is leaving responsible and committed physicians "increasingly frustrated and despairing."[37]

Managed care may be a monstrous system, but it is not immune to the pressures of public opinion. Since the failure of the Clinton health care reforms in the early 1990s, the comprehensive reform of U.S. health care has not been on the national political agenda. But below the Washington horizon, the managed care industry has been losing ground to a coalition of the patient population, the medical profession, and the state legislatures. These retreats have weakened such pillars of managerial medicine as utilization review and the control of a patient's access to his or her doctor. But this permanent guerrilla warfare is leaving health care in a no man's land in which managed care has forfeited the confidence of the U.S. patient population but in which there is as yet no successor in sight to replace it, since neither physicians nor patients are calling for a return to the old fee-for-service system of health insurance. We will discuss what might be done in the book's final chapter.

9

FOUCAULT'S TOWER

A STRONG CASE CAN BE MADE that the products of the German software maker SAP have had as great an impact on the lives of working Americans as that of any IT company—Microsoft, Intel, IBM, and Hewlett Packard included. But outside the highly specialized world of enterprise resource planning (ERP) software, SAP is almost totally unknown, as indeed are most of SAP's U.S. competitors, companies such as Peoplesoft, J. D. Edwards, and Siebel Systems. Only SAP's leading U.S. competitor, Oracle Corporation, has escaped such anonymity, but this is due more to the intense rivalry and personal animosity between Oracle's CEO Larry Ellison and Microsoft's Bill Gates than to Oracle's strong presence in the field of what has come to be known as "enterprise computing."

As we have seen, ERP grew out of the reengineering of the early 1990s, taking the single business processes that were the concern of reengineers, and then joining them together to form giant megaprocesses. Early versions of SAP software comprised three chief elements. The first was labeled logistics and included the main manufacturing processes: materials management, production planning, quality assurance, and plant maintenance. The second, financials, pulled together procedures such as financial and asset accounting. The third element was labeled human resources and included such things as personnel administration, planning, and development.

From the mid-1990s onward, SAP's success in marketing software products that integrate these three functions gave rise to the new acronym ERP. It has remained a convention of the industry that ERP refers to the integration of these activities—logistics, accounting, and human resource management. Processes whose integration with this inner core has come later, such as customer relations management (CRM) and supply chain management (SCM) are usually described as add-ons to the original ERP. In a 1999 report on ERP, Deloitte Consulting estimated that in 1998 SAP had a 66 percent share of the U.S. market, and Oracle an 11 percent share.[1]

Despite its obscurity, ERP is therefore a driving force in the reshaping of American business, particularly in service industries. In its year 2000 report on the ERP industries, the Boston IT consultancy AMR Research states simply, "Most companies now consider core ERP applications as part of the cost of doing business, a necessary part of the organization's infrastructure."[2] In July 2000, Karl Heinz Cypris, director of SAP solutions at Compaq Computer, told the *Financial Times* that "ERP business is saturated" because "all of the big customers are set up now." The ERP market, he said, will "stay and grow" as "attention is switching to other things," such as the "web, Customer Relations Management and e-commerce."[3] With 80 percent of Americans working in service industries, the bread and butter of ERP, the productivity of U.S. labor and the productivity of ERP are now inextricably linked.

For a business, the implementation of ERP is expensive, disruptive, and very time-consuming. In its 1999 survey of ERP, Deloitte Consulting writes of a "massive change like ERP" that takes "up to four years" to complete.[4] Thomas Davenport writes of "the huge investment required to implement [ERP] at large companies—typically ranging from $50 million to more than $500 million."[5] The testimony of consultants, and of surveys conducted by consulting firms, provides strong evidence that, so far, ERP has been a poor performer. In a 2000 report on basic ERP, PA Consulting Group has come up with an astonishing statistic: 92 percent of its European respondents "were dissatisfied with the results achieved to date," while "only 8 percent had achieved a positive improvement in performance." Fifty-three percent of the surveyed companies had looked for improvements in productivity, but only 5 percent had gotten them. Fifty percent had aimed for "streamlined business processes," but only 5 percent had found them. Forty-five percent were banking on "improved information flows," but on this score only 13 percent were satisfied.[6]

PA concluded that "ERP implementation has represented a massive area of spending for companies in which limited functionality is being enjoyed and where the return on investment falls far short of expectation." On the American side, Computasoft Consulting came up with a similar result, finding in a 1999 survey that "two thirds of companies have failed to realize the benefits they expected from the leading ERP solution, from SAP."[7] In yet another survey of basic ERP, which also appeared in 1999, Cambridge Information Networks found that 22 percent of surveyed companies "never" expected to recover the cost of their ERP investments, with some respondents commenting that "if time and payback are as long—or nonexistent—as the survey results indicate, then something is really wrong."[8] Tony Friscia, president and CEO of AMR Research, told the *Financial Times* at the end of 1999 that "most companies are not doing business differently and have not achieved a result on their [ERP] investment."[9]

ERP's greatest problem is that it is simply the old reengineering of the early 1990s writ large. First-generation reengineering took single business processes such as "order fulfillment" and subjected them to an assembly line discipline. "Basic ERP" takes these single, stand-alone processes, joins them together, and is followed by "advanced ERP," which extends this digital welding to the structure of entire businesses. The mediocre record of basic ERP suggests that reengineers have embarked upon this advanced variant of their practice without having first solved the problem that has dogged the practice of reengineering from the start: A practice based upon the discipline and control of the assembly line does not do well in contexts in which human agents discuss, argue, negotiate, and strike deals, as they habitually do in service industries.

The English-language version of Gerhard Keller and Thomas Teufel's exhaustive manual on SAP's ERP software, *SAP R/3 Process Oriented Implementation* (1997), conveys the overwhelmingly industrial, assembly line quality of ERP.[10] Keller and Teufel were both employees of SAP when they wrote the book. With Keller and Teufel, we know we are back in familiar reengineering territory the moment the two authors describe how SAP's ERP software permits the elaborate preplanning of work by managers and software engineers, opening up new fields for the digital assembly line. The testing and setting up of ERP's processes is a strictly engineering affair, with the human element lost amid the digital levers and pistons. Keller and Teufel's language is difficult to follow for anyone outside the narrow world of ERP specialists:

> Next to the basic constructs already implemented in programming languages, such as sequences, conditional branching, and unconditional branching and loops, additional more complex flow constructs are required to specify the control flow between workflows.[11]

A careful deciphering of this language reveals the reengineer/scientific manager's determination to have preplanned responses ready for every possible contingency on the line. This is the common purpose of the "sequences," "conditional branching," "unconditional branching," and "more complex flow constructs. . . . required to specify the control flow between workflows." We have already encountered such language at the call center, where scripting experts created loops and branches in their digital scripts to deal with all the twists and turns that could arise in conversations between agents and customers. Now this planning is applied to the whole gamut of corporate process. As in the call center, SAP software also allows managers to monitor and control the work of employees in as much detail as they want.

Writing from the perspective of the frontline worker, one of SAP's Internet essayists explains, "not only are you informed of the tasks that you need to do as they occur, but these tasks are also prioritized and accompanied by an exact description of what has to be done."[12] Each task comes with an attached target time for its completion, along with a "deadline monitoring" system that records whether the employee indeed meets his or her deadline. If the deadline indeed is not met, the system, using automatic escalation procedures, takes the work away from the delinquent employee without the manager's "having to intervene on the neglected process."[13] The manager can then do the work himself or herself or assign it to someone else.

But if managers do want to intervene, the software allows them to "look in detail at what work has been done by [his or her] department," with the "on line" work of employees also leaving a "precise audit trail" that managers can trace.[14] The software gives managers the power to "drill down" so that they can also look at the work of a particular employee in "real time." The manager can "view the execution of individual work steps" or "view information on the current work item at any point." There is also a "historical aspect" to this monitoring, which consists of the "logging of a workflow's [past] execution data."[15]

All these features of SAP's ERP systems mark them as very close cousins of the original reengineering of the early 1990s. But there is one aspect to the whole ERP phenomenon that has no parallel in the old reengineering. In these new surroundings, the management theorist Thomas Davenport is a helpful guide. As an advocate of reengineering, Davenport has had a somewhat checkered career. In 1993 he produced one of the first textbooks on the subject, but just two years later he wrote a reengineering mea culpa for the Internet business magazine *Fast Company*, accusing reengineers, himself included, of treating employees "as if they were just so many bits and bytes."[16]

However, by 2000, Davenport had rejoined the reengineering camp and wrote *Mission Critical*, his second textbook on the subject, and one that deals extensively with ERP.[17] The book was sponsored by Andersen Consulting (now Accenture), and at the time of the book's publication, Davenport was director of Andersen's Institute for Strategic Change. Davenport is still a critic of the old reengineering, but as an Andersen employee, his criticisms are more tempered and in-house than they once were. Like Keller and Teufel, Davenport is also a heavy user of ERP's impenetrable jargon, and translation is often needed.

Whereas in 1995 Davenport got close to writing off reengineering altogether, he now offers a more technical criticism that focuses on the flawed methods used by the early reengineers to create their processes.

First, then, Davenport's criticism, expressed in the language of ERP. Egged on by reengineering zealots (Davenport evidently now sees himself as a reengineering "moderate"), the typical early reengineering project involved "very ambitious changed goals in the design phase." With such an approach, little thought was given to "the limits that [information systems] would place on process designs." But "what happened when companies took the revolutionary new process designs and tried to build information systems to support them?" Too often there was a "big gap between the design of a reengineering project, and its implementation," and this was because "the available software. . . . did not support the companies'. . . . process designs."[18]

In plain English: Carried away by reengineering's promise of soaring productivity, the early reengineering zealots too often drew up their plans for a process, such as customer relations management, without first giving enough thought to the software systems that might manage the newly designed process. Once planning was complete, the reengineers then looked around for the needed software, buying it from a variety of sources and putting it together themselves. But when this marriage of process and software actually took place, the reengineers all too often found that the new processes were too complex for the software to handle, and the project failed. The SAP authors Keller and Teufel are also strongly critical of this freelance design of processes by companies. The user (i.e., the company)

> composes his individual process. . . . a paradise? Unfortunately not. In this method the egotism of individual people carrying out the functions will dominate the project work. The resulting business process will not be lean, nor will it deal responsibly with the resources.[19]

Davenport and the SAP authors agree about how the new, hyper-reengineering should be saved from this error of the old. Companies should give up trying to create their own reengineered processes and instead buy them off the shelf from ERP vendors such as SAP and Oracle. In the words of Chris Deacon, a senior ERP specialist at the consultancy Computer Science Corporation (CSC), "SAP does not sell software—it sells best-practice business processes."[20] So, instead of "starting from scratch" in their design of processes, companies, according to Davenport, "start from what is possible or easily accomplished in SAP, Oracle or PeopleSoft."[21]

When U.S. companies start buying their processes "off the shelf" from companies like SAP and Oracle, then these companies and their leading software designers suddenly find themselves with a great deal of power. Their decisions about how processes should be embedded in their software will shape the ways in which millions of workers do their jobs. Neither the SAP authors nor Davenport, despite his earlier misgivings, now have any qualms about vesting such power in the hands of small groups of software designers. They are confident that this power will be wisely exercised.

Davenport writes that the "process designs" supported by SAP and Oracle are based on a generic set of "best practices" that are in fact better than the process designs that most firms create for themselves and this is because "the software vendor's business knowledge, which is conveyed through the standard software. . . . makes it possible to implement the latest business developments."[22] The client therefore "no longer receives just a piece of software" but also "adaptable process oriented organization" containing "insights from business management science," which "the companies themselves may have overlooked."[23]

In scope and ambition, this new version of the "one best way" surpasses anything we have so far come across in this new age of scientific management. With ERP's off-the-shelf processes, whole segments of business life can now be prefabricated according to the dictates of "business management science." But outside the narrow community of ERP vendors and their consultants, there are those who have asked whether companies such as SAP have always shown good judgment about how business processes should be put together. In December 1999, Alan Davies, then group marketing director of the U.K. software developers

J.B.A., told the *Financial Times* that the ideas of "most ERP vendors are based on mid-twentieth century business management attitudes" that "become less and less relevant as we enter the 21st century."[24]

Nigel Town, U.K. manager for the software developers Pick Systems, also told the *Financial Times:*

> We all know that they [the ERP developers] need years and years and millions and millions of dollars so they can beat the client into submission and force them to reinvent their organization in their own image.[25]

With this hyper-reengineering, the distance between those who wield power and those who are its objects has never been greater. At least with the old reengineering, those who created the new processes and those who operated them worked for the same company, even though in practice there was scant communication or consultation between the higher and lower echelons. But now that the core processes of ERP need no longer be designed in house, senior managers cannot consult with their employees even if they want to. To his credit, Thomas Davenport makes no attempt to hide any of this, and in his latest reengineering textbook he does not use the misleading rhetoric of employee teamwork, empowerment, and autonomy to describe what is going on.

He seems to have concluded that the gains in productivity to be had from the new hyper-reengineering outweigh the disadvantages of the passive, subordinate workforce that this reengineering creates. Early in the book, Davenport faces up to the criticism that ERP systems impose a "hierarchical, command and control perspective on organizations"— and admits that the criticism is well founded. ERP systems "do presume that information will be centrally monitored and that organizations have a well defined hierarchical structure."[26] Later in the book, Davenport raises the issue of employee empowerment. For employees, "the space for free action is admittedly limited" as "ERP systems won't work very well if individual workers or even departments have a say as to how key information elements should support a particular business function."[27]

That kind of empowerment "would place severe restrictions on the function of a system across disparate parts of an organization." It is therefore "important to make clear from the beginning of an [ERP] implementation that workers and individual departments won't be able to design their own systems."[28] Davenport provides an example of workers at a manufacturing company who were "excited about the new [ERP] system their company was installing." So "several plant groups put together lists of their information preferences and of employees who volunteered to work with the new system." But, unfortunately, "managers had to inform the plant workers that their inputs were not particularly helpful, and that no such local empowerment was possible with the new system."[29]

Despite all their problems with ERP's first phase, companies and their consultants are determined to push on into its second and third phases. Tony Friscia of AMR Research, the Boston IT consultancy, told the *Financial Times* that companies "were now extending the capabilities of these ERP systems to implement the concept of the extended enterprise," though Friscia himself had found that "most companies. . . . have not achieved a result on their [ERP] investment."[30] Despite its clients' 92 percent "dissatisfaction rate" with ERP, PA Consulting is still advising clients "to view their ERP systems as solid building blocks" for future ERP projects.[31] But first prize for rallying the shell-shocked corporate troops for the big push into the no man's land of extended ERP goes to Deloitte Consulting, a company described by the *Financial Times* as having "SAP experience coupled with the right reengineering methodology."

In its own ERP survey, Deloitte found that the average ERP implementation takes "up to four years" so that when companies "go live" with their basic ERP system "they've run a marathon."[32] Deloitte's chief message to its clients is that, despite the strain and exhaustion of the marathon they have just run, they should not expect too much from their "going live" with basic ERP. Like mountaineers attempting the ascent of Everest, by "going live" they have simply reached base camp, where the real mountaineering begins: "The rewards go to those who venture into the wave where the greater benefits lie—not the First

Wave of going live, but the post-implementation Second Wave." Continuing in this over-heated vein, Deloitte tells its clients that it is not "by simply turning the system on, but by forcefully moving into the deeper journey [that] the full capabilities and benefits of the ERP-enabled enterprise are found."[33]

In its early stages, at least, this "deeper journey" passes through some of the flattest topography of the business landscape—customer relations management (CRM) and supply chain management (SCM). In both spheres, scientific management is firmly established as the controlling philosophy of management, so the closer integration of these two processes with the existing processes of ERP simply reinforces the already dominant role of scientific management in the workings of ERP. With CRM, there are, as we have seen, ways of bringing software and employees together that can enhance the skill, judgment, and earning power of employees. Workers can be properly trained to make use of all the information that CRM software can bring to bear when an agent deals with the customer. But this opportunity is being pushed aside by the juggernaut of scientific management, with its digital scripts, multiple techniques of monitoring and control, and micromanagement of the employees' working life.

Supply chain management is perhaps the most familiar of ERP's new phases because basic ERP itself already contains a strong supply chain element. A basic ERP system that automatically links the sales, production scheduling, and credit checking of a business qualifies as a segment of the supply chain. The supply chain of extended ERP lengthens the chain to include a company's customers and suppliers, and also brings in the Internet as a possible means of communication between the three parties. Thus, the customer of a manufacturing company can check into the manufacturer's ERP systems and find out whether the company can supply a quantity of goods by a certain date. Similarly, the manufacturer himself can, with extended ERP, automatically notify a supplier when components or raw materials are required.

The one certain member of the supply chain hall of fame is Henry Ford, whose setting up of a chain linking raw material and finished product at his Highland Park and River Rouge plants remains the most remarkable achievement of supply chain history. Anyone reading Horace Arnold's 1916 account of the Highland Park supply chain will be at home with the product manuals of companies like i2 Technologies and Manugistics, today's market leaders in supply chain technology. The manuals of the latter are heavy on technical jargon, but the unchanging nature of supply chain management often shows through. Sanjiv Sidhu, former CEO of i2 Technologies and an uncrowned king of the modern supply chain, told the *Financial Times* of how i2's systems "optimize the purchase of both mission-critical and maintenance, repairs, and operations (MRO) products"—in plain English, "we get the goods to the right place on time." Sidhu's narrative comes firmly down to earth when he lists the timely delivery of "office furniture and cleaning fluid" as an example of the "supply chain optimization" possible with i2 software.[34]

The supply chain is a virtual machine whose operations have to be governed by an elaborate set of rules, though the rules set out and enforced by i2's or Manugistics' systems are a good deal more complex than those that governed the supply chain of Ford's day. Supply chains can be shortened and lengthened, formed and reformed, rejigged and replanned, with a speed and ease inconceivable in Ford's time. But this does not mean that the job of supply chain management has grown more complex. In Ford's time, the supply chain manager had to set up his own system of runners to monitor the supply chain and make sure that it was working properly.

If the chain was in danger of coming apart, the manager had to work out the solution on the spot. If shifts in market conditions required that the supply chain be recalculated, the manager had to do the recalculating. Among the skills of a contemporary supply chain manager, with the help of user-friendly graphs and charts, is to make sense of the information the system sends to his workstation. The manager has to recognize when the system is flagging that something is wrong, and he then has to evalaute the system's recommendations about what remedial action should be taken. However, in one critical respect, the contemporary supply chain manager is much more an object of scientific management than his counterparts of Ford's time.

With the working universe of the manager focused on templates that the system conjures up on his workstation screen, the manager's working life becomes visible to the gaze of his superiors in much the same way that the work of the call center agent is visible to his all-seeing supervisor. Senior managers can set targets for the speed and efficiency of the supply chain, and then, at any time, activate the system to find out whether the supply chain manager is meeting his goals. This brings us to the third phase of ERP which, no less than the reengineering of CRM and SCM, has a very significant impact on the nature of business organization. This third phase of ERP is built around systems that gather and analyze information about all aspects of company activities at virtually every level. By subjecting managers to the disciplines of process, ERP's third phase begins to erode the ancient distinction between the manager and the managed.

On the very first page of *Mission Critical*, Davenport writes that "for the first time since large businesses were created, managers will be able to monitor the doings of the company in near real time." Later he goes on to explain that for managers and employees at multiple levels of the company "there is no more hiding when performance is poor, and no more ex post facto revisions."[35] However, in this newly transparent enterprise, some managers are more equal than others. The managers who cannot hide when performance is poor are the kind of managers who deal with supply chains. But one group of managers escapes this real-time surveillance—the CEO and his senior colleagues. They are not objects of the electronic eye, because they are the electronic eye.

With the introduction of reporting and analytical systems encompassing the entire structure of the enterprise, we need to reach beyond the language of economics and "business science" and find a vocabulary equal to the challenge of describing what is going on now. The great French historian, sociologist, and philosopher Michel Foucault has provided such a language. In his book *Discipline and Punish: The Birth of the Prison* (1979) Foucault develops the concept of "panoptic power" and its embodiment in an institution, the panopticon. As the title of Foucault's book suggests, the archetypal panopticon is a prison, and Foucault's definition of panoptic power is shot through with the vocabulary of punishment. The panoptic prison was to be a "twelve-sided polygon formed in iron and sheathed in glass" in order to create the effect of what the nineteenth-century English philosopher Jeremy Bentham called "universal transparency."[36]

A central tower, with wide windows, "opened onto the inner wall of the surrounding polygonal structure, which itself was divided into narrow cells extending across the width of the building." Each cell "had a window on both the inner and outer walls," allowing light to cross the cell, thus illuminating "all the inhabitants to an observer in the central tower, while that observer could not be seen from any one of the cells." Mirrors were also fixed around the tower to "direct extra light into these apartments." Of course, the modern, high-security prison becomes a high-tech panopticon the moment closed-circuit television cameras are placed on or near the ceiling of its cells and passageways.[37] Foucault analyzes the psychological effects of this "universal transparency."

"The major effect of the panopticon," Foucault writes, was "to induce on the inmate a state of conscious and permanent visibility that assured the automatic functioning of power."[38] For power to be exercised in this automatic way, the inmate does not have to believe that he is under constant observation, but only that the possibility of his being under observation is constantly present. In Foucault's words:

> Visible: the inmate will constantly have before his eyes the tall outline of the central tower from which he is spied upon. Unverifiable: the inmate must never know whether he is being looked at at any one moment; but he must be sure that he may always be so. . . . In the peripheric ring, one is totally seen, without ever seeing; in the central tower, one sees everything, without ever being seen.[39]

Foucault then deepens his analysis of the state of mind of those who are the objects of panoptic power:

> He who is subjected to a field of visibility, and who knows it, assumes responsibility for the constraints of power; he makes them play spontaneously upon himself; he inscribes in himself the power relation in which he simultaneously plays both roles; he becomes the principle of

his own subjection. By this very fact the external power may throw off its physical weight. . . . It is a perpetual victory that avoids any physical confrontation and which is always decided in advance.[40]

In her book *In the Age of the Smart Machine*, Shoshana Zuboff shows how Foucault's analysis and language can very easily be transferred to the non-penal setting of the business enterprise. The attainment of panoptic power has been a goal of scientific managers ever since Taylor created his shop floor planning departments, with their hordes of "functional foremen." But it is only with the coming of the computer, and the computer's empowerment with the attachment of monitoring software, that panoptic power has become a real and overwhelming presence in offices and factories. The empowered computer that confronts the employee at the beginning of every working day is nothing less than Foucault's "tall outline of the central tower from which he [the employee] is being spied upon." Once the computer is up and running, so too is the possibility of managerial monitoring and control, though at any given moment the employee can never know whether this power is actually being exercised.

The concept of "panoptic power," however, needs to be looked at in the context of the whole business, the panoptic corporation, and not just in the context of those parts of the business inhabited by frontline workers. With the coming of the panoptic corporation, much of the managerial workforce also now finds itself to be the object, as well as the beneficiary, of panoptic power. The top executive of an anonymous paper manufacturer outlined to Zuboff his vision of a future "panoptic corporation," that turns out to have been remarkably prescient:

> My vision is that one wall of my office will be a screen. I can hit buttons and see my reports or any other data I want. The data base will integrate the entire organization, and all the data will be in agreement. . . . I want the president of the company to have a screen on his wall. We should be able to look at the data on a minute-by-minute basis, and the screen should be continuously updated.[41]

In the mid-1980s, when Zuboff did most of her research, this vision may have had the look of science fiction. But today, companies like

SAP are marketing monitoring and control systems that occupy not one but all four office walls within the executive suite, giving the CEO and his fellow executives a panoptic view of the entire enterprise, including the detailed activities of all levels of management—save the highest. The appearance of a piece entitled "Managing by Wire," in the September–October 1993 edition of the *Harvard Business Review,* marked an important milestone in the intellectual gestation of the corporate panopticon.[42] The authors, Stephen Haeckel and Richard K. Nolan, give an account of panoptic power that has clearly had a strong influence on companies like SAP. Haeckel was, at the time, director of strategic studies at IBM's Advanced Business Institute, and Nolan was on the faculty of the Harvard Business School.

Haeckel and Nolan's choice of the title "Managing by Wire" was intended to link the corporate panopticon with one of the more reassuring images of contemporary life, the aircraft pilot sitting in his cockpit and piloting a modern jet airliner to safety. Haeckel and Nolan explain that when today's pilots do their job, they no longer rely, as they once did, on the evidence of what they see, feel, and hear. Instead, pilots rely on an "informational representation" of the aircraft created by an onboard computer, and are thus "flying by wire."[43] In the same way, "managing by wire" requires that top managers create an "informational representation" of the entire company. This representation will be made up of "expert systems, databases, software objects," and other "technical components" that are integrated to "do the equivalent of flying by wire." Once this happens, "the executive crew. . . . pilots the organization, using controls in the information cockpit of the business. Managers respond to readouts appearing on the console."[44]

Haeckel and Nolan's linking of the corporate panopticon and the "friendly skies" is a deft piece of public relations, but as the controlling metaphor of panoptic power, Foucault's powerful and sinister image of the "tall outline of the central tower" is much to be preferred. Foucault's metaphor conveys the essential point that the principal objects of panoptic power are human beings, and not the inanimate gauges and engines of Haeckel and Nolan's airline fantasy. The moment Haeckel and Nolan start describing in detail the "informational representation" of the company they'd like to see installed in their panoptic cockpit, the unmistakable outline of Foucault's tower looms in the murk:

> To faithfully represent management's design, a robust enterprise model must consistently characterize any process at any scale, exhaustively account for the possible outcomes of every process, and unambiguously specify the roles and accountability of employees involved in carrying them out.[45]

SAP has now brought Haeckel and Nolan's vision to life with its own real-life version of the "management cockpit." This is a top-level conference room whose four walls are covered with illuminated charts dealing with every conceivable aspect of corporate performance. Each wall contains 6 rectangles, with each rectangle containing 6 charts, making a total of 36 charts per wall, and 144 charts for the whole cockpit. But the number of charts that can be displayed on the four walls of the cockpit is virtually unlimited, because the "management cockpit officer" manning the "flight deck" can "drill down" and conjure up charts dealing with the minute-by-minute activities of plants, offices, machines, assembly lines, managers, groups of employees, and even single employees.[46]

The coming of SAP's real-life management cockpit suggests that the corporate mania for monitoring and control has now reached a point at which the dialogue between the managerial pilots in their cockpit could become promising material for some future Kubrikesque film. Embedded in each of the management cockpit's four walls is a "corporate performance monitor" providing for the "definition, analysis, visualization and interpretation of key performance indicators."[47] To this end, the four walls of the cockpit are color coded. A black wall shows the "main success factors and financial indicators." A red wall displays "market performance," a blue wall "the performance of internal processes and employees," and a white wall "the status of strategic projects."[48] The cockpit supports the "top down translation of enterprise strategy" as well as "bottom-up performance monitoring." The CEO and his leading colleagues can examine the key performance indicators for the business as a whole and then "drill down" and get "detailed data from the

ERP "transaction systems," including data on employee performance gathered by SAP workflow software.[49]

John Seely Brown, preeminent philosopher of technology and former Director of Xerox PARC, has described the top-heavy, elaborate creations of ERP as "monolithic blocks of concrete" that are "so cumbersome and difficult to change that the structure of the enterprise is in effect set in stone."[50] But such inflexibility is characteristic of the entire universe of reengineering and ERP: from SAP's slabs of organizational concrete, to the pre-packaged treatments drawn up by MCOs and their "disease management" satellites, to the digital scripts which govern every utterance of the call center agent. The chief casualty of all these forms of scientific management is what John Seely Brown calls "practice": the employee's accumulated skill, knowledge and experience which, applied to the daily problems of the workplace, enable employees to do their jobs well.

Reengineers rely on IT's all-seeing eye to narrow the scope of practice, honoring a strategy which has been at the heart of scientific management since the time of Taylor and Ford. With the coming of ERP in its most advanced forms this campaign has entered a new phase, pushing aside the accumulated experience of entire company workforces. We have already come across this digital hubris in health care, where MCOs have targeted the practice of physicians, relying instead on case managers armed with data bases and expert systems. Now ERP's own digital version of Foucault's tower, with management cockpit at the top, fulfills the reengineer's vision of the corporation as machine, renewing the values of the machine age for the new century.

10

THE ECONOMICS OF UNFAIRNESS

THE CHRONOLOGY OF THIS BOOK spans almost two centuries of American history. In 1824, John Hall first achieved the automatic machining of metal components at the Harpers Ferry arsenal, and Hall's new methods were the American ancestors both of mass production and of scientific management. By another convenient accident of history, one of the pivotal events in this narrative, the beginnings of mass production at Ford's Highland Park plant in 1913, stands near the midpoint of this 200-year narrative. If time travel allowed us to look back from the perspective of 1913, we could see how Henry Ford and Frederick Winslow Taylor pulled together the technical and organizational achievements of the nineteenth century and welded them into a productive machine of commanding power and efficiency.

Looking forward from 1913, and with the advantage of hindsight, we can see how Ford's and Taylor's methods were elaborated by the technologies of the mid- and late twentieth century, and continue to shape profoundly today's U.S. economy. From their base in manufacturing, these methods have, under the rubric of reengineering, launched an invasion of the service economy in which 80 percent of Americans work. Herein lies perhaps the central paradox of the information age. On one side is a group of companies, epitomized by the successful software start-up, that embodies the virtues of the new economy, businesses that really are flexible and "flattened" in their structure,

170

with little or no hierarchy, with a truly skilled workforce, and with a pro-lific record of technological innovation. Yet the products of many of these companies, once installed in companies of the "old" economy, too often strengthen a business culture embodying values that are the exact opposite of those that have made possible the success of the start-ups themselves.

Every reengineering expansion has been sustained by software sys-tems spawned by companies that exemplify the virtues of the "new economy." The control and monitoring systems of reengineered auto plants are provided by a group of software companies, many located in the midwestern industrial heartland; the control systems of the call cen-ter industry are the work of another group of software companies, many located in California. "Managerial medicine" is heavily dependent on the database software of a handful of specialist vendors. The lumbering, unwieldy structures of ERP could not hold together without the glue of software provided by ERP specialists such as Oracle and SAP.

Although the alliance between information technology and scientific management is at work throughout the economy, its roles in manufac-turing and services differ in important ways. In manufacturing, mass production and scientific management have been powerful presences for more than a century. After twenty years of renewal, mostly at the hands of the Japanese, the industrial variants of the two systems have a new lease on life. Such bastions of the old industrial economy as the U.S. automobile, steel, and household appliance industries are now able to compete with Japanese and German producers in a way that they could not fifteen years ago. The strong productivity growth achieved by these and other manufacturing industries in the 1990s is evidence of this success.

But in the service industries, the presence of mass production and sci-entific management in their current forms is a much more recent phe-nomenon. Their origins can be traced back seventy years to Leffingwell's developments of Taylor's ideas for use in the office. But it has been the technological surge of the past ten to fifteen years that has powered the advance of reengineering, a particularly aggressive form of service-sector Taylorism. The record of this service-sector reengineering has been consistently unimpressive. There has been the acknowledged failure of the old reengineering, and the poor record of its successor, ERP. There is also strong anecdotal evidence of reengineering's shortcomings in sectors such as health care and customer service.

The differing histories of manufacturing and services in the contemporary American economy bear upon the reforms appropriate to each of the two sectors. In manufacturing, scientific management and mass production are so deeply rooted that it is probably utopian to believe that an alternative industrial culture, such as the skill-based culture of Germany and northern Europe, can now take root in the United States at such a late phase of the industrial era. The renewal of the old industrial model by Japanese companies such as Toyota further weakens the impetus for reform. Nevertheless, as long as mass production and scientific management remain dominant forces in U.S. manufacturing, there are still battles to be fought there.

In manufacturing, scientific management works by speeding up the pace of work in very small increments. Computers and their software have powers of measurement and control that make them formidable weapons of scientific management and speed up. In manufacturing, and in services that resemble manufacturing, such as call centers, there has to be a force to balance the scientific manager's drive for speed. Without such a countervailing force, the drive for speed too often continues until employee exhaustion and stress impose their own final limits on productivity. Indeed, as we have seen, Mike Parker and Jane Slaughter coined the phrase "management by stress" to describe the kind of overheated work regime that I saw at Nissan's Sunderland plant in the north of England.[1]

For seventy years, labor unions have been the worker's best defense against excessive speed up, and they still are. In the auto industry, the UAW has been carrying on the fight against speed up since the 1930s. I myself only fully grasped the importance of this union role when I visited the joint GM-Toyota assembly plant in Fremont, California, in November 1997. Named New United Motor Manufacturing Inc., (NUMMI), the Fremont plant is a former GM plant that has become a manufacturing showcase in which GM executives and workers can learn firsthand how the Toyota production system works. At first glance, the assembly line at Fremont did not look very different from what I had seen at Nissan.

Workers performed their repetitive tasks as car bodies moved slowly down the line. At rest areas, there were the familiar plastic-covered worksheets specifying tac for each worker on the line, down to the nearest fraction of a second. But the atmosphere of the plant was quite different from what I had found at Nissan. Workers had time to perform their tasks free of stress. I was even able to discuss quality-control problems with an assembly line worker as she fixed front fenders to the moving car bodies. At Nissan, this would have been quite inconceivable. The difference between Nissan and NUMMI is the union. At Fremont, the labor-management contract gives the UAW a formal, consulting role in fixing the pace of production, and the union has used this power to good effect.[2]

The auto industry is one of the last great bastions of union strength in U.S. manufacturing, and the industry provides important examples of fruitful labor-management cooperation on the shop floor. At GM's Saturn plant in Spring Hill, Tennessee, there is a formal structure of labor-management consultation that approaches the German model of industrial codetermination. GM, however, has not extended the methods of the Fremont and Spring Hill plants to its remaining "conventional" plants. But of the Detroit Big Three, Ford has had the most success in achieving labor-management collaboration at all its U.S. plants. Proof of Ford's commitment to this collaboration came in March 1997 when Johnson Controls, one of Ford's chief U.S. suppliers, was fighting unionization at three of its U.S. plants. Alex Trotman, then CEO of Ford, told top managers at Johnson Controls that they should recognize the UAW and work with it, as Ford had done. This advice was much resented by Johnson Controls administration.

This particular Ford model, however, is not necessarily the wave of the future as far as U.S. manufacturing is concerned. Statistics starkly show that only 9 percent of private sector workers and 15 percent of workers in manufacturing belong to unions. Even the auto industry is evolving in ways that are unfavorable to the UAW. As the Detroit Big

Three outsource more and more of their assembly work to their suppliers, a rising percentage of autoworkers find themselves employed by antiunion companies such as Johnson Controls. But there is one way of reversing these trends, not only in the auto industry but throughout the U.S. economy, and that is by reforming U.S. labor laws in ways favorable to the union side.

Strengthening the workplace rights of organized labor is not a fashionable cause today, even among liberals. The past abuses of labor's most powerful constituents—the Teamsters, the construction unions—are not yet ancient history. But the legal pendulum can also swing too far in the direction of union impotence, as my visit to the Iowa call center shows. The National Labor Relations Act of 1935 (NLRA), also known as the Wagner Act, forms the backbone of federal labor legislation in the United States. The current NLRA also includes significant amendments to the original NLRA, most notably those of the Labor Management Relations Act of 1947, or Taft-Hartley Act. The NLRA upholds the rights of employees to form unions, a right also guaranteed by the U.S. Constitution. The NLRA therefore outlaws acts by employers that might interfere with this right.

Employers may not fire employees who want to form a union and who may have begun canvassing their coworkers for this purpose. Employers may not threaten or intimidate employees once an election for union representation is under way. If employees vote for a union, the employer must enter into contract negotiations with the union side. Once contract negotiations have begun, the employer must negotiate in good faith. Human Rights Watch's October 2000 report, "Unfair Advantage," is an indispensable guide to how the NLRA actually operates in the workplace. The report describes the lengths to which companies will go to prevent employees from forming unions.[3]

Between 1992 and 1997, a total of 125,000 workers received payments from their employers as compensation for unlawful dismissal or discrimination suffered for pro-union activities. For 2000, the most recent year for which statistics are available, the figure was 30,590. By the late 1990s, one out of every eighteen workers involved in an organizing campaign was a victim of workplace discrimination at the hands of an employer.[4] A compiler of these statistics, Professor Charles Morris, concludes that "a substantial number of employers involved in union [organizing] campaigns deliberately use employment discrimination against employees as a device to remove union activists and thereby inject an element of fear in the process of selecting or rejecting union representation."[5]

The NLRA provides an elaborate process of litigation to deal with such cases, but a determined employer can exploit the immense inertia of the system to draw out litigation for years. The employer can appeal the decision of the NLRA's court of first instance, an administrative judge, first to the National Labor Relations Board (NLRB) in Washington, the body that acts as the NLRA's court of appeal. The employer can also appeal a decision of the NLRB to the federal courts, and the legal journey from administrative judge to federal judge can last for years. When I visited the UAW's East Peoria local in the summer of 1997, there were Caterpillar workers who had been fired in 1993 and whose cases were still pending before the federal courts.

Even if a company's legal marathon fails and it is convicted of an unfair labor practice, it faces no penalty. All the company must do is reinstate the worker in question and pay the difference between what the worker had earned during the years of litigation and what he would have earned had he never been fired by the company. Ernest Duval, a Haitian immigrant unfairly dismissed in 1994 by the King David Nursing Home in West Palm Beach, Florida, in 1999 received $1,793 in back pay for the five years it took to litigate his case.[6] Few workers have the stamina for these legal marathons, and even those vindicated by the NLRB or the federal courts often do not seek reinstatement with their original employer.

The illegal firing of pro-union workers is one among a battery of lawless acts that companies use to defeat union-organizing campaigns. Others include the use of threats and intimidation during the run up to an election; the manipulation of wages and benefits to penalize union supporters and favor opponents; the refusal to bargain with a newly established union committee, even if the validity of a union election has been upheld by the NLRB; and a refusal to bargain in good faith once negotiations do get under way. Caterpillar's conduct during most of the 1990s was an example of this cumulative lawlessness, moving the NLRB to rule that "Caterpillar's pattern of unlawful conduct convinced us that, without proper restraint, [it] is likely to persist in its attempt to interfere with employees' statutory rights."[7]

The NLRA's chief flaw is that it does not permit the NLRB or the courts to punish an employer for breaking the law. In the words of the Human Rights Watch report, the NLRB can only "order a make-whole remedy restoring the status quo ante as the remedy for unfair labor practices." Persistent corporate lawbreakers such as Caterpillar should be punished as repeat offenders, liable for fines that rise with each new violation of the law. Unions and employees guilty of breaking the law would be liable for the same penalties. Amendments to the NLRA are also needed to correct the severe imbalance of power in the workplace.

Employees who are fired for pro-union activity should be reinstated once an administrative judge rules in their favor, and should be discharged only if and when the NLRB rules that a dismissal was justified on grounds of misconduct. With this change, employers could no longer keep unions out simply by firing the union suppporters, as they now frequently do. The NLRA should also be amended to establish strict legal standards for court review of NLRB decisions. This would draw a distinction between exceptional cases in which an appeal to the federal courts might be justified and the many routine cases in which employers appeal all the way to the federal courts simply to waste time and wear down the union side, as in the Caterpillar case.

Labor unions empower employees when they negotiate with employers on pay and benefits. But unions also perform the mundane but critical task of checking the reengineers' and the scientific managers' drive for speed, monitoring, and control. Strong labor unions are therefore essential when scientific management and mass production still drive the performance of a manufacturing economy, as they do in the United States. Unions are also needed in service sector workplaces—the call center, the Toyota-model clinic—in which the drive for speed has taken over and needs to be checked. But while the presence of labor unions is a necessary antidote to the practice of scientific management in manufacturing, the strengthening of labor's hand does not address the root problem of the service industries. This is the practice of scientific management and mass production in sectors of the economy in which neither belongs and in which their presence is particularly damaging to the interests of both employees and consumers. Nowhere is this presence more damaging than in health care.

The industrialization of health care has failed because neither the U.S. patient population nor the medical profession are prepared for the speeded-up medicine MCOs have tried to introduce. The public is not yet ready to allow aggressive business practices to intrude into a sphere that it still regards as largely personal and private, and in which the private virtues of compassion and kindness have a role to play. From this perspective the worst practices of managed care constitute a collective violation of the Hippocratic oath and its most famous injunction: "Whatever houses I may visit, I will come for the benefit of the sick, remaining free of all intentional injustice and of all mischief."[8]

A basic requirement of any health care reform must be that it simplify the existing system, not add to its complexity, as did the Clintons' failed reform of the early 1990s. It is here that the advantages of a single-payer system are so compelling. The single-payer system embodies a fundamental principle of social equity, that access to quality, affordable health care is the right of every citizen, no less than the right to education and the right to equal protection under the law. By providing quality health care for all citizens, irrespective of income levels and employment status, the single-pay system would also end a great social evil whereby between a quarter and a third of the U.S. population has to live with the fear either that it will not receive adequate care when seriously ill, or that the cost of such care will destroy its financial security. A single-payer system would also restore the relationship between physicians and their patients to the center of the health care universe, permitting physicians to take care of their patients free of constant interference from MCO case managers and medical reengineers.

In practice all Americans over the age of sixty-five already belong to a single-payer system, Medicare, which despite its shortcomings still gets high approval ratings from the American public. The version of a single payer system put forward by leading advocacy groups such as Physicians for a National Health Program (PNHP) improves on Medicare by curtailing such time-wasting practices as the individual billing of patients.[9] Neither Medicare nor the version of National Health Insurance (NHI) advocated by PNHP are systems of "socialized medicine." Physicians would continue to work for themselves, or they would be members of group practices, as they are now. There would still be publicly and privately owned hospitals, as now. What does change is the financing and disbursement of health insurance.

As insurers' MCOs disappear, they would be replaced by a single national insurance authority which levies premiums from the entire population through the tax system. The proceeds are then distributed to state insurance agencies or, in the case of larger states such as California or New York, to regional agencies. These agencies would be responsible for the detailed administration of the system. They would provide hospitals with their annual budgets, negotiated on the basis of the size and needs of the population served. Physicians could choose to be compensated by salary, fee for service, or a combination of the two, with rates negotiated between physician representatives and the state agencies.

A great advantage of a single-payer system is that it would improve dramatically the efficiency of U.S. health care by eliminating at a single stroke the farrago of bureaucracies created by managed care, something the Clintons' reforms of 1993 conspicuously failed to do. There would be no further need for utilization reviewers and disease managers, and they would depart the scene. In 1999 the General Accounting Office (GAO) estimated that a bureaucratic purge along these lines could save as much as $100 billion, enough, in the GAO's estimate, to finance the additional cost of universal coverage.[10] The Medicare system already demonstrates the efficiencies of a single-payer system with administrative costs, expressed as a proportion of total Medicare spending, at one-quarter the level of the private sector.[11]

The introduction of a single-payer system would not of itself resolve the problem of how to limit the resources the nation devotes to health care. But reform would place the issue fully within the public policy arena, where it belongs. MCOs have lost control of health care costs principally because the public will not accept limits on its access to care when it suspects that the money saved accrues to the MCO's bottom line. With national health insurance the public itself funds health care through the tax system, and in the permanent debate on the allocation of public funds, health care would be in direct competition with defense, homeland security, education, and the environment. If the public came to feel that the provision of health care was inadequate, then the public could either pay the higher taxes needed to make things better or accept cutbacks in other areas of spending such as defense.

The recent history of health care reveals the power of public opinion to force businesses to weaken or abandon practices that the public finds objectionable. But these reengineering methods are at large throughout the economy and, in the case of ERP, are being applied to entire businesses. If public opinion can modify such practices in health care, why not in the other sectors in which reengineers have been at work? Such a widespread backlash against reengineering is unlikely as long as an economy can deliver strong growth, low inflation, and low unemployment. But the Achilles' heel of the reengineered economy has been its failure to deliver real wage increases for a majority of Americans. How long this inequality can continue before it finds strong political expression is one of the great imponderables of the new century. As of early 2003, the politics of inequality were being held in check by a consensus that the slow growth of real incomes experienced by most Americans is a passing phenomenon that the economy's future expansion is likely to rectify.

The Democratic party, despite its ambivalent relationship with its own progressive past, is still the political force best placed to challenge this illusion and bring the politics of inequality to life. Ruy Teixeira and Joel Rogers's book *America's Forgotten Majority: Why the White Working Class Still Matters* (2000) describes how the politics of inequality have been playing out in the Democratic party and may continue to play out in the run-up to the 2004 election. In 2002, Teixeira brought his analysis up to date with a second book, *The Emerging Democratic Ma-*

jority, coauthored with John Judis.[12] Teixeira and Judis give an illuminating account of the battle for Vice President Al Gore's political soul, which took place during the two-year run up to the presidential election of 2000. On one side were those still loyal to the ideas of Bill Clinton and his chief political tactician, Dick Morris; they urged Gore to eschew the rhetoric of "class warfare" and the New Deal, and instead stick with such safe topics as the protection of the environment and the economic achievements of the Clinton administration. But there was also a group that looked to renew the legacy of the New Deal for the information age.[13]

From the start of his campaign in early 1999, Gore vacillated between the two sides, but by the time of the Democratic National Convention in August 2000, the progressives were ascendant. Here the key figure was Stan Greenberg, a former Yale political scientist and pollster for Bill Clinton's 1992 campaign, who was fired by Clinton after the November 1994 elections. In contrast to Morris and to Clinton himself, Greenberg believed that the party's "flirtation with soccer moms" and suburban swing voters was "a distraction from the real task at hand— winning back the affections of the majority of working Americans,"[14] and particularly the loyalty of white middle-income voters living in the less-fashionable suburbs who had missed out on the late-1990s boom.

In his convention speech, Gore therefore put aside the soccer moms and addressed the problems of Greenberg's working families. He spoke of an embattled middle class, struggling to make ends meet, besieged by over-mighty corporations, and on whose behalf he as president would fight.[15] Gore's economic proposals focused on tax credits and subsidies that would help these working families in areas such as child care, health insurance, retirement, and the college education of their children. This was a very different account of recent U.S. economic history from the one given to the convention the night before by Bill Clinton, and indeed from the account give by Gore himself as Clinton's vice president for the previous seven and a half years.

One of Gore's errors as a candidate was to spring this "new populism" on the Democratic party, and indeed the nation, without much preparation or warning. For this reason, Gore's convention speech got a very mixed reception from the media. I remember the senior pundit David Gergen describing Gore's economic analysis as "wrong," and the liberal pundit Michael Kingsley describing it as a "hard left" position that had prevented Gore from taking credit for the achievements of the "Clinton-Gore economy." After the election, the pollsters and pundits who had lost out to Greenberg in the battle for Gore's ear also weighed in. The New York pollster Mark J. Penn claimed that Gore had "missed the target of the twenty-first century, the wired workers" and that Gore's "old-style message sent him tumbling in key border states. . . . They were turned off by populism."[16]

However, in the days immediately following the election, Greenberg conducted an extensive poll that proved that he had been right to reconnect Gore to the progressive traditions of the Democratic party. Gore had done particularly badly among white working-class males, a group of voters that should have rallied to his progressive message. But Greenberg did not find that these voters had been put off by Gore's populism; in fact, quite the opposite:

> When Greenberg asked these voters what three factors most contributed to their voting, or considering voting, for Gore, the one that far outnumbered all the others—mentioned by 49 percent of these respondents—was his New Deal-style promise to protect Social Security and add a prescription-drug benefit for seniors.[17]

What cost Gore their vote were his "exaggerations and untruthfulness" (29 percent of respondents), his support for "legalizing the unions of gay couples" (19 percent), and "his being too close to Bill Clinton" (17 percent).[18] To appreciate the force and relevance of Greenberg's findings one has to go back to Teixeira and Rogers' original 2000 text, *America's Forgotten Majority: Why the White Working Class Still Matters*. This "white working class" comprises many of the groups discussed in this book: the old blue-collar industrial working class and their white-collar equivalents in the service industries, and lower-level managers and administrators with less than a four-year college education, the kind of middle-income workers who have found themselves on the wrong side of reengineering and ERP.[19]

This "forgotten majority" of white voters has an annual family income clustering around the national median ($42,228 in 2001), and comprising about 55 percent of the electorate.[20] By confining their analysis to this white working class, Teixeira and Rogers exclude black and Hispanic workers at lower income levels, but the grounds for this exclusion are political, not economic. Rogers and Teixeira, like Greenberg, are interested in the white "forgotten majority" as a group that is politically up for grabs, in a way that the black and Hispanic voting population, predominantly loyal to the Democratic party, is not. But, economically, both the white and minority working classes are in the same boat.

Both are subject to what Teixeira and Rogers call the New Insecurity, the predicament of middle- and lower-income families who have stagnant or barely rising real incomes, are less and less able to rely on long-term job security, and face rising costs for health care, retirement, child care, and the college education of their children—the very issues addressed by Gore in his convention speech. In 2002 and 2003, the New Insecurity has been on the rise, largely due to the corrosive effects of the health care crisis on middle- and even upper-middle-income groups. The relevant census data only goes as far as 2001, but with health care premiums now rising at rates of 15 to 20 percent a year, the trends revealed in the 2001 figures will almost certainly have persisted into 2003. Of the 1.4 million Americans who, in 2001, lost their health insurance, 800,000 had incomes in excess of $75,000, and among the 40.9 million Americans without health insurance in 2001, 24.2 percent had family incomes of $50,000 or more, the largest single group defined by income.[21]

Like Gore, Teixeira and Rogers want to help the struggling middle class with tax cuts and subsidies, only on a more generous scale. However, there is a limit to what can be achieved with this fiscal generosity. Teixeira and Rogers estimate that 55 percent of American employees and their families belong to their "forgotten majority," the white working class. Another 25 percent of employees and families, mostly minorities, can be classified as "lower-income." Around 80 percent of American employees and their families are therefore vulnerable to the

New Insecurity. This 80 percent figure also happens to coincide with the percentage of the U.S. workforce that the Bureau of Labor Statistics classifies as "production and non-supervisory workers."[22]

As defined by the Bureau of Labor Statistics, this group broadly co-incides with workers outside the higher executive, managerial, and professional ranks. However, Teixeira and Rogers do not explain why such a very high percentage of the U.S. workforce should be in such a state of chronic insecurity despite the strong performance of the economy during the late 1990s. Specifically, they do not discuss the causes of the long-term stagnation of real incomes in the United States. Policies that address the consequences of this stagnation, but not the causes, are unlikely to succeed. If the stagnation of wages and salaries continues unchecked, the size of the tax bailout needed to keep the middle class afloat has to increase over time.

With the coming retirement and aging of the baby boom generation certain to strain existing programs such as Social Security and Medicare, the use of the tax system to support the working middle class is likely to run up against the fiscal buffers sooner rather than later—and particularly if the slowdown of 2001–02 portends a period of slower growth for the U.S. economy, with lower tax revenues. Another drawback of failing to identify and remedy the causes of inequality is that the opportunity to do so is left open to those advocating policies that are damaging and ill conceived. Before the Asian financial crisis put paid to it in the fall of 1998, there was, for example, a theory of "globalization" that looked beyond the American shores for the causes of inequality within the United States.

With the improbable duo of Pat Buchanan and Lester Thurow as its leading protagonists, this version of globalization had the American middle class diminished by the emergence of new industrial economies in the Third World.[23] Because this theory had the potential to feed protectionist sentiment in Congress and among the voting public, the then-MIT economist Paul Krugman wrote a series of furious polemical essays, published in 1997 under the title "Pop Internationalism," exposing the muddled economics of the new globalism.[24] Krugman won the technical argument, but it was the Asian financial crisis that really showed Buchanan and Thurow's Third World economies to have feet of clay.

The protectionist virus has inhabited the American polity since its birth, always available to a public suffering through hard times. But public opinion is the indispensable catalyst of beneficial change, as the politics of health care demonstrate. The health care battle has been fought on technical issues such as the right to external review, but it has been the public's refusal to accept the industrialization of health care—the intrusion of mass production and scientific management into the hospital ward and the doctor's office—that has framed the conflict and forced the managed care industry to give ground. The thesis of this book has been that this alliance of mass production and scientific management has been responsible not simply for the poor treatment of employees as patients, but also for their poor treatment in the workplace, and particularly for the stagnation of their real incomes.

The public's opposition to the health care variants of mass production and scientific management needs therefore to extend to the role of these practices throughout the economy. But this will only happen if the debate on the new mass production economy gets beyond technical workplace issues and is placed in its broader political and historical context. Many elements of this broader political context already exist. The September 2000 *Business Week* poll that found Americans so discontented with the performance of MCOs was published under the banner headline "Too Much Corporate Power?" Sixty-three percent of respondents judged the way big companies treated their employees as "poor to fair," and 64 percent judged them as "poor to fair" in providing job security. Seventy-four percent believed that big companies had too much political influence. Ninety-five percent endorsed a code of corporate conduct that has been fading away for the past thirty years: companies "owe something to their workers and the communities in which they operate, and they should sometimes sacrifice some profit for the sake of making things better for their workers and communities."[25]

As if on cue, the Enron scandal and the ensuing corporate crime wave of 2001–2002 provided compelling evidence of the corrupting effects of excessive corporate power. The cry of "too much corporate power" evokes the politics of the first Roosevelt era rather than the second, the politics of turn-of-the century progressivism rather than the politics of Depression-era liberalism, though the NLRA itself was legislation in the Progressive tradition. It would be appropriate if a political philosophy born in the age of Ford and Taylor were revived at a time when their methods are enjoying such a revival. The essence of progressivism is to use the law to shrink excessive concentrations of corporate power. Progressivism is therefore free of the stigma of fiscal extravagance that has crippled New Deal liberalism since the decline of Lyndon Johnson's Great Society in the late 1960s.

There is already a strong progressive current in contemporary American politics. Two major candidates in the 2000 election, Bill Bradley and John McCain, both attacked the excessive political power of business and advocated campaign finance reform as a way to deal with it. As we have seen, Vice President Gore took up the anticorporate theme in his 2000 convention speech, even though in the run up to the 1996 presidential election he had been one of the Clinton administration's chief emissaries to the Democratic party's big corporate donors. Another issue feeding the progressive current is the threat to privacy posed by business's use of digital technology and the Internet to accumulate a mass of information about citizens and consumers.

This corporate snooping targets the citizen in the privacy of his own home. But scientific management armed with digital technology is a form of extreme corporate snooping in the workplace. We have therefore reached a point at which issues that are already of concern to citizens and consumers in their private lives are pushing right up against almost identical issues that ought to be of concern to citizens and employees in the workplace. Even if the New Taylorism could be shown to enhance productivity, it should nonetheless be opposed on the grounds that it subjects employees to a degree of monitoring and control that, outside the workplace, would be considered demeaning and a gross violation of privacy.

However, to argue that the drive for increased labor productivity must be firmly balanced by a concern for employee dignity and welfare may seem to threaten what has become the jewel in the crown of the "new economy." The acceleration of U.S. productivity growth in the second half of the 1990s is perhaps the defining accomplishment of that economy, proof that U.S. businesses' huge investment in IT has at last paid off. Some economists, notably Robert J. Gordon of Northwestern University, have questioned whether such an acceleration of productivity growth has actually taken place,[26] but there is a mass of detailed evidence suggesting that output per worker may indeed have been growing faster than it did in the 1970s and 1980s.

As we have seen, in manufacturing Japanese production methods—the Single Minute Exchange of Die (SMED), the "just in time" replenishment of the assembly line—can add to output per worker, whatever their impact on the quality of working life. There are also major segments of the service economy, notably retail, wholesale, and distribution, whose activities are highly susceptible to the methods of mass production and where increases in productivity take place much as they do on the factory floor. One thinks of WalMart's "perpetual inventory system," the digital machines that are beginning to displace the checkout clerk at the supermarket, the satellites and sensors that monitor every moment of the trucker's working day, and the handheld computers that enable supervisors to micromanage the work of FedEx and UPS deliverymen.

But the productivity picture darkens once the focus shifts from these industrialized services to what I'll call core services—services such as health care and customer service, where there is an irreducible human element that cannot be displaced by automated or expert systems. Here the productivity record is poor and testifies to the reengineer's failure to make scientific management work in contexts where human agents must talk, listen, and bargain. In health care the bureaucratic bloat chronicled by Drs. Himmelstein and Woolhandler points to one of the great productivity fiascos of recent times.

David Levine, formerly chief economist at Sanford Bernstein and Co., estimates that for the years 1972–1994 productivity in the hospital sector fell at an average annual rate of around 1.75 percent a year, making a cumulative decline of nearly 40 percent over the twenty-two-year period.[27] Himmelstein and Woolhandler's latest research shows that the bureaucratization of health care has continued unabated into the new century, so that a reversal of this dismal productivity record is unlikely to have occurred.[28] Similarly Frederick Reichheld's detailed, statistical analysis of the customer service side of business provides powerful evidence of how the "disloyalty effect" of scientific management cripples the productivity of customer-facing employees.

The poor productivity of core service industries suggests that the improved productivity record of the late 1990s will be difficult to sustain. Over time the economy's employment mix will continue to shift away from manufacturing and the industrial side of services, where productivity has improved, and in favor of core services, where the productivity record has been unimpressive. Manufacturing's shedding of labor shows up in the employment statistics month after month, and such service sector industrialization as the automation of the wholesale and retail supply chain will increasingly produce the same effect in these service industries. But in core services the human element places a limit on this displacement of labor, and sometimes requires its reversal. There is, for example a shortage of trained nurses in hospitals, and an acute shortage of teachers in inner cities and poor rural areas.

It is a commonplace of economics that the increased productivity of workers will be matched by increases in their real wages and benefits. When firms invest in new capital equipment, so the argument goes, the productive potential of the new equipment will not be realized unless the skills and pay of the workforce are upgraded. Similarly, when output per employee increases, employers can more easily reward their workers because, with costs per unit of output falling, higher wage costs need not be passed on to the consumer in the form of higher prices. As with most propositions of economics, these are not laws of science with predictive value, they are simply empirical observations of how economic actors may have behaved in the past, with no guarantee that they will continue to act that way in the future.

Recent economic history is proof of just how tentative such propositions can be. An overriding goal of *The New Ruthless Economy*, and of the reengineering that underpins it, has been to turn these ideas on their head so that increases in employee productivity are *not* matched by increases in employees' real wages and benefits, with the fruits of increased productivity diverted elsewhere—to shareholders, senior managers, and CEOs. The link between higher productivity and higher real wages and benefits breaks down when technology is used in ways that deskill most workers, undermine their security in the workplace, and leave them vulnerable to employers possessed of overwhelming power.

In such an economy one would expect the figures for the growth of labor productivity and figures for the growth of real wages and benefits to grow far apart, and that is exactly what the statistics do show. Between 1989 and 2002 the American worker's total compensation—wages plus benefits—grew at any average annual rate of .43 percent. But during the same period output per hour for employees in private, nonfarm business increased at an annual average rate of 2.07 percent. The record of the golden years of 1995–2000 was no different, with worker productivity increasing at an annual average rate of 2.48 percent, and worker's real compensation increasing at an average annual rate of .7 percent. In 1989–2002 the average annual growth of productivity exceeded the growth of real compensation by 481 percent, and by 354 percent in 1995–2000.[29]

It is not difficult to think of reforms that are needed to correct the imbalance of power in the American workplace, and to protect American workers from the exploitation and unfairness which is a consequence of that imbalance. There is a need for employees to have a much stronger voice in deciding how technology is used, whether through employee-owned businesses, through unions, or, where unions are absent, through some other body. There is also a need for laws to prohibit the constant surveillance of employees by their managers. But something more is called for. In this new age of scientific management and mass production, the evolving relationship between man and digital machine is now a great issue of culture and society, comparable in importance to civil rights, the equality of women, the future of medicine, and the practice of genetic engineering in the era of the Human Genome Project.

In the wake of the first machine age a century ago, western societies, including the United States, tamed the harshness of industrialization with a social contract binding management and labor which was broadly accepted by both sides. The contract is now in urgent need of repair and renewal, but the debate as to how this should be done is only just beginning.

NOTES

CHAPTER 1. A NEW ECONOMY?

1. Figures on growth and investment from U.S. Department of Commerce, Bureau of Economic Analysis, "Real Private Gross Fixed Investment by Type 1959–2000." Available at http://www.bea.doc.gov, and in the statistical annex of "The Economic Report of the President, 2001" (Washington, D.C., 2001).

2. "Economic Report of the President, February 2003," Statistical Section, Table b–2: "Real Gross Domestic Product 1959–2003." Available at http://w3.access.gpo.gov/eop.

3. U.S. Department of Labor, Bureau of Labor Statistics: "Average Hourly Earnings of Production and Non-Supervisory Workers, 1982 Dollars, January 2003." Data extracted April 10, 2003.

4. Milt Freudenheim, "Small Employers Severely Reduce Health Benefits," *New York Times,* September 6, 2002.

5. Jared Bernstein, "The Jobless Recovery," Economic Policy Institute Issue Brief 186, January 24, 2003, p. 6. Available at www.epinet.org.

6. Lawrence Mishel, Jared Bernstein, and Heather Boushey, *The State of Working America, 2002–2003* (Washington, D.C., 2003), p. 120, Table 2.3: "Growth in private-sector hourly wages, benefits, and compensation, 1987–2001 (2001 dollars)."

7. Mishel, Bernstein, and Boushey, *The State of Working America, 2002–2003,* pp. 211–13.

8. See Lester Thurow, *Head to Head: The Coming Economic Battle among Japan, Europe and America* (New York, 1992) for a discussion of Germany and Japan as agents of competitive globalization. See also Lester Thurow, *The Future of Capitalism* (New York, 1996) for a discussion of the Asian tiger economies in the same role.

9. See, for example, Alan B. Krueger, "How Computers Have Changed the Wage Structure: Evidence from the Microdata 1984–1989," *Quarterly Journal of Economics* 108 (1): 33–61 (February 1993); Eli Berman, John Bound, and Zvi Griliches, "Changes in the Demand for Skilled Labor Within U.S. Manufacturing Industries: Evidence from the Annual Survey of Manufacturing," National Bureau of Economic Research Working Paper no. 4255, January 1993; Paul Krugman, "Technology's Revenge," in *Pop Internationalism* (Cambridge, Mass., 1997), p. 197.

10. For a discussion of this wider definition of technology, see Paul Krugman, "Technology's Revenge," p. 195.

11. For a discussion of reengineering see, for example, Michael Hammer and James Champy, *Reengineering the Corporation: A Manifesto for Business Revolution* (New York, 1993); Michael Hammer, *The Reengineering Revolution* (New York, 1995); James Champy, *Reengineering Management* (New York, 1995); Thomas Davenport, *Process Innovation, Reengineering Work through Technology* (Cambridge, Mass., 1993). For a discussion of enterprise resource planning (ERP), see Thomas Davenport, *Mission Critical, Realizing the Promise of Enterprise Systems* (Cambridge, Mass., 2000). See also *Financial Times* (London), *FT* Surveys: *Enterprise Resource Planning*, May 26, 1999; *Enterprise Resource Planning*, December 15, 1999; *E-Business: ERP and Beyond*, July 19, 2000.

12. Michael Hammer, *The Reengineering Revolution*, p. xi.

13. AMR Research (Boston), "The Enterprise Applications Report, 1999–2000," p. 11.

14. *Encyclopaedia Britannica*, 14th ed., s.v., "Henry Ford, 'Mass Production.'"

15. Geoffrey Hounshell, *From the American System to Mass Production* (Baltimore, 1984), p. 224.

16. *Encyclopaedia Britannica*, 14th ed., s.v., "Henry Ford, 'Mass Production.'"

17. See, for example, David H. Autor, Frank Levy, and Richard J. Murnane, "The Skill Content of Recent Technological Change: An Empirical Exploration," National Bureau of Economic Research Working Paper no. 8337, June 2001, 32.

18. See the discussion of this issue by Susan Helper of Case Western Reserve University in National Bureau of Economic Research, "NBER/Sloan Project Report: Industrial Technology and Productivity: Incorporating Learning from Plant Visits and Interviews into Economic Research" (Papers presented at the Annual Meetings of the American Economic Association, January 2000), p. 5.

19. An updated version of *The American Way of Death* was published in 1998: Jessica Mitford, *The American Way of Death Revisited* (New York, 1998).

The variety and sophistication of trade literature differs considerably from one industry to another. In the case of the call center industry, which I discuss in chapters 7 and 8, one source dominates: the industry's leading trade journal, *Call Center Solutions*. But in the case of health care (chapters 9 and 10), the industry literature is vast and varied. There are the trade journals of the managed care industry, such as *Health care Business* and *Healthplan Magazine*. There are quasi-academic journals closely aligned with the managed care industry, such as *Managed Care Quarterly*. There are books on the theory and practice of managed care put out by consultancies such as Andersen Consulting and Ernst and Young.

20. Michael L. Dertouzos, Richard K. Lester, Robert M. Solow, and the MIT Commission on Industrial Productivity, *Made in America: Regaining the Productive Edge* (Cambridge, Mass., 1989), p. 48.

21. The Conference Board, *HR Executive Review* (New York) 3(1):2 (1995).

22. Timothy H. Bresnahan, Erik Brynjolfsson, and Lorin M. Hitt, "Information Technology, Workplace Organization and the Demand for Skilled Labor: Firm Level Evidence," National Bureau of Economic Research Working Paper, no. 7136, May 1999, p. i.

23. Paul A. David, "Understanding Digital Technology's Evolution and the Path of Measured Productivity Growth: Present and Future in the Mirror of the Past," in *Understanding the Digital Economy: Data, Tools, and Research*, ed. Erik Brynjolfsson and Brian Kahin (Cambridge, Mass., 2000), p. 54.

24. Quoted by Alan Greenspan in "Remarks at the 81st Annual Meeting of the American Council on Education," Washington, D.C., February 16, 1999, p. 2. Available at www.federalreserve.gov.

25. Daniel Aaronson and David G. Sullivan, "The Decline of Job Security in the 1990s: Displacement, Anxiety and Their Effect on Wage Growth," prepared for the Federal Reserve Bank of Chicago, *Economic Perspectives*, first quarter 1998, pp. 17–43. Available at www.frbchi.org/pubs-speech/publications/periodicals.

26. Alan Greenspan, "Education, Technology, and Economic Growth," Remarks at the Building Dedication Ceremonies at the Kenan-Flagler Business School, University of North Carolina, Chapel Hill, September 12, 1997, p. 1. Available at www.federalreserve.gov.

CHAPTER 2. THE ROOTS OF MASS PRODUCTION

1. Alfred D. Chandler, Jr., *The Visible Hand, The Managerial Revolution in American Business* (Cambridge, Mass., 1977), pp. 253–56, 259–62.

2. Ibid., pp. 249–53.

3. Merritt Roe Smith, *Harpers Ferry Armory* (Ithaca, N.Y., 1977), pp. 219, 249.

4. Hounshell, *From the American System,* p. 42.

5. Smith, *Harpers Ferry Armory,* p. 239.

6. Hounshell, *From the American System,* pp. 89, 161.

7. Ibid., pp. 47–50.

8. Ibid., pp. 91–123.

9. Frederick Winslow Taylor, *Shop Management* (New York, 1911), p. 110.

10. Ibid., p. 159.

11. See for example, David Nelson, *Frederick W. Taylor and the Rise of Scientific Management* (Madison, Wisc., 1980), p. 174.

12. Frederick Winslow Taylor, *Principles of Scientific Management* (New York, 1911; paperback ed. 1967), pp. 48–49.

13. Frederick Winslow Taylor, "The Art of Cutting Metals," in *Scientific Management, A Collection of the More Significant Articles Describing the Taylor System of Management* (Cambridge, Mass., 1914), p. 245.

14. Ibid., p. 252.

15. Ibid., p. 262.

16. Ibid., p. 263.

17. Taylor, *Shop Management,* p. 113.

18. Ibid., p. 102.

19. Nelson, *Frederick W. Taylor and the Rise of Scientific Management,* p. 85.

20. David Montgomery, *Fall of the House of Labor* (New York, 1987), p. 247.

21. Chandler, *The Visible Hand,* p. 278.

22. Hounshell, *From the American System,* pp. 220, 224.

23. Stephen Meyer, *The Five Dollar Day: Labor, Management, and Social Control in the Ford Motor Company, 1908–1921* (Albany, N.Y., 1981), p. 25.

24. Hounshell, *From the American System,* p. 251.

25. Meyer, *Five Dollar Day,* pp. 11, 20–21.

26. Horace Arnold, *Ford Methods and the Ford Shops* (New York, 1915), p. 246. Available at the New York Public Library, on microfilm, call number, *XMQ–428.

27. Ibid., p. 174.

28. Ibid., p. 349.

29. Henry Ford, in collaboration with Samuel Crowther, *My Life and Work* (New York, 1922), quoted in Alfred D. Chandler, *Giant Enterprise, Ford, General Motors and the Automobile Industry, Sources and Readings* (New York, 1964), p. 39.

30. Meyer, *Five Dollar Day,* p. 32–35.

31. Ford, *My Life and Work,* quoted in Meyer, *Five Dollar Day,* p. 21.

32. See, for example, Arnold, *Ford Methods and the Ford Shops*, pp. 117–27.
33. Ibid., p. 144.
34. Charles Reitell, "Machinery and Its Effect Upon the Workers in the Automobile Industry," *Annals of the American Academy of Political and Social Science* 116 (November 1924), quoted in Chandler, *Giant Enterprise*, p. 183.
35. Quoted in Meyer, *Five Dollar Day*, p. 64.
36. Emma Rothschild, *Paradise Lost, The Decline of the Auto-Industrial Age* (New York, 1973), p. 40.
37. Chandler, *Giant Enterprise*, pp. 13–14.
38. Ibid., p. 153.
39. Ibid.
40. Stephen Meyer, "The Persistence of Fordism: Workers and Technology in the American Automobile Industry, 1900–1960" in *On the Line: Essays in the History of Auto Work*, ed. Nelson Lichtenstein and Stephen Meyer (Urbana, Ill. 1989), p. 83.
41. Ibid., p. 82.
42. Louis R. Eltscher and Edward M. Young, *Curtiss-Wright: Greatness and Decline* (New York, 1998), p. 103.
43. Peter F. Drucker, *Post Capitalist Society* (New York, 1994), p. 36.
44. Roger E. Bilstein, *The American Aerospace Industry: From Workshop to Global Enterprise* (New York, 1996), pp. 73–74, 77.
45. Michael J. Piore and Charles F. Sabel, *The Second Industrial Divide: Possibilities for Posterity* (New York, 1984).
46. Ibid., chap. 7.
47. Ibid., pp. 205–8.

CHAPTER 3. THE PAST ALIVE: AUTOMOBILES

1. Dertouzos et al., *Made in America*, p. 48.
2. National Center on Education and the Economy, Commission on the Skills of the American Workforce, *America's Choice: High Skills or Low Wages!* (New York, 1990), p. 2.
3. Dertouzos et al., *Made in America*, p. 49.
4. National Center on Education and the Economy, pp. 37–38.
5. Paul A. David, "Understanding Digital Technology's Evolution and the Path of Measured Productivity Growth: Present and Future in the Mirror of the Past," in *Understanding the Digital Economy*, ed. Brynjolfsson and Kahin, p. 54.
6. Thomas H. Davenport, *Process Innovation: Reengineering Work through Information Technology* (Cambridge, Mass., 1993), p. 17.

7. Phillip Garrahan and Paul Stewart, *The Nissan Enigma: Flexibility at Work in a Local Economy* (London, 1992), p. 78.

8. Taylor, *Shop Management,* p. 28.

9. Taylor, *Principles of Scientific Management,* p. 128.

10. Garrahan and Stewart, *Nissan Enigma,* pp. 79–80.

11. James P. Womack, Daniel T. Jones, and Daniel Roos, *The Machine that Changed the World* (New York, 1990).

12. Ibid., p. 11.

13. Shigeo Shingo, *A Revolution in Manufacturing, the SMED System* (Portland, Ore., 1985).

14. Ibid., p. xv.

15. Ibid., p. 343.

16. Ibid., p. 66.

17. Ibid., p. 14.

18. Womack, Jones, and Roos, *The Machine that Changed the World,* p. 53.

19. Shingo, *A Revolution in Manufacturing,* pp. 36, 76.

20. Ibid., pp. 42, 116.

21. Ibid., pp. 53–55.

22. Ibid., p. 48.

23. Ibid., pp. 73–75.

24. Ibid., pp. 46–47.

25. Ibid., back cover.

26. Ibid., pp. 122–23.

27. Ibid., pp. 58–59.

28. McKinsey Global Institute, *Manufacturing Productivity* (Washington, D.C.: 1993).

29. Ibid., Case Studies, "Automobile Assembly," p. 1 (facing), "Automobile Parts," p. 1 (facing).

30. McKinsey, "Automobile Assembly," p. 8.

31. Ibid., p. 2.

32. McKinsey, "Synthesis," p. 9.

33. McKinsey, "Automobile Assembly," pp. 6–7.

34. Ibid., p. 8.

35. Ibid., pp. 6, 10 (facing).

36. McKinsey, "Synthesis," p. 8.

37. Ibid., p. 8 (facing).

38. Ibid.

39. McKinsey, "Automobile Assembly," p. 6.

40. National Center on Education and the Economy, p. 24.

41. McKinsey, "Synthesis," p. 8 (facing).

42. Available at www.bls.gov.

43. The UAW has organized the workforce at a joint GM-Toyota plant in Fremont, California, known as NUMMI (New United Motor Manufacturing, Inc.). However the UAW's presence at NUMMI is due to its past relationship with GM, not Toyota.

44. Mike Parker and Jane Slaughter, "Choosing Sides: Unions and the Team Concept," *Labor Notes* (Detroit, 1988); "Working Smart: A Union Guide to Participation Programs and Reengineering," *Labor Notes* (Detroit, 1994). *Labor Notes* is a pro-union monthly newsletter available at 7435 Michigan Avenue, Detroit, MI, 48210; (313) 842-6262.

CHAPTER 4. THE RISE OF THE REENGINEERS

1. Quoted in Shoshana Zuboff, *In the Age of the Smart Machine* (New York, 1988), p. 117.

2. William Henry Leffingwell, *Scientific Office Management* (Chicago, 1917), p. 5.

3. William Henry Leffingwell, *Textbook of Office Management* (New York, 1932), p. 78.

4. Leffingwell, *Scientific Office Management,* p. 5.

5. Ibid., p. 20.

6. Ibid., pp. 20–21.

7. Ibid., p. 218.

8. Ibid., pp. 32, 219–20.

9. Ibid., p. 38.

10. William Henry Leffingwell, *Office Management, Principles and Practice* (New York, 1925), p. 62.

11. Leffingwell, *Scientific Office Management,* p. 39.

12. Ibid., p. 4; Leffingwell, *Textbook of Office Management,* p. 411.

13. Leffingwell, *Textbook of Office Management,* p. 72.

14. Leffingwell, *Scientific Office Management,* pp. 46, 48.

15. Ibid., p. 48.

16. Ibid.

17. Leffingwell, *Textbook of Office Management,* p. 25.

18. Ibid., p. 367.

19. See www.mtm.org.

20. Paul Mulligan, "The Manual of Standard Time Data for the Office," quoted in Daniel Bell, *The End of Ideology: On the Exhaustion of Political Ideas in the Fifties* (New York, 1962), p. 237.

21. International Labour Organization, "Effects of Mechanization and

Automation in Offices: III," *International Labour Review* 81 (4): 351–52 (1960), quoted in Zuboff, *In the Age of the Smart Machine*, p. 120.

22. "Measuring How Office Workers Work," *Business Week*, November 14, 1970, p. 54, quoted in Zuboff, *In the Age of the Smart Machine*, p. 122.

23. Association for Systems Management, "A Guide to Office Clerical Time Standards for Manual Operations" (Toledo, Ohio, 1972), quoted in Zuboff, *In the Age of the Smart Machine*, p. 122.

24. James Duncan, "Clerical Work Needs Engineering," *The Office* (July 1969): 30–34, quoted in Zuboff, *In the Age of the Smart Machine*, p. 121.

25. Hammer and Champy, *Reengineering the Corporation*, pp. 22–30; Davenport, *Process Innovation*, pp. 5–15, 50–61.

26. Leffingwell, *Office Management*, p. 54.

27. Hammer and Champy, *Reengineering the Corporation*, p. 26.

28. Zuboff, *In the Age of the Smart Machine*, p. 119.

29. Davenport, *Process Innovation*, p. 275.

30. Ibid.

31. Hammer and Champy, *Reengineering the Corporation*, pp. 36–39, 67–71.

32. Michael Hammer, "Reengineering Work: Don't Automate, Obliterate," *Harvard Business Review* (July–August 1990): 106.

33. Hammer and Champy, *Reengineering the Corporation*, p. 93.

34. Thomas Davenport and James E. Short, "The New Industrial Engineering: IT and Process Redesign," *Sloane Management Review* (Summer 1990): 15.

35. Hammer and Champy, *Reengineering the Corporation*, p. 76.

36. Davenport, *Process Innovation*, p. 261.

37. Frederick Winslow Taylor, *Shop Management* (New York, 1911), p. 28.

38. Ibid., p. 51.

39. Ibid., pp. 17, 257; Hammer and Champy, *Reengineering the Corporation*, p. 65.

40. Zuboff, *In the Age of the Smart Machine*, pp. 9–11.

41. Ibid., p. 57.

42. Champy, *Reengineering Management*, pp. 125–26, 165–66.

43. Davenport, *Process Innovation*, p. 62.

44. Taylor, *Principles of Scientific Management*, p. 83.

45. Hammer and Champy, *Reengineering the Corporation*, pp. 207–8.

46. Davenport, *Process Innovation*, p. 12.

47. Taylor, *Principles of Scientific Management*, p. 83.

48. Hammer, *Reengineering Revolution*, p. 23.

49. Ibid., p. 29.

50. Ibid., p. 124.

51. Ibid., p. 40.

52. Ibid., pp. 40, 50.

53. Ibid., p. 129.

54. Hammer and Champy, *Reengineering the Corporation*, p. 106.

55. Hammer, *Reengineering Revolution*, p. 66.

56. Ibid., p. 60.

57. Ibid., pp. 61, 122.

58. Joseph B. White, "Reengineering Gurus Take Steps to Remodel Their Stalling Vehicle," *Wall Street Journal*, November 20, 1996.

CHAPTER 5. THE CUSTOMER RELATIONS FACTORY

1. Robert Griggs, "Managing Customer Relations for E-Commerce Business," *Call Center Solutions* (hereafter *CCS*) (June 1999): 89.

2. Lou Volpe, "Distributed Call Centers Move into the Decade of Intimacy," *CCS* (May 1999): 92.

3. Tom Peters, *The Circle of Innovation* (New York, 1997), pp. 253, 465.

4. Rosabeth Moss Kantor, *On the Frontiers of Management* (Cambridge, Mass., 1997), p. 14.

5. Bill Gates, *Business @ the Speed of Thought* (New York, 1999), p. 24.

6. Davenport, *Process Innovation*, pp. 16, 270.

7. Hammer and Champy, *Reengineering the Corporation*, p. 130.

8. Louis Uchitelle, "For Answerers of '800' Calls, Extra Income but No Security," *New York Times*, March 27, 2002.

9. Ed Arnold and Michael Hoffman, "Training Drivers and Opportunities in Call Centers," A Study Conducted by Omnitech (Boston, 1998); see also Arnold and Hoffman, "Banish the Barriers to Personalized Customer Service," *CCS* (November 1998): 116–20, 122, 124.

10. Arnold and Hoffman, "Training Drivers and Opportunities," p. 4.

11. Ibid., p. 20.

12. *CCS* (April 1999): 118.

13. Greg Stack, "The New Business Environment, CTI in ECM Architecture," *CCS* (July 1999): 2. Available at www.tmcnet.com/articles/ccsmag/ 0799/0799toc.htm.

14. Volpe, "Distributed Call Centers," p. 97.

15. Stack, "New Business Environment," p. 3.

16. Volpe, "Distributed Call Centers," p. 97.

17. Rita Dearing, "Not the Same Old Script," *CCS* (July 1999): 1. Available at www.tmcnet.com/articles/ccsmag/0799/0799toc.htm.

18. Sharna Kahn, "Redefining Call Center Metrics: The Quality Connection," *CCS* (January 1999): 2. Available at www.tmcnet.com/articles/ccsmag/ 0199/0199kpmg.htm.

19. Dearing, "Not the Same Old Script," p. 2.

20. Ibid., p. 1.

21. Ibid., p. 2.

22. Rich Tehrani, "PC-Based Solutions Help Small Call Centers Stand Tall," *CCS* (November 1998): 138.

23. Alan Kessler, "Bringing Knowledge to Customer Service," *CCS* (July 1999): 2. Available at www.ccsmag.com/articles/ccsmag/0799/0799e feature2.htm.

24. Ibid., p. 1.

25. Ibid.

26. Jack Whalen and Erik Vinkhuyzen, "Expert Systems in (Inter)Action: Diagnosing Document Machine Problems over the Telephone," in *Workplace Studies: Recovering Work Practice and Information Systems Design,* ed. Christian Heath, Jon Hindmarsh, and Paul Luff (Cambridge, U.K., 2000), pp. 92–140.

27. See, for example, Charles H. Ferguson and Charles R. Morris, *Computer Wars: The Fall of IBM and the Future of Global Technology* (New York, 1994), pp. 105–7; see also Claudia H. Deutsch, "The Fading Copier King: Xerox Has Failed to Capitalize on Its Own Innovations," *New York Times,* January 19, 2001.

28. Simon London, "A Visionary and His Big Picture," *Financial Times,* September 6, 2002.

29. Whalen and Vinkhuyzen, "Expert Systems in (Inter)Action," p. 92.

30. Ibid., p. 103.

31. Ibid.

32. Ibid., p. 98.

33. Ibid., p. 99.

34. Ibid.

35. Gary Shearer, "Voice/Screen Capture System Boosts Quality and Productivity," *CCS* (November 1998): 100.

36. Ibid., p. 201.

37. Ibid.

38. Ibid.

39. Shearer, "Voice/Screen Capture System," p. 103.

40. "Teloquent Offers Extended Reporting Capabilities," *CCS* (November 1998): 36.

41. Dan Ater, "Teleservicing the Needs of the Health-Care Industry," *CCS* (June 1998): 94.

42. Stephen Pace, "Customer Interaction Software: Three Critical Steps Lead to the Right Purchase," *CCS* (June 1998): 44.

43. Tony Procops, "Call Logging and Monitoring: Essential for Teleservices," *CCS* (June 1998): 64.
44. "Upgraded Telemonitoring System from CBSI," *CCS* (November 1998): 40.
45. Don McCormick, "The Emerging Face of Outbound Teleservices," *CCS* (April 1999): 93.
46. Ibid., p. 94.
47. "Funk Software Shifts Proxy Remote Gateway," *CCS* (June 1999): 28.
48. Ibid.
49. Shearer, "Voice/Screen Capture System," p. 103.
50. Procops, "Call Logging and Monitoring," p. 64.
51. Christopher Botting, "Building the Virtual Call Center," *CCS* (May 1999): 98.

CHAPTER 6. ON THE DIGITAL ASSEMBLY LINE

1. See Mike Parker and Jane Slaughter, "Choosing Sides: Unions and the Team Concept," *Labour Notes* (Detroit, 1998); see also Mike Parker and Jane Slaughter, "Working Smart, A Union Guide to Participation Programs and Reengineering," *Labor Notes* (Detroit, 1994).
2. "Tac" is Japanese industrial parlance for a target time set by management for the performance of a task see my discussion in chapter 3.
3. RuthAnn Hogue, "Why Do They Come?" *Arizona Daily Star* (hereafter *ADS*), November 17, 1998: available at www.azstarnet.com/growing pains/tues02.htm, p. 2; RuthAnne Hogue, "Tucson Poised for Growth," *ADS*, November 18, 1998: available at www.azstarnet.com/growing pains/plusminus.htm.
4. RuthAnn Hogue, "Your Feedback," *ADS*, November 16, 1998.
5. RuthAnn Hogue, "Centers a Target for Union Effort," *ADS*, November 17, 1998: available at www.azstarnet.com/growingpains/tues06.htm, p. 2.
6. Ibid.
7. RuthAnn Hogue, "Couple Fell into Call Jobs: It's a Way to Get By," *ADS* (November 15, 1998), pp. 1–3. Available at www.azstarnet.com/ growingpains/8hours.htm.
8. Hogue, "Centers a Target for Union Efforts," pp. 1–2.
9. RuthAnn Hogue, "Fighting for Benefits, Workers Find It Hard to Get Help after Firing Injury," *ADS*, November 16, 1998.
10. Interviews with Gayle Brown and Gary Johnson, Steward (now president) of Fairhaven CWA Local, January 29, 1998. AT&T refused my request for an interview to discuss the Gayle Brown case.

11. The Radclyffe Group, "Call Center Culture: The Hidden Success Factor—Achieving Service Excellence" (Fairfield, N.J., June 1998): 1–10. See also follow-up report, June 1999.

12. Ibid.

13. Ibid.

14. 9-5, "Stories of Mistrust and Manipulation: The Electronic Monitoring of America," February 1990, p. 11. 9-5 is a lobbying group for working women, now based in Milwaukee, Wisconsin.

15. Arnold and Hoffman, "Training Drivers and Opportunities in Call Centers," p. 11.

16. Dina Vance, "Call Centers Lead the Wave of Banking's Future," *CCS* (February 1999): 3. Available at www.tmcnet.com/articles/ccsmag/0299/0299hr.htm.

17. Author's telephone interview with Mike McGrath, January 14, 2000.

18. Rodney Kuhn, "Using Quality Monitoring to Enhance Performance and Improve Morale," *CCS* (June 1999): 116.

19. Whalen and Vinkhuyzen, "Expert Systems in (Inter)Action," pp. 92–140.

20. Ibid., pp. 96–126, for Whalen and Vinkhuyzen's discussions of CasePoint's shortcomings.

21. Frederick Reichheld and Robert G. Markey Jr., "Loyalty and Learning; Overcoming Corporate Learning Disabilities," *Bain and Company Essays: The Relations between Loyalty and Profits # 1* (Boston, undated), p. 1.

22. Frederick Reichheld, "Loyalty-Based Management," *Harvard Business Review*, Reprint 93210 (March–April 1993): 71.

23. Frederick Reichheld and W. Earl Sasser Jr., "Zero Defections: Quality Comes to Services," *Harvard Business Review*, Reprint 905081 (September–October 1990): 107.

24. Reichheld, "Loyalty-Based Management," p. 68.

25. Frederick Reichheld, *The Loyalty Effect: The Hidden Force behind Growth, Profits, and Lasting Value* (Cambridge, Mass., 1996), pp. 1–21, 91–116.

26. Ibid., pp. 101–2.

27. Ibid., pp. 100–105.

28. Whalen and Vinkhuyzen, "Expert Systems in (Inter)Action," pp. 126–32.

29. Ibid., pp. 132–38.

30. Ibid., p. 137.

31. Author's telephone interview with Jack Whalen, January 8, 2003.

CHAPTER 7. THE SCIENTIFIC MANAGEMENT OF LIFE—AND DEATH: PART I

1. Walter A. Zelman and Robert A. Berenson, *The Managed Care Blues and How to Cure Them* (Washington, D.C., 1998), p. 16.

2. Ibid., p. 25.

3. Ibid., p. 1.

4. For succinct definitions of HMO and PPO see www.investorwords.com.

5. Zelman and Berenson, *The Managed Care Blues,* p. 11.

6. Ibid., p. 10.

7. "Too Much Corporate Power?" *Business Week,* September 11, 2000, pp. 148–49.

8. Quoted in Laura Landro, "Costs, Politics of Health Care Will Dominate Debate in '03," *Wall Street Journal,* January 2, 2003.

9. National Conference of State Legislatures, "Managed Care"; see "U.S. Supreme Court Upholds Authority to Protect Patients," p. 3. Available at www.ncsl.org/programs/health/managed.htm.

10. See Robert Pear, "Spending on Health Care Increased Sharply in 2002," *New York Times,* January 8, 2003; Sarah Lueck, "Health-Care Spending Rises 8.7%, Fastest Expansion in 10 Years," *Wall Street Journal,* January 8, 2003.

11. For 2001–2003 figures, see "Data Update," Physicians for a National Health Program, Newsletter (fall 2002), p. 4.

12. Rebecca Knight, "Aetna Positive Despite Posting Higher Losses," *Financial Times,* April 26, 2003.

13. Dr. David Himmelstein et al., "Quality of Care in Investor-Owned *vs.* Not-For-Profit HMOs," *Journal of the American Medical Association* (hereafter *JAMA)* 282 (2): 159–63 (July 14, 1999).

14. Drawn from a data series known as HEDIS, a "set of standardized, quality, utilization, financial and other indicators" put together by the National Committee on Quality Assurance and designed to permit comparisons of MCO performance. See www.ncqa/Programs/HEDIS.

15. Himmelstein et al., "Quality of Care," p. 160.

16. Ibid., p. 161.

17. Andersen Consulting, *Changing Health Care: Creating Tomorrow's Winning Enterprise Today* (Santa Monica, 1997).

18. Ibid., biographical information inside book jacket.

19. Ibid., p. 55, 127.

20. Ernst and Young, *Information Technology for Integrated Health Systems, Positioning for the Future* (New York, 1996), p. 44.

21. Ibid., p. 37.

22. "Idealized Design of Clinician Office Practice; An Interview with Donald Berwick and Chuck Kilo of the Institute for Health Improvement," *Managed Care Quarterly,* 7 (4): 66 (1999).

23. Erica Drazen and Jane Metzger, *Strategies for Integrated Health Care;*

Emerging Practices in Information Management and Cross-Continuum Care (San Francisco, 1999), p. 92.

24. Ibid.
25. Ernst and Young, *Information Technology for Integrated Health Systems,* p. 141.
26. J. D. Kleinke, *Bleeding Edge, The Business of Health Care in the New Century* (Gaithersburg, Md., 1998), p. 173.
27. Charles Ornstein, "Kaiser Clerks Paid More for Helping Less," *Los Angeles Times,* May 17, 2002.
28. Dr. Kenneth Ludmerer, *Time to Heal, American Medical Education from the Turn of the Century to the Era of Managed Care* (New York, 1999), p. 384.
29. Ibid., p. 367.
30. Ibid., p. 359.
31. Ibid.
32. Ibid., p. 361.
33. Ibid., p. 376.
34. Ibid.
35. Ibid., p. 365.
36. Kleinke, *Bleeding Edge,* p. 156; see also pp. 151–55, 157–80.
37. Dr. Stephen D. Boren, "I Had a Tough Day Today, Hillary," *New England Journal of Medicine* (hereafter *NEJM*) 330 (7) (February 17, 1994).
38. Andersen Consulting, *Changing Health Care,* pp. 46, 48.
39. Carl Peterson, "The Technology of Disease Management," *Healthplan Magazine* (March–April 1999): 78.
40. Health care Business Roundtable, Special Section on Disease Management, *Health care Business* (September–October 1999): 22.
41. Dr. Edward H. Wagner, Brian T. Austin, and Michael Von Korff, "Improving Outcomes—Chronic Illness," reprinted in *Managed Care and Chronic Illness,* ed. Peter D. Fox and Teresa Fama (Gaithersburg, Md., 1996), pp. 108–9; Rebecca Voelker, "Population Based Medicine Merges Clinical Care, Epidemiological Techniques," *JAMA* 271 (17): 1301-2 (May 4, 1994).
42. Wagner et al., "Improving Outcomes in Chronic Illness," p. 108.
43. Voelker, "Population Based Medicine," p. 1301.
44. Wagner et al., "Improving Outcomes in Chronic Illness," p. 108.
45. Voelker, "Population Based Medicine," p. 1301.
46. Andersen Consulting, *Changing Health Care,* p. 116; Ernst and Young, *Information Technology for Integrated Health Systems,* p. 147.
47. Dennis J. Streveler, "How Information Technology Will Give Patients

Unprecedented Control over their Futures," *Health care Business* (January– February 1999): 80.

48. Karen Niemi et al., "Integrating Clinical and Support Process Design for Effective Health Services," *Managed Care Quarterly* 5 (3): 5 (1997).

49. Dr. William C. Schumacher, "Give Peace a Chance," *Health care Business* (July–August 1999): 80.

50. "That's Dr. Provider to You," *Health care Business* (July–August 1999): 11.

51. Ibid.

52. Paul Ellwood et al., "Health Maintenance Strategy," *Medical Care* (9): 291–98 (1971).

53. David U. Himmelstein and Steffie Woolhandler, "The Corporate Compromise: A Marxist View of Health Maintenance Organizations and Prospective Payment," *Annals of Internal Medicine* (15): 498 (September 1988).

CHAPTER 8. THE SCIENTIFIC MANAGEMENT OF LIFE—AND DEATH: PART 2

1. Dr. Jerome Kassirer, "Clinical Problem Solving, a New Feature in the Journal," *NEJM* 326 (1):60 (January 2, 1992).

2. Dr. William P. Peters and Dr. Mark C. Rogers, "Variation in Approval by Insurance Companies of Coverage for Autologous Bone Marrow Transplantation for Breast Cancer," *NEJM* 330 (7): 473–77 (February 17, 1994).

3. Mark Hagland, "25 Years Later, an Unfinished Revolution, Interviews with Alan Enthoven, Ph.D., and Paul Ellwood, M.D.," *Healthplan Magazine* (November–December 1999): 46.

4. Dr. David U. Himmelstein, Dr. James P. Lewontin, and Dr. Steffie Woolhandler, "Who Administers? Who Cares? Medical Employment in the United States and Canada," *American Journal of Public Health* 86 (2): 173 (February 1996).

5. Ibid., p. 174.

6. Dr. David U. Himmelstein, Dr. James P. Lewontin, and Dr. Steffie Woolhandler, "Administrative Costs in U.S. Hospitals," *NEJM* 329 (6): 401 (August 5, 1993).

7. Dr. Steffie Woolhandler and Dr. David U. Himmelstein, "When Money Is the Mission—The High Cost of Investor Owned Care," *NEJM* 341 (6): 445 (August 5, 1999).

8. Dr. Steffie Woolhandler and Dr. David U. Himmelstein, "The Deteriorating Administrative Efficiency of the U.S. Health Care System," *NEJM* 324 (18): 1257 (May 2, 1991).

9. Ibid., p. 1255.
10. Dr. Steffie Woolhandler and Dr. David U. Himmelstein, "Costs of Care and Administration at For-Profit and Other Hospitals in the United States," *NEJM* 336 (11): 774 (March 13, 1997).
11. Institute of Medicine, "To Err Is Human: Building a Safer Health System" (Washington, D.C., 1999).
12. Harris Interactive, "Fear of Litigation Study: the Impact on Medicine," Final Report, April 11, 2002, Table 6: "Conducted for Common Good," p. 17.
13. Wagner et al., "Improving Outcomes—Chronic Illness," pp. 108–9; Rebecca Voelker, "Population Based Medicine Merges Clinical Care, Epidemiological Techniques," *JAMA* 271 (17) : 1301–2 (May 4, 1994).
14. Kassirer, "Clinical Problem Solving," pp. 60–61.
15. Ibid., p. 60.
16. Dr. Ronan Jaffe and Dr. Doron Zahager, "The Domino Principle," *NEJM* 335 (5): 341 (August 1, 1996).
17. Eric Cassell, *The Nature of Suffering and the Goals of Medicine* (New York, 1991), p. 223.
18. See, for example, Dr. Jerome Kassirer, "A Report Card on Computer-Assisted Diagnosis, the Grade –C," *NEJM* 330 (25) (June 23, 1994); Stephen B. Soumerai and Helen L. Lipson, "Computer Based Drug Utilization Review—Risk, Benefit or Boondoggle?" *NEJM* 332 (24) (June 15, 1995); Richard A. Garibaldi, "Computers and the Quality of Care—a Clinician's Perspective," *NEJM* 338 (4) (January 22, 1998).
19. Cassell, *The Nature of Suffering*, pp. 148–53.
20. Ibid., pp. 149–52.
21. Ibid., p. 151.
22. Dr. Paul G. Shekelle et al., "The Reproducability of a Method to Identify the Overuse or Underuse of Medical Procedures," *NEJM* 338 (26): 1888 (June 25, 1998).
23. Dr. Ralph I. Horwitz, "Complexity and Contradiction in Clinical Trial Research," *American Journal of Medicine* 82: 498–510 (March 1987).
24. Ibid., pp. 501–4.
25. Dr. Claudia A. Steiner, Dr. Neil R. Powe, Gerald F. Anderson, and Abhik Das, "The Review Process Used by U.S. Health Care Plans to Evaluate New Medical Technology for Coverage," *Journal of General Internal Medicine* 11: 294 (1996).
26. Ibid., pp. 299–300.
27. Ibid.

28. Dr. Jerome Groopman, *Second Opinions: Stories of Intuition and Choice in the Changing World of Medicine* (New York, 2000). Groopman is a professor of medicine at the Harvard Medical School and chief of experimental medicine at Beth Israel Deaconess Medical Center in Boston. He is also, unusually, a staff writer for the *New Yorker*, and some chapters of his book originally appeared as pieces in that magazine.

29. Groopman, "A Routine Case of Asthma," in *Second Opinions*, pp. 69–96.

30. Ibid., p. 71.

31. Ibid., pp. 88–89.

32. Ibid., pp. 79–83.

33. Ibid., p. 80.

34. Ibid., p. 81.

35. Ibid., p. 80.

36. Ibid.

37. Ibid., p. 81.

CHAPTER 9. FOUCAULT'S TOWER

1. Deloitte Consulting Report, "ERP's Second Wave: Maximizing the Value of ERP-Enabled Processes" (New York, 1998), p. 1.

2. AMR Research, "The Enterprise Applications Report" (Boston, 1999–2000), p. 11.

3. Philip Manchester, "Customer Relations Management," in *Financial Times Survey: E-Business: ERP and Beyond*, July 19, 2000, p. viii.

4. Deloitte Consulting Report, "ERP's Second Wave," p. 1.

5. Thomas Davenport, "Putting the Enterprise into the Enterprise System," *Harvard Business Review* (July–August 1998): 126.

6. PA Consulting Group Report, "Unlocking the Value in ERP, Realizing Value for Investments in Integrated Business Systems" (London, 2000), pp. 6–9.

7. Mark Vernon, "Going Live Is the End of the Beginning," in *Financial Times Survey: Enterprise Resource Planning*, January 19, 2000, p. ii.

8. Cambridge Information Network Report, "The Transformation of ERP: From Money Pit to Money Pot" (Cambridge, Mass., 1999), p. 7.

9. Rod Newing, "ERP and the Supply Chain," in *Financial Times Survey: Enterprise Resource Planning*, December 15, 1999, p. vii.

10. Gerhard Keller and Thomas Teufel, *SAP R/3 Process-Oriented Implementation* (Reading, Mass., 1997).

11. Ibid., p. 47.

12. SAP E-Business Solutions, "How Does It Make Life Easier for my

Operational Users?" Undated; downloaded from www.sap.com/ solutions/technology/workfl__users.htm July 2001. No longer available at SAP's website but can be obtained from the author at sihead@aol.com.

13. SAP E-Business Solutions, "SAP Business Workflow: What is Workflow?" Undated, downloaded from www.sap.com/solutions/technology/ workfl__users.htm, July 2001. No longer available at SAP's website but can be obtained from the author at sihead@aol.com.

14. Ibid.

15. Keller and Teufel, *SAP R/3 Process-Oriented Implementation*, p. 105.

16. Thomas Davenport, "The Fad that Forgot People," *Fast Company*, November 1995, p. 1. Available at www.fastcompany.com/online/01/ reenging.html.

17. Thomas Davenport, *Mission Critical, Realizing the Promise of Enterprise Systems* (Cambridge, Mass., 2000).

18. Ibid., p. 143; also pp. 137–42.

19. Keller and Teufel, *SAP R/3 Process-Oriented Implementation*, p. 56.

20. Philip Manchester, "Rich Rewards Yet to be Unlocked," *Financial Times Survey: E-Business and Beyond*, July 19, 2000, p. i.

21. Davenport, *Mission Critical*, p. 21.

22. Ibid., p. 22.

23. Keller and Teufel, *SAP R/3 Process Oriented Implementation*, p. 57.

24. Mark Vernon, "Going Live is the End of the Beginning," *Financial Times Survey: Enterprise Resource Planning*, December 15, 1999, p. ii.

25. Geoffrey Wheelright, "Heavyweights Attempt to Learn New Business Tricks," *Financial Times Survey: Enterprise Resource Planning*, December 15, 1999, p. viii.

26. Davenport, *Mission Critical*, pp. 18–19.

27. Ibid., pp. 126–27.

28. Ibid., p. 126.

29. Ibid., pp. 126–27.

30. Rod Newing, "ERP and the Supply Chain," *Financial Times Survey: Enterprise Resource Planning*, December 15, 1999, p. vi.

31. PA Consulting Group Report, "Unlocking the Value of ERP," p. 11.

32. Deloitte Consulting Report, "ERP's Second Wave," p. 2.

33. Ibid., p. 18.

34. Geoffrey Nairn, "Supplier Profile, i2 Technologies," *Financial Times Survey: E-Business: ERP and Beyond*, July 19, 2000, p. viii.

35. Davenport, *Mission Critical*, p. 1.

36. Quoted in Zuboff, *In the Age of the Smart Machine*, p. 320.

37. Ibid., p. 320.
38. Ibid., p. 321.
39. Ibid., p. 321.
40. Ibid., p. 321.
41. Ibid., chaps. 9 and 10.
42. Ibid., p. 338.
43. Stephan Haeckel and Richard Nolan, "Managing by Wire," *Harvard Business Review* (September–October 1993): 122–32.
44. Ibid., p. 122.
45. Ibid., p. 123.
46. Ibid., p. 127.
47. "SAP, Strategic Enterprise Management with my SAP.com: Translating Strategy with Actions," pp. 2–7; SAP White Paper, "Welcome to the Strategic Enterprise Management Community, Join the Collaboration to Master the Changes of the New Economy," pp. 1, 8–9, 11; "SAP in Focus; Management Cockpit—Improve Your Enterprise Performance." All papers undated; downloaded from www.sap.com July 2001. No longer available at SAP's website but can be obtained from the author at si-head@aol.com.
48. "SAP, Strategic Enterprise Management with my SAP.com," p. 4.
49. "SAP in Focus," p. 1.
50. Simon London, "A Visionary and His Big Picture," *Financial Times* (London), September 6, 2002.

CHAPTER 10. THE ECONOMICS OF UNFAIRNESS

1. See Mike Parker and Jane Slaughter, "Choosing Sides: Unions and the Team Concept," chap. 3; also Mike Parker and Jane Slaughter, "Working Smart, A Union Guide to Participation Programs and Reengineering," *Labor Notes* (Detroit, 1994).
2. Roger Alcaly, "A New, Better Kind of Corporation," *New York Review of Books,* April 10, 1997, p. 42.
3. Human Rights Watch (HRW), "Unfair Advantage: Workers' Freedom of Association in the United States under International Human Rights Standards" (New York, 2000). Available at www.hrw.org/reports/2000/uslabor.
4. HRW, "Unfair Advantage," chap. 5, "Case Studies of Violations of Workers' Freedom of Association," p. 2. Available at www.hrw.org/ reports/2000/uslabor/USLBR008-03.htm. Latest figure on dismissals

provided by Lance Compa, author of "Unfair Advantage," and are based on National Labor Relations Board data.

5. Ibid.

6. Ibid., p. 8.

7. National Labor Relations Board, Decision and Order, Caterpillar Inc. *v.* UAW, Cases 33-CA-10414 and 33-CA-10415, December 10, 1996, p. 2.

8. Translation from the Greek by Ludwig Edelstein, available at www.pbs. org/wgbh/nova/doctors/oath__classical.html.

9. See, for example, Dr. Marcia Angell, "Dispelling the Myths about Single-Payer Health Care," Physicians for a National Health Program (PNHP, undated); "National Health Insurance, Single Payer Fact Sheet"(PNHP, 2001); Dr. Gordon Schiff and Dr. David U. Himmelstein, "Questions and Answers about Single Payer National Health Insurance" (PNHP: 1996). Ad Hoc Committee to Defend Health Care, Cambridge, Mass., "For Our Patients, not for Profits, a Call to Action," *JAMA* 278 (21): 1733–38 (December 3, 1997); Dr. David U. Himmelstein and Dr. Steffie Woolhandler, and the Writing Committee of the Working Group on Program Design, "A National Health Program for the United States: A Physician's Proposal," *NEJM* 320 (2): 102–8 (January 12, 1989).

10. PNHP, "National Health Insurance, Single Payer Fact Sheet," p. 1.

11. Woolhandler and Himmelstein, "The Deteriorating Administrative Efficiency of the U.S. Health Care System," p. 1257.

12. Ruy Teixeira and Joel Rogers, *America's Forgotten Majority: Why the White Working Class Still Matters* (New York, 2000); John B. Judis and Ruy Teixeira, *The Emerging Democratic Majority* (New York, 2002).

13. Judis and Teixeira, *The Emerging Democratic Majority,* pp. 136–43.

14. Teixeira and Rogers, *America's Forgotten Majority,* back jacket.

15. Al Gore, "Remarks as Prepared for Delivery at the Democratic National Convention," August 17, 2000. Available at www.algore.com/speeches/ s__08172000__dnc.html.

16. Judis and Teixeira, *The Emerging Democratic Majority,* p. 141.

17. Ibid., p. 142.

18. Ibid.

19. Teixeira and Rogers, *America's Forgotten Majority,* pp. 15–18.

20. Ibid., p. x.

21. Quoted in John M. Broder, Robert Pear, and Milt Freudenheim, "Problem of Lost Health Benefits is Reaching into the Middle Class," *New York Times,* November 25, 2002.

22. Katherine G. Abraham, James R. Spletzer, and Jay C. Stewart, "Trends in

Worker Pay, What Do the Data Show," *American Economics Association Papers and Proceedings* 89 (2): 37 (May 1999).

23. See, for example, Lester Thurow, *The Future of Capitalism*, chaps. 4, 8; Patrick J. Buchanan, *The Great Betrayal* (Boston, 1998).

24. Paul Krugman, *Pop Internationalism*.

25. "Too Much Corporate Power," *Business Week*, September 11, 2000, pp. 148–49.

26. See, for example, Robert J. Gordon, "Does the 'New Economy' Measure up to the Great Inventions of the Past" *Journal of Economic Perspectives* 14 (4): 49–74 (Fall 2000).

27. David Levine, "The Productivity Mystery Unraveled—The Case of Hospitals" (Sanford Bernstein and Co., unpublished company memorandum, June 1997), p. 1.

28. Forthcoming in the *NEJM,* Summer 2003.

29. U.S. Department of Labor, "Major Sector Productivity and Costs Index: Output per Hour Nonfarm Business, percent change year ago, 1989–2002." Available at www.bls.gov, downloaded May 6, 2003; see also Mishel, Bernstein, and Boushey, *The State of Working America,* p. 120, table 2.3.